Fiddler Crabbe

G. R. Dixon

Fiddler Crabbe, 2'nd Edition

Contact author at noxid100@cox.net

ISBN 978-0-615-45096-4

<u>Part 1</u>

<u>The Early Years</u>

Chapter 1

In springtime there are places in Ireland that can seem achingly beautiful to a young man in his twenties. Lester Crabbe was awash with such feelings one Saturday morning in May. He sat on the slope of a dune that looked out across the Irish Sea. The sun glinted and danced on the waves like a billion diamonds. Seagulls drifted effortlessly over the beach in their perpetual quest for stranded fish and sun-stricken clams. Below him Coot, his old dog, ranged up and down the beach, scattering the gulls before him as he went. Now and then the dog would stop and dig furiously in the hard, wet sand.

Lester couldn't know it then, but at twenty-four he was at the height of his powers. He would never again feel so alive. The sun beat down on his forearms, already beginning to lose their winter pallor. Sweet, balmy sea breezes ruffled the thick shock of red hair on his head. An old man might have wished only to stay there in that spot forever. But Lester felt restless and vaguely tormented by ancient siren songs … songs that had stirred young males since the dawn of time.

He wondered why, even on calm and balmy days like this one, the waves rolled faithfully in. The sea had always been mysterious to him.

"Where do they come from?" he mused. He knew there was probably a scientific explanation for it all. But he as much liked some of the Irish myths that had come down from old. Whatever the truth might be, one could not help but be lulled by the muted roar of the surf, punctuated here and there by thuds as the breakers fell over themselves and spent themselves on the beach.

Lester reveled that he had this day and the next off. Some of his friends had to work on Saturday's. But his truck-driving job required his presence only five days a week. He loved the job. Indeed he had loved the feel of a steering wheel in his hands from the first time his father had held him on his lap, letting him help steer the family car to his grandparents' place. He knew then that he would drive a truck when he grew up. As a teen he had read everything he could find about internal combustion engines, drive trains, transmissions and the like. Even now, after several years behind the wheel, he got a thrill out of controlling all that power.

Lester leaned back on his elbows and let his mind drift back to high school days. It was then that he first met Emma. With a smile he remembered how pretty he'd found her to be, even while she acted as though he didn't exist. It had taken every ounce of his courage to ask her to the prom in their senior year. And he'd been numb and walking on air for the rest of the day when she smiled and agreed to be his date. From that time on there had really been no one else for either of them.

After graduation Emma's family had sent her to vocational school in Dublin. For the two years she was away he had drowned his loneliness in hard work here in the village. But the summer between Emma's first and second years in Dublin had been theirs. And sometime during that golden season it became clear to both that they were more than high school sweethearts. The love they discovered together was so beautiful that it never occurred to him to confess it as a sin.

After completing her training, Emma had returned to an accounting job at the meat processing plant. It was the region's biggest employer. A year after her return they were married. Lester had lived frugally during Emma's two years away. And after her return they saved money by going for long walks on the beach, rather than go out for intimate dinners. He had never really proposed to her. It seemed that both knew they were mates for life. By the time the date for their wedding drew nigh, Lester had saved enough to make a down payment on the cottage.

"Thank God for this sainted place," he thought. Belfast, with all its unrest, seemed a million miles away. Here in the village life was as peaceful as it ever gets in Ireland, notwithstanding the donnybrooks that occasionally spilled out of one pub or another on Saturday nights.

Lester winced now at the state of anxiety he'd existed in while Emma was away. Would she meet someone else? Would she change? In fact she *had* met other people, and time changed her as it inevitably changed him. She had left for Dublin a pretty girl, but had returned a beautiful woman. And during the same period, he had matured from a callow youth into a man.

Why did he feel so restless? It was a beautiful day! He should be dissolving in a puddle of contentment. He knew that Emma would have the cottage's windows open, and the bedroom curtains would be billowing inward like the sails of a ship. Perhaps he yearned for an afternoon nap back there in their bed. Although gone for only an hour, he longed to see her.

"Coot!" he shouted, rising and brushing the sand from the seat of his pants. Down on the beach Coot's head snapped up.

"Come on, boy!" he shouted, turning toward home, secure in the knowledge that before he'd gone a dozen steps Coot would race past him and take the lead. On the walk back to the cottage the old dog paused frequently, adding his own marker to bushes along the path. Lester marveled that he could do it so often between drinks. At last they broke free of the dunes and were on the cottage's street.

When Lester entered the kitchen, Emma was on her knees pulling pots and pans out of the lower cabinets. It was a fetching sight.

"Hello the house," he greeted.

"Hi!" she smiled over her shoulder.

On an impulse, Lester lifted her to her feet and turned her to face him. He pulled her against himself and smiled down at her pretty face. Her blue eyes seemed to divine the hungry look in his own.

"And what's this then, Mr. Naughty?" she teased.

"What are we doing?" Lester mumbled thickly.

"Cleaning the cupboards," she shrugged, smiling shyly.

Lester kissed her long and hard on the mouth until her body began to go limp.

"Can they wait a bit?" he mumbled huskily.

Emma didn't answer, but took him by the hand and led him into their bedroom.

"I love you, Mrs. Crabbe," he whispered, wrapping his arms around her and kissing the graceful curve of her neck. Emma pulled away and moved toward their closet, undoing the top button of her blouse. With a happy sigh Lester sat on the bed's edge and began unlacing his shoes. Outside there was only the sound of the sea breeze in the trees. The sweet scent of roses, planted by Emma along the back wall of the house, wafted through the open bedroom window.

"Remember these moments," he thought to himself. "They'll warm your heart when you're old and all the world's gone cold."

Chapter 2

In what would eventually become the state of Wisconsin, in the land destined to be called America, the woolly mammoth raised its shaggy head. Muck and vegetation hung from the great beast's tusks. Far above, a distant star spewed a million tons of elementary particles into space every second. One of them started on a long journey to the mammoth's home planet. By the time it arrived, the mammoth's kind would have been extinct for tens of thousands of years.

Through the millennia the tiny particle sped through the vastness of the cosmos at speeds close to that of light itself. Only a few days after the Saturday when Lester had interrupted Emma's spring cabinet cleaning, the particle plunged through Earth's atmosphere, passing between the atoms of the cottage's roof and into Emma's abdomen. Finally, after its trip of more than a hundred thousand years without incident, the particle collided with an atom deep inside Emma's body. But it was not one of her own atoms that took the hit. Still unknown even to her, a tiny cluster of guest cells had embedded itself in the wall of her womb. It marked the beginning of new life. By the time the tiny projectile collided with one of the microscopic cluster's cells, the cluster had begun differentiating left and right halves. The star-particle smashed into the nucleus of one of the tiny speck's left-side atoms, making subtle changes to a strand of DNA.

This was of course not a unique event. Science tells us that such genetic mutations are intrinsic to the process of evolution. Sometimes the changes are advantageous, and sometimes they aren't. It's all part of the great genetic game of chance that has populated Earth with countless forms of plant and animal life.

Five weeks later Emma suspected that she might have conceived. A visit to Doc Fitzsimmons confirmed it. Lester nearly fell to the floor when she told him that there would soon be three of them in the cottage. His joy at becoming a father filled Emma with a warmth she had never experienced before.

In the ensuing months the two busied themselves, converting the cottage's second bedroom into a nursery. Emma's mother arranged for a baby shower, ensuring no lack of clothing for the family's new addition. Lester and Emma spent many an evening trying boy and girl names out on each other. Eventually it was decided that the baby would be called 'Sean' (pronounced *Shawn*) if it were a boy, and 'Catherine' if a girl.

Little Sean arrived on schedule nine months later. Doc Fitzsimmons presided over the baby's entry into the world, as he did at all such events in the village. It was a routine birth. Lester became light-headed when the doctor came out to the waiting room and told him that he had a son. Mother and child were doing fine. Lester thanked Doc Fitzsimmons at least five times. Doc Fitzsimmons smiled and patted him on the shoulder. Over the years he had grown used to the wild gratitude of fathers.

"You can go in and see her in twenty minutes," the Doc said. "We're movin' her into Room 225."

"225 ... 225," Lester kept repeating in his mind, watching the minutes click by agonizingly slowly on the wall clock. At last the time passed and he ventured out of the waiting room, his heart pounding and his mind full of fear that he wouldn't know what to say.

When Lester found Room 225 Emma was already nursing the baby. Her face was blotchy from the strain of delivery; yet she never looked more beautiful. Indescribable feelings filled Lester to the core of his soul. He crept into the room and sat next to the bed, kissing Emma on her soft shoulder and gazing with rapt eyes at the tiny person sucking on her breast. Emma searched out his eyes.

"I love you," he whispered.

"Me too," she answered.

"My son ... my son!" kept coursing through Lester's mind like a mantra. Philosophical thoughts flooded his brain ... thoughts that had never occurred to him before. For the first time he felt his own mortality. Just as his grandfather had passed on, leaving his father and him behind, so one day would he leave Sean and his children. What would Sean grow up to be? So much depended on him and

Emma. He vowed that they would not fail to provide Sean with every advantage.

Two days later Emma was brought out to the hospital's curb in a wheelchair. With great care Lester helped her into their car. A nurse handed her little Sean, wrapped in a soft blanket. In all his years behind the wheel, Lester had never driven with greater care than he did that day on the way home. Once at the cottage, Emma handed him the baby to hold while she got out of the car. It was the first time Lester had held him. It was the first time he had held *any* baby. He was stiff and afraid. It brought a smile to Emma's lips.

Slowly they wended their way up the sidewalk and into the cottage's front door. Once inside Lester couldn't hand the small bundle back to Emma quickly enough.

"Let's lie down in our new crib," she cooed, taking the infant into the nursery.

"When does he eat?" Lester whispered.

"Oh, not for an hour," Emma smiled. "Let's lie down ourselves."

Lester followed her into their bedroom and stretched out on the bed next to her. He held her in his arms and kissed her chastely on the lips. She dozed off while he whispered over and over, "I love you."

Six weeks after Lester brought Emma and little Sean home, the time for Sean's first doctor appointment rolled around. Doc Fitzsimmons was his usual, outgoing self when they arrived.

"Let's have a look at this big boy," he said softly, taking Sean from Emma and leading the way into his small clinic's examination room. After Emma had removed Sean's baby clothes the Doc seemed to grow pensive.

"Hm-m-m," he muttered, turning the baby this way and that. He placed a finger in each tiny hand and tested its grip. He felt the baby's legs.

"OK," he said at length. "Go ahead and get him dressed and bring him into my office. It's down at the end of the hall."

Lester watched silently as Emma pulled the tiny togs over their son's arms and legs.

"What do you think?" he whispered. Emma remained silent. When she'd gotten Sean dressed, she looked up at Lester.

"Shall we join the doctor?" she murmured. The office door was open and Doc motioned them in.

"Have a seat," he bade them, motioning at some chairs in front of his big, polished desk.

"Well, he's a fine boy," Doc began. "Everything seems to be OK."

Emma and Lester relaxed visibly.

"Have you noticed anything … unusual?" Doc continued.

"No," Emma answered, thinking it to be a routine question. But Lester felt his stomach tighten.

"I, ah … I feel there are signs of a slight asymmetry," Doc continued, looking them both squarely in the eye.

"Asymmetry?" Lester answered. "I don't understand. Asymmetry where?"

Doc's eyes seemed to admonish Lester not to get excited.

"His left side," Doc replied at length. "His left side seems to be a wee bit larger than his right side. It may be nothin'. It may have been there at birth and I didn't notice it at the time."

Lester looked at Emma. She seemed to be blocking the whole conversation out, being more intent on fussing with little Sean than listening to the Doc.

"What would cause such a … an asymmetry?" Lester asked.

Doc looked candidly at Lester.

"I don't know," the old man replied. "It could have happened in the womb. The right side might catch up with the left side in time. It's hard to say. I've never seen it before, and I've never read about it. But I'll nose around a bit."

"What do we … what should we do?" Lester asked.

"Nothin' unusual," Doc answered. "Just treat him like a baby. We'll wait and see how it goes."

Doc rose, signaling the end of the conference. Lester helped Emma to her feet. He clasped Doc's extended hand across the desk.

"And don't worry!" Doc charged them both. "He's a fine, healthy boy!"

As Lester and Emma walked out the door, Doc called after them.

"Tell the nurse I want to see Sean again in three months."

That night Lester watched intently as Emma washed the baby and prepared him for his crib. It did indeed seem that the left side was slightly bigger.

"What do you think, do you see anything?" he asked Emma.

"Oh, it's nothin'," she answered, wrapping Sean in a fresh diaper. "Doc Fitzsimmons is just an old dope, isn't he? He's just an old dopey dope," she cooed.

Lester put the thought out of his mind and joined Emma.

"Hi, Seanie boy," he sang in his best falsetto, squeezing one tiny foot between his thumb and forefinger. "How's Daddy's boy?"

The baby smiled and stiffened all four limbs, waving them about in the air.

"Asymmetry my foot!" Lester thought. Maybe there was a small size difference there. But he was confident that in a few months everything would even out.

Chapter 3

Lester and Emma settled comfortably into the routines of parenthood. Four weeks after bringing little Sean home, Emma returned to her job. Her own mother and Lester's mother happily took turns, watching the baby during the day and taking him to the processing plant midway through each morning and afternoon. While her coworkers took coffee breaks, Emma came out to the car and nursed Sean.

In no time at all little Sean's follow-up appointment with Doc Fitzsimmons arrived. Again Lester took some time off from work to drive Emma and the baby to the doctor's office.

Doc Fitzsimmons pursed his lips after removing Sean's baby clothes and scanning the tiny body. Lester's heart skipped in his chest.

"Any change?" he prodded.

Doc Fitzsimmons nodded slightly, looking up over his wire-rimmed spectacles.

"Um hm-m-m," he said in a tone designed not to arouse alarm. "Maybe a little more asymmetry … maybe a tiny bit more. But he still appears to be a perfectly healthy little boy."

Lester bent and stared at Sean. There was undeniably a small size difference between the baby's left and right sides. Afterward, in his office, the Doc apprised Lester and Emma of a theory he'd read about. This theory suggested that many of the changes wrought by chance genetic alterations were of a repressive nature, merely masking traits no longer advantageous in a changing world.

"Did you know that we all have gill slits early on, when we're still in the womb?" he asked.

"No! Whatever for?" Lester exclaimed. "Is it to breathe under water while we're in there?"

"No, no," Doc laughed. "We get our oxygen through the placenta and the umbilical cord while we're in the womb. The gill slits are believed to be genetic artifacts from our ancestors' days in the sea. It's believed that they're masked and closed over as the embryo develops into an air-breathin' creature."

"The repression theory," Lester mumbled, his voice trailing off.

"Yes, I think so," Doc confirmed.

"And Sean's asymmetry?" Emma interjected. Doc gazed at her, appreciating her decision to participate in the conversation.

"Possibly some ancestral traits that escaped repression because of a genetic change. You know that the Earth emits low levels of radiation constantly.   That and cosmic rays are believed to be responsible for these random changes at the root of evolution."

"Ancestral traits?" Lester murmured. "What does that mean? Are we supposin' that Sean is half cavema … half cave child?"

Doc laughed.

"Oh, that's a droll one," he said. "Cave child indeed. You've a wild imagination, Lester Crabbe. He's a lovely, modern boy, he is. But there's no denyin' his left side is already showin' greater strength than his right."

Doc rose again and shook Lester's hand.

"Tell the nurse that I want to see Sean again in six months," he smiled. "And don't worry. He's as healthy as any baby I've ever examined."

In the months that followed, little Sean's lopsidedness persisted and even (Lester secretly thought) increased. The baby's left and right arms and legs seemed to be the same length. But everything on the left side was more massive and, as Lester and Emma soon discovered, a good deal stronger. It wasn't a bit easy to extricate one's hair from little Sean's left hand once he'd grabbed a handful. Lester and Emma quickly learned to duck away from such small catastrophes.

All of the asymmetry appeared to be below the neck, and Lester and Emma both said more than one silent prayer of thanks for that. The baby's face seemed to be perfectly symmetrical, and there was every reason to believe that he'd grow up to be a handsome lad.

At ten months Sean was on his feet, pulling himself around the inside of his playpen. And just after his first birthday he took his first real steps. His relatively massive left leg never seemed to impede his toddling. But by the time he was two, he had the strength of a six-year-old in his left side. In the normal course of banging his toys on the floor he destroyed many of them, and his parents quickly learned which toys had a reasonable chance of surviving through the first few play sessions.

By his fifth birthday Sean was playing out in the backyard. Fruit trees grew there, and he climbed easily up into their topmost branches.   Other mothers in the neighborhood were more sympathetic than alarmed at Sean's condition. They readily allowed their own children to play with Sean. From the start he seemed to know that he had to go easy with his left side, and not give his playmates the same treatment he gave to his toys.

With a nagging sense of dread, Emma brooded as Sean's first day at school loomed on the horizon. Children could be so cruel! She shared her fears with Lester after they'd retired for the night.

"I know … I know," he agreed. "There might be tough moments for him. But what's to be done? I really think he's better off in the local school, home with us at night, than bein' shipped off to a special school out of the county."

"Sure and I agree with that," Emma concurred. "We shan't be sendin' our boy away!"

But still, she worried. It was as if Sean's condition fanned the flames of her maternal protective instincts. Happily, it turned out that much of her worrying was for naught.

Chapter 4

In the days preceding Sean's first day at school Emma strove mightily to hide her fears. She went to great lengths to tell Sean how much fun school was going to be. Sean of course had no clue that he was different from other children. And by the time the dreaded day arrived he was full of enthusiasm. Emma took the morning off from work in order to walk to school with him. At first he strode purposely along, feeling very grown up. But when the schoolhouse came into view he slowed and it was clear that his confidence was giving way to anxiety. Once inside the schoolhouse, however, his confidence seemed to return. He could see that many of his new classmates were also tense. Two were actually crying and this, oddly enough, made him feel better. He told himself that he was braver than that, and resolved to give them words of encouragement before the day was out.

The infant class teacher asked for everyone's attention and told the children to find seats. Sean ended up sitting behind a pretty girl with long, black curls. He sat rigidly upright in an attempt to be as tall as she, but when they stood up it was clear that he fell short of that goal by two inches. Nonetheless he was drawn to her from the first.

Emma joined the other parents … mostly mothers … in the back of the room. The children quickly settled down and gave Mrs. O'Shaughnessy their undivided attention. She introduced herself and gave a little welcoming speech. Then she showed the youngsters how to fold their hands on their desks, how to lay their heads down on the desks during "quiet time," and so on. The children were all very eager to please, and it occurred to Emma that her memories of schoolyard cruelties were from a later time. Infant class students were, for the most part, angels. With a sigh of relief she silently filed out of the back of the room along with the other mothers when Mrs. O'Shaughnessy signaled them that it was safe for them to go. Sean smiled over his shoulder at her as she left. She began to feel good about things. Everything was going to be all right.

As the year progressed Emma was delighted at how readily Sean was accepted by his schoolmates. Children at that tender age seem to be all but blind to any deformities in one of their peers. By the end of the first month Sean had made many new friends.

There were swings and a jungle gym in the schoolyard, and Sean became somewhat celebrated for the feats he could pull off with ease on the latter. Using his mighty left arm he maneuvered through the bars more like a chimpanzee than like a six year old boy. He developed two great crushes in that first year. One was on Mrs. O'Shaughnessy, who he thought was quite the most wonderful teacher in the world. And the other of course was on Kathleen, the pretty girl who sat in front of him. She, in turn, found his mighty left half to be extremely admirable, and was quite in love with him. Their attachment carried over into the first and second classes, but tapered off in the third by mutual consent.

By the time Sean entered the fourth class life had become rough and tumble. Football … what is called soccer in America … was the sport of choice. Sean's lopsidedness didn't affect his ability to run, and he was a welcome participant in the games during recess and after school. The one thing that set him apart at such times was the inordinate power in his left leg. He had to restrain himself from kicking the ball clear out of the school grounds, and cultivated the habit of using his right leg for ball kicking purposes.

Most of the same faces turned up for class every year. But at the start of the fifth class there was a new one. It belonged to a big youth with a cruel glint in his eye. Sean would learn later that this boy was a year older than he and his classmates. Rumor had it that he'd been held back a year in his former school.

His name was Michael Lister, and it soon became apparent that he was a bully of the first order. Sean, with his asymmetric physique, was a natural target. Like a shark, young Lister approached Sean cautiously at first, but then with increasing confidence. He would purposely collide with Sean as they filed out for recess.

"Watch it, stupid," he'd snarl. And the truth was that Sean was cowed by the bigger boy, quite as the other students were.

Michael took to body-blocking Sean harder and harder during the football games. By then, refraining from using the great strength in his left side during rough and tumble had become second nature to Sean. Naturally Michael soon concluded that the man-sized musculature in Sean's left side didn't amount to anything.

All of the fifth class boys, except for Michael Lister, had bicycles. No doubt Michael's father would have bought one for his son if apprised of the situation. But Michael hated asking his father for anything. Mr. Lister was more powerful than his son was, and Michael resented that. And so it was that Michael decided to take Sean's bike.

"I'll be needin' this, freako," he told Sean after school one day. He took hold of the handlebar and pulled it with such force that Sean nearly fell to the ground. The other boys instantly understood what was going on and averted their eyes. To a one they felt sorry for Sean. But what could they do?

"Would you like to take a little ride, then?" Sean asked meekly, hoping to sow the idea that this was only a temporary matter.

"Would I like to take a little ride," Lister sang out in a mocking voice. "Get off, you freak, this is my bike now. Find another."

By now Sean was standing next to the bike. Without really thinking about it, he lifted the heavy bike off the ground and held it at arm's length behind him. The other boys gasped at this display of strength. The move jerked the handlebar from Lister's grip with a force that startled him. But many weeks of submission on Sean's part had convinced the bully that he had nothing to fear.

"Give it here, gimpo, or I'll smash your ugly face," he commanded.

"I can't. It was a present from me mother and father," Sean pleaded.

"You're askin' for it," Lister snarled, and punched Sean in the face. It was the first time Sean had ever been struck. With a strange but fleeting buzz in his head he staggered backward and fell on top of the bike.

"Get the picture, dummy?" Lister growled, grabbing Sean's shirt and pulling him off the bike. Blood trickled out of Sean's nose and down his upper lip. The old inhibitions vanished and he grabbed Lister's wrist in his man-sized left hand. The muscles in his meaty left forearm knotted.

"I said no," he stated quietly, applying pressure to Lister's arm. Michael cried out in pain and he was forced to his knees. So powerful was the vise-like grip on his arm that it seemed to be either yield or have the bones in his arm snapped. Despite himself, he cried out.

"Ow! You're breakin' me arm, Crabbe."

Sean was pleasantly amazed. It was the first time he had ever used his abnormal strength on another boy in anger. He had not realized until this moment just how much stronger the left half of him was.

"No more trouble from you, then," he more stated than asked.

"All right, all right," Lister answered in a tone rapidly admitting defeat.

"For any of us," Sean added.

"Sure, sure. Let go, man, you're breakin' me bloody arm!"

The other boys sat on their bikes, taking the amazing incident in with wide eyes. Those who missed the show would make the ones who were there recount the whole scene in minute detail for weeks afterward.

Sean released his iron grip on Lister's arm, mounted his bike and rode off without further comment. The other boys fell in behind him, leaving Michael Lister sitting in the dirt.

At first young Lister tried to block the truth from his mind. He got up and morosely slapped some of the dirt from his pants. By the time he had shuffled doggedly home, however, his initial denial had been displaced by the acceptance of a painful and inescapable new reality. For as long as Sean Crabbe was around, his bullying days were over.

Chapter 5

Sean finished primary school without further incident. Michael Lister, initially shunned after his losing encounter with Sean, changed his ways. In time the other boys accepted him. Several years later, as an adult, he would look back and realize that Sean Crabbe had done him a great favor the day he had all but snapped the bones in his forearm.

In Ireland, as everywhere, the girls grow up before the boys. And in the sixth class Sean began to sense a subtle change in his female peers. It seemed that they no longer accepted him so freely and without question. Some might argue that deep instincts were beginning to kick in. As the girls approached childbearing age, they became repelled by Sean's asymmetry. The great strength that had once excited them now made them feel uneasy. Although Sean sensed this change, it didn't unduly upset him. For although he had the strength of a grown man in his left side, physically he remained a boy. Indeed he would remain a boy up through his second year in high school.

Unhappily for him, some of his boyhood chums also seemed to become distant when their voices cracked and deepened. For reasons less obvious than in the girls' case, they too seemed for the first time to feel that Sean was not part of "the group." Sean was much more keenly aware of such changes in the case of the boys, and it wounded him. Fortunately there were a few other late bloomers in the old gang, and they continued being blind to Sean's deformity.

Most of the people in the village attended mass every Sunday. Sean's family was no exception. After the services it became a tradition for either Lester's or Emma's parents to come over to the cottage for Sunday dinner. And, about once a month, Sean and his parents would have dinner at one of the grandparents'.

On those Sundays when Emma's parents came to the cottage, Sean loved to sit at the feet of Grandma Mary while Emma busied herself in the kitchen. Lester and Emma's father would usually go out into the backyard, weather permitting, to enjoy a pipe. Sean and

Grandma Mary would settle into the parlor for a chat. They'd start out by discussing the day's sermon, and would then move on to other topics. Sean loved these times and opened up to Grandma Mary as he did to no one else. While he sat with his great, muscular arm lying on her lap, he would expound on many topics while she listened and rubbed her fingers through his head of thick red hair. She always seemed to be interested in his opinions.

One Sunday the sermon had been on the time honored idea that "No man is an island."   Afterward Grandma Mary had an interesting, related thought:

"You know, Sean, every man who ever lived has had some one special island that he feels is his home," she said.

Sean was silent for a bit.

"What about people who live on continents?" he challenged. "What about Canadians, or Europeans?"

"Well … what are continents? They're just big islands, aren't they?"

"Australia is," he granted.

"But they all are. All are surrounded by the sea."

"Europe isn't," he argued.

"Sure and it isn't. But the distinction between Europe and Asia is man's work. The land mass they occupy is an island, as is every scrap o' dry land risin' above the oceans of the Earth!"

"I guess I think of an island as bein' somethin' small," Sean mused.

"Faith and many are," Grandma answered. "But some are larger, like Ireland. And some are enormous, like the America's."

"Yes, I guess you could say that," Sean thought aloud. "I guess that makes Ireland me island home."

"Perhaps. Perhaps not," Grandma answered cryptically. Sean gave her a puzzled look.

"Sure and it is!" he protested.

"It is for now," the old woman answered. "But who knows what the future holds?"

"You mean I might one day leave Ireland?" Sean asked.

"Many have," she answered. Sean pondered that fact and wondered what the future held for him. At length he spoke again.

"What is home, if not where a man lives?"

"Ah!" Grandma answered. "Home isn't so much where a man lives, as where he *wants* to live."

"I'll bet there are lots of people not livin' at home, then," Sean snorted.

"And you'd be right," she answered.

"How does a man … how will I know when I've found me island home?" Sean wondered.

"You'll know," the old woman answered. "You'll know it when you gaze into the right woman's eyes."

Sean grew uneasy at this thought. He was beginning to believe that a relationship with a woman was not in the cards for him. Grandma Mary sensed the reason for his silence.

"Oh, you and she will find each other one fine day," she said, rubbing Sean's head a little harder. "I don't know where or when. But I know it will happen."

"And how do you know that?" Sean muttered, still convinced that no woman would ever want him.

"I just know," she answered gently. "I feel it in me bones. And when that happy day arrives, think of our talk today, won't you?"

"Aye, I will that," Sean promised. And indeed the day *would* come when he'd not remember anything else about that day, but he'd remember Grandma's promise. And he'd wonder how she could have known.

"Dinner!" Emma called from the dining room. With a sigh Sean rose and helped Grandma to her feet. It would be several weeks before they talked again, and indeed not many more of those enchanting sessions remained. Grandma Mary died unexpectedly in Sean's second year of high school. It was the first time he had lost anyone dear to his heart, and at first he was in full denial. He had touched her face as she lay in her casket and had felt only a vague sense of cynicism. He knew he should be sad, but there had been no tears.

Two days later, at the church's funeral services, the priest had spoken.

"Mary Flannagan had a full life. She shared nearly fifty years of marriage with Shamus Flannagan. I'm told that she never left our island home…"

And suddenly the only grief Sean had ever known filled him to the depths of his soul. He collapsed in tears, burying his face in his hands. "Grandma … Grandma…" his mind cried silently. "Where are you?" And then he felt his father's arm on his shoulders, comforting him. On the other side of his father he heard Emma softly weeping. With tears streaming down his face, he looked across at his mother. His father's other arm was around her. Sean reached across his father's lap and squeezed Emma's hand. She looked up at him and smiled through her tears, taking comfort in his own sadness. And through it all he heard the priest's words float, as in a dream:

Sunset and evening star, and one clear call for me. And may there be no moaning at the bar when I put out to sea.

Chapter 6

In the beginning of his third year in High School, adolescence hit Sean like a ton of bricks. There were the usual changes of course. But in his case there was something more. Whereas his right half became more manly, his left half nearly doubled in size. It was undeniably grotesque. The strength in his left arm became prodigious. Weightlifting in the school gym was a favorite pastime. With one hand Sean easily lifted weights above his head that no grown man in the village could match using both arms. Not only was he the only one in anyone's memory who could do a one-armed pull up, but he broke the Guinness record for the number he could do without letting go of the bar.

As these changes in his body occurred, Sean of course became interested in girls. And it was now that the lack of interest on the girls' part became painfully obvious. A few girls went out of their way to be nice. But it was clear that their intentions were not romantic.

"It makes them feel good to be nice to the freak," he thought bitterly.

Virtually all of the late-blooming males, who had stuck by him during his eighth and ninth years, also lost their boyhood by the tenth year. And more than ever Sean was odd man out. Group outings on the weekends now inevitably included both sexes, and Sean was not invited.

Lester's father, Grandpa Joe, sensed the void created in Sean's life when Emma's mother died, and he took steps to remedy the situation. He owned a small shop and asked Sean to come by after school to help him out. Sean eagerly accepted, and they shared many an interesting conversation during lulls between customers.

"Life is a game, me boyo. 'Tis a great game," Grandpa Joe would say. "And a man will not fail if he plays the game straight."

"Even if he loses his life by playin' things straight?" Sean half teased.

"Even then," the old man answered without hesitation. "Everyone dies. It's how a man feels about himself when his time comes … that's the important thing."

Sean pursed his lips and nodded agreement. All of his sensibilities affirmed that his Grandpa was right.

Toward the end of his eleventh year Sean applied for a summer job at the meat processing plant. He was thrilled when they notified him that he'd be hired. Whereas his classmates reveled in the free time summer vacation afforded them, Sean could scarcely wait for the new job to begin.

He was tasked with washing down the floors and cleaning the equipment used in the slaughter of steers and hogs. It was the least desirable job in the entire operation, but he pitched into it with a vengeance. With his left arm … now bigger by far than the strongest man's … he could wield the big push broom with the greatest of ease, scouring the concrete floors for hours without tiring. Men who had worked at the plant their entire adult lives whispered to one another of his strength and stamina.

Midway through the summer, three strange men held up the plant payroll office. The company cashier, a slight man named Leroy Farnsby, was a good fellow, active in the community and well-liked by all. He complied with the robbers' demands, quite as upper management had instructed him. Nonetheless, after he had handed over two canvas bags of money, one of the thieves pointed his pistol at Leroy's head and pulled the trigger. The gun clicked but nothing happened. The robber looked at the pistol in disbelief. He pointed the gun at Leroy again and pulled the trigger twice more. Again, click, click and nothing more.

"Come on!" the others shouted at him as they bolted from the office.

"You are a lucky bloke," the thief muttered to Leroy, chasing the others out the door.

They were never caught, but their getaway car was found twenty miles south of town. In it were the bags they had taken from the cashier's office, empty of course, and the three guns they'd used in the holdup. Leroy readily identified the one that had been unsuccessfully fired at him, it being the only revolver.

The police checked the pistol. It was in good working order. They fired two of its five bullets into special wadding at the police station. But the other three … the three that had failed to blow Leroy's brains out … were duds. Everyone marveled at the odds of that happening.

Sean still sought Grandpa Joe out for conversation whenever he could.

"What are the chances o' that?" he mused aloud when the talk turned to Leroy Farnsby.

"I'm not sure chance played a role," Grandpa answered.

"No role? How else can you explain it?" Sean demanded belligerently.

Grandpa Joe looked over his spectacles at his grandson. He knew how tough life must be getting for Sean.

"Leroy Farnsby was a God fearin' man … he was a *good* man, Bubby," the old man allowed.

"To be sure," Sean agreed. "But…"

"I'm goin' to tell you a secret," Grandpa continued. "Some say it's blarney and nothin' more. But I know from experience that it's true."

Sean looked at the old man attentively. His eyes begged him to continue.

"Every God fearin' man…" the old man went on, "…every man who loves and honors God gets at least one miracle in his life, and I expect Leroy got his when that pistol misfired. Not once, mind you, but three times in a row."

Sean nodded in somber agreement. There was no denying that the whole business did smack of a miracle.

"And you, Grandpa, what was your miracle?" he asked.

"I'll no say," the old man answered. "But I'll tell you this: when you get yours, you'll know it. Make no mistake about that."

Sean pondered his grandfather's words that night as he lay waiting for sleep to come. What would his miracle be? He doubted that he would ever be made symmetric. And if that were possible, then which half would he want to change? He fell asleep debating the question.

The summer drew to a close, and the awe over Leroy Farnsby's incredible escape from an untimely end wound down. Sean's classmates more or less eagerly prepared to return to high school. But Sean was less than enthusiastic. The men at the plant seemed to accept his deformity quite as his peers in primary school had done. It was only the other adolescents in high school who depressed him in a thousand ways. He even thought about telling his parents that he wasn't going to return, but was going to stay on at the processing plant. However, he knew they'd have none of that! With the greatest reluctance he bade goodbye to summer vacation. Emma sensed his pain, and many a night she shed bitter tears into her pillow while Lester lay breathing deeply beside her.

Chapter 7

Sean's senior year in high school turned out to be not as bad as he'd anticipated. He avoided disappointment largely by remaining a loner. Occasionally he would overhear comments from other students, but as often as not they were complimentary in their way, marveling at the enormous strength in his left shoulder and arm. His Saturdays were taken up by a weekend job at the processing plant, and of course Sundays were family time.

The one great threat to Sean's self esteem turned out to be the high school queen bee. Her name was Lillian Scully, and without question she was physically striking in every way. Unfortunately, years of being deferred to by virtually every man she'd been around since childhood had not made for a sensitivity to match.

All Sean knew was that he was hopelessly smitten with her. There must be something to the old saying that love is blind, for he pushed his deformity out of his mind whenever he fantasized about her. Nor was he discouraged by the fact that she was the steady girlfriend of Peter Connolly, the captain of the football team.

Like many of his contemporaries, Sean had been bombarded with the idea that a troubled teen should talk his problems over with his parents. And so late one Sunday afternoon in November he caught Lester alone in the living room and sought his counsel. Lester listened intently as his son pulled the curtain back and bared a corner of his young soul. And as Sean spoke of his infatuation with Lillian Scully, Lester felt his heart sink. What should he say? How should he respond? He would die rather than wound his boy. Yet all his instincts told him that Sean was headed for a great fall. Perhaps if he de-glamorized the object of Sean's affection…

"Well, you know, son, if there's one thing I've learned in life, it's that physically beautiful women don't always have the *inner* beauty that makes for a good relationship."

Sean looked at Lester with surprised eyes.

"O' course your Ma is one of them that does," he added hastily.

Lester studied Sean's face. Clearly that approach was falling on deaf ears. What advice could he give Sean that would at least minimize his heartbreak? Suddenly it hit Lester that perhaps the best advice would be no advice at all.

"But then," he continued, "the truth is that no man can advise another on his dealin's with the fair sex."

Sean swelled with pride. It was the first time his father had hinted that he was becoming a man.

"How did you and Ma get together?" Sean asked.

"Ah! Well now, there's a bit of a story there!" Lester laughed. "When I was your age I thought she was the prettiest girl in the world. But she wouldn't give me the time o' day."

"Really!" Sean exclaimed, obviously fascinated.

"On my oath. I was dead certain she'd laugh in my face if I asked her to the senior dance. But I also knew I'd hate myself if I didn't chance it."

"So you asked her?" Sean pressed eagerly.

"Aye, I did, I did," Lester smiled, fishing out his pipe. "It took every drop of courage the Lord gave me, but I popped the question."

"And?" Sean cried.

Lester smiled, his eyes seeming to drift back twenty years. He tamped tobacco into the pipe's bowl.

"And…" he said, striking a match and sucking flame into the tobacco, "And, she said 'Yes'."

He looked at Sean with twinkling eyes. Sean's own eyes glowed with the boundless idealism of youth.

"And the two o' you fell in love," he murmured, gazing wistfully out of the window.

"Aye," Lester answered gently. "We did."

Sean heaved a mighty sigh, and Lester snapped back to the present reality.

"But you know, Sean," he continued, striving his best to sound casual, "more often than not things don't work out that way."

"No?" Sean answered absently.

"No, they don't. More often than not a young man's crush on a young woman is one-sided. Maybe she's interested in someone else."

Lester again watched Sean closely.

"Or o' course as often it's a young woman who's infatuated with a young man, but he doesn't know she exists."

Sean nodded, glancing sideways at his father. He seemed to be considering the possibility in his own case. But then his face took on a resolved look.

"Only one way to find out, isn't there?" he half-smiled. "Ask her."

Lester sucked hard on his pipe, sending a veil of smoke up in front of his face.

"Well ... I guess..." he murmured. "But you should remember ... *every* young person should remember ... more often than not things don't work out the very first time. Your Ma and I were the exceptions to that rule."

Sean nodded.

"If things don't go well," Lester continued, "rest assured that you've got lots o' company!"

"What would you have done if Ma had told you to get lost?" Sean asked, looking carefully at his father. Lester looked away.

"Oh," he sighed at length, "I'd have survived, I'm sure. I'd have got over it. Time heals all hurts and disappointments."

"Someone else would've come along," Sean said soothingly, seemingly trying to ease a case of broken heart that had never occurred.

Lester smiled at Sean.

"I expect so," he said. "But aren't you glad things turned out the way they did?"

"Yes, I guess I am!" Sean laughed.

But that night, as he lay in bed, Sean wondered, "What if Ma and Da' had never got together? Would I never have been born?" A tear squeezed out of the corner of one of his eyes.

"And would that have been so bad?"

Chapter 8

It was Monday, the last week in November, and the senior prom was only a week away. Totally blocking out the thought that Lillian Scully no doubt already had a date, Sean decided to make his move at lunchtime in the school cafeteria. Lillian sat on the other side of the room, at a table with a handful of other girls. All of them were cheerleaders, and they were all school royalty.

"Well, here goes," Sean thought, rising from his solitary lunch. His brain felt numb. Voices of doom screamed inside of him that he was on a fool's errand. Yet other voices prodded him not to lose his nerve.

"Nothin' ventured, nothin' gained," he muttered in an attempt to bolster his courage. As he approached the table there was a distinct ebb in the chattering of students in the vicinity. The girls' incessant laughter died away and they all looked up at him curiously. One or two smiled, but Sean took no notice. He was completely focused on Lillian.

"Hi, Lillian," he tried to smile, bowing slightly and immediately realizing how stupid that must look. Lillian Scully only nodded. What on earth could this freak want?

"I was wonderin' if you … if I could take you to the prom," he forced himself to say. Sean's entire body was suddenly drenched in sweat.

A few of the girls secretly admired Sean for his courage. But Lillian looked like he had touched her in some inappropriate way. She laughed out loud. The other girls looked at her in mild disdain. Their eyes seemed to soften in sympathy for Sean.

"I'm afraid I'm booked," Lillian answered curtly.

"Oh … too bad," Sean mumbled lamely. Waves of mortification swept over him. What could he have been thinking? His embarrassment only roused the killer instinct in Lillian.

"Too bad? Too *bad*?" Lillian laughed. "Even if I weren't, I wouldn't be your date for a million quid."

Sean felt the blood drain from his face. Indignation began to crowd the embarrassment from his mind. By now the entire cafeteria had gone silent. A couple of the other girls at the table now looked with disgust at Lillian. Their eyes seemed to ask her how she could be so cruel.

"And how about for two million?" Sean asked quietly. He had no idea why he said it. The question just popped out of his mouth.

Lillian's eyes lost some of their cruel mirth. She really didn't know anything about this odd young man or his family. For all she knew, he might come from rich people. And her mother, also a shrew of the first order, had drummed it into her head from girlhood that her highest priority should be to snag a rich man.

"Maybe," Lillian answered demurely. "Why? Have you got two million to pay for a date?"

Sean smiled. Suddenly he knew that he had her!

"No," he answered, "I'm just tryin' to establish your price."

Several students within earshot stifled strangled laughs. Lillian's cheeks blanched with rage.

"You cheeky scum!" she shouted, jumping to her feet and throwing a glass of punch into Sean's face. Sean smiled and pulled a handkerchief from his pocket.

"Have a nice day," he smiled. Dabbing at the punch, he began to move away just as Peter Connolly approached the table. Lillian's face flushed red when she saw her boyfriend.

"Smash his ugly face!" she shouted. Now the entire room went totally silent. Peter looked at her in surprise. When he glanced at the other girls, a couple of them shook their heads almost imperceptibly. Little warning flags went up in young Connolly's head.

"What's the problem then?" Peter asked tentatively.

"Smash him!" Lillian yelled. "He called me a whore!"

Peter Connolly looked at Sean. Sean in turn had paused a few tables away and was looking back at him. Peter didn't know much about Crabbe, but he could scarcely believe that Sean could be so callous.

Sean instinctively felt it would be a sign of weakness to deny it. So he raised his left arm, bare to above the elbow, and made a great fist, slowly rotating it back and forth. Huge muscles, like the cables that anchor a large ship, rolled over each other beneath the skin.

Now Peter Connolly would in time become a political figure at the national level. And he had made it his habit early in life not to get into fights he could not win.

"Did he?" he asked the other girls at the table.

"No-o-o," three of them said quietly. Lillian looked at them, her eyes flashing anger.

"He did … he implied it!" she shouted.

Emily, the one girl who had never been cowed by Lillian, rose to take her tray to the drop-off window.

"Whatever he said, you had it comin', dear," she smiled sweetly, walking away with swishing hips.

Peter Connolly put his hand on Lillian's shoulder and gently pushed her down into her chair.

"Calm down," he chided her. "We'll talk about it later."

"Oh, so you're goin' to let him get away with it then," she cried. Her eyes filled with angry tears. "Maybe I should o' accepted his bloody invitation."

She rose to her feet, sending her chair skidding back against the next table with a bang, and stomped up to the tray collection window. Without a backward glance she threw her tray onto the conveyor belt and stormed out of the cafeteria.

"What really happened?" Peter asked the other girls.

"He asked her to the prom, and she laughed at him," one of girls began.

Sean continued back across the room to gather up his own tray. Underclassmen … some of them late bloomers like he had been … looked up in wide-eyed awe as he passed. Before the day's end the whole scene would be told and re-told a hundred times.

In a sense, the legend of Fiddler Crabbe began on that day. But Sean had mixed emotions. He kicked himself for having been fool enough to think that Lillian Scully would have anything to do with him. On the other hand he couldn't help being pleased at how he'd returned her cruelty.

"It probably isn't the last slap you'll be gettin' from the fair sex," he thought to himself. He'd have to be careful. In his case, romance could be expected not to be without pain. One thing became clear to him: a relationship had to be as much her idea as it was his. He resolved never to delude himself again on that score.

Chapter 9

Lillian Scully was not finished with Sean. Not by a long shot. She knew that her three older brothers would be coming home for Christmas, and she hatched up a plan to put Sean in his place. Two of her brothers lived in Belfast and were, in fact, active in the IRA. The other was a junior stockbroker and had emigrated to London. They were a tough lot. All three of them were strapping young men, and they all liked a good fight --- especially when the odds favored them.

On the Monday after the prom, Lillian approached Sean before classes.

"Hi!" she smiled brightly.

Sean looked at her in surprise.

"Hello," he answered warily.

"Sean, I want to apologize for the terrible way I behaved a week ago," she said. "I'm really sorry."

Sean felt slightly stunned and embarrassed.

"Oh, it's OK," he smiled. "No harm done here." The thought flitted through Lillian's mind that the cripple actually had a rather handsome face.

"Listen," she continued excitedly, "we're plannin' a little pre-Christmas party at the community center this Saturday night, and we'd like you to come. Could you?"

Little warning bells went off in Sean's mind. If nothing else, the scene in the cafeteria had been a reality check for him. He no longer harbored any illusions about Lillian Scully and himself. But he decided to play along and see where Lillian was going with this thing.

"I think I could," he answered, smiling weakly.

"Oh, good!" Lillian beamed. "The party's at 8 PM, but I could use some help doin' a bit of decoratin' beforehand. Somebody to hold the chair while I'm up on it hangin' balloons and the like. D' you think you could meet me there at 7?"

"I could," Sean said, rationalizing to himself that 'could' didn't mean 'would.'

"Great! See you then!" Lillian smiled seductively, giving his left shoulder a little squeeze. Feeling its mammoth size through the cloth of his shirt disconcerted her for an instant. But she quickly rallied and walked away.

Later that day Lillian confided with one of the other cheerleaders. She gleefully described how Sean Crabbe was going to get his block knocked off on Saturday night. Of course before the day was done the word had spread throughout the cheerleader squad and even to Peter Connolly. Although Peter didn't understand it at the time, a little switch tripped in his head. As a result he would eventually distance himself from Lillian Scully. She would never become Mrs. Peter Connolly. But that all lay in the future. For now he only felt that he should somehow warn Sean Crabbe.

The next morning, after physical education, Peter sauntered past Sean's locker. Sean was seated on a bench taking off his sneakers.

"Sean," Peter said quietly, pausing in front of Sean but not looking at him.

Sean looked up curiously, hoping that Peter wasn't going to pick a fight. He really seemed to be a decent sort, and Sean didn't want to get into it with him.

"Don't go," Peter suggested in a barely audible voice. Somehow Sean knew exactly what Peter was talking about.

"I wasn't plannin' to," he answered.

"Good," Peter nodded approvingly as he walked away. Although he didn't know the details, Sean was moved by the warning.

"But thanks anyway, Peter," he called softly. Without answering or looking back, Connolly raised his arm and made the victory sign with his fingers.

Lillian's brothers all arrived Friday afternoon for the Christmas holiday. After being properly hugged and kissed by their mother, they were pulled aside by Lillian. In low tones she told them how this freak at school had called her a whore when she tried to tell him, in the gentlest possible terms, that she couldn't be his date for the prom.

The three brothers listened intently and exchanged hard glances. They told Lillian that they'd take care of him. It was a matter of family honor.

"I thought you would," she smiled. "I've arranged to meet him Saturday night outside the community center."

And so the plan was set. The three brothers would wait in the shadows across the street, and when the cripple showed up they'd give him a beating he'd never forget.

"There's just the one thing," she added. "He is massively developed in his left side. They say he's stronger than two men on that side."

The brothers were fascinated and even eager to see this. But they assured Lillian that there wasn't a man alive the three of them couldn't handle, no matter how strong he was.

Saturday night at 6:45 the brothers and Lillian took their positions. Lillian wore a miniskirt that showed off her shapely legs. She was mindful of her promise to let Sean hold a chair while she stood on it. Even though he'd never get the chance to check her out, the idea excited her.

7:00 o'clock came and went with no sign of Sean. It was chilly outside and Lillian began to shiver. At 7:10 one of the brothers sauntered over and suggested that perhaps there had been some sort of mix up.

"Oh, he'll be here all right," Lillian snapped. "It's the best offer he's had in his entire, miserable life."

The brother shrugged and went back across the street. By 7:30, with no sign of Sean, the brothers had had enough. Together the three of them crossed over and told Lillian that they were going to the pub for a night of celebrating with some old friends.

Lillian felt tears of rage sting her eyes. Someone had warned Crabbe! She kicked herself for having confided in one of her so-called friends.

"It looks like beauty's been stood up by the beast," the brother from London teased. Lillian wheeled on him and punched him savagely on the ear.

"Here, now," one of the other brothers scolded, wrapping his arms around her and pinning her arms to her sides. "We'll have none o' that!"

Lillian twisted free from his bear hug and stomped away. The brothers could see that she was crying bitterly.

"Hell hath no fury…" the brother from London said, rubbing his reddened ear.

"Aye," one of the others agreed. "Especially when the fury is a conceited colleen."

"I wonder if the cripple ever actually called her a whore," the third remarked.

"I doubt it," the brother with the smarting ear answered. "Lill has never had any qualms about bendin' the truth when it suited her purposes."

Chapter 10

By the time classes re-convened after New Year's, Lillian's feelings of rage toward Sean had mollified somewhat. All of her girlfriends swore that they had not tipped Sean off. The idea that Sean might not be so stupid as she'd initially thought began nagging Lillian's mind. She couldn't help remembering how he had raised his mighty arm that day in the cafeteria. Despite herself the memory thrilled her. But of course she avoided Sean for the rest of the school year. When the "friend" she'd confided in asked her about Saturday night, she answered that she'd thought better of the idea and had never shown up.

The rest of the school year played itself out without incident for Sean. In midyear Lester and Emma began to press him about what his plans were. They had put aside a sizable sum over the years and wanted him to continue on with his education. But Sean told them that he wanted to take a year off from school. He promised to think about going to college or university the following spring.

And so, after graduating from high school, Sean went to work full time at the meat processing plant. He would ride to work with Emma every morning. She'd go into the offices to her company finance officer job, and he would walk down to the stockyards and into the slaughtering rooms at the back of the plant.

It was good to be back full time with the rough and tumble men who worked there. As always, none of them looked askance at Sean's deformity. If anything they were thankful for it. He contentedly resumed his job of scrubbing down the slaughtering floors … a job that they found tiring. As usual they would glance at one another and shake their heads in wonder as Sean scrubbed the floors for hours on end, swathing the great push broom back and forth effortlessly.

The processing plant slaughtered steers, hogs and sheep. There were areas where each of these animals was killed. In the case of hogs, the animals' hind legs would be shackled and they'd be unceremoniously hauled into the air. Once the pigs had been hoisted by their hind hocks, one of the men would expertly stick them in the throat with a long knife. After their blood had drained out into a trough in the floor, they'd be pushed along the conveyer for further processing. It was always a noisy time, since the pigs screamed bloody murder when pulled off their feet.

The much larger steers necessarily had to be handled differently. Hauling a conscious animal that weighed over a thousand pounds into the air was too risky, especially when the animal had horns. In the steers' case the animals were led into stanchions where their heads were secured. Their rear hocks were then shackled as in the case of the pigs. But before a steer was hoisted off its feet it was dispatched with a stunner. This was a device that fired a retractable, stainless steel pin into the steer's skull, rendering it unconscious and in many cases instantly killing it. Once this had been done the stanchion would be opened and the steer would be hoisted up.

On the days when steers were slaughtered, the screams of the hogs were replaced by the reports of the stunner. For the skull-piercing pin of this device was fired into the steers' heads using blank pistol cartridges. The steers, aligned in a long row, would jump at the first couple of shots, but then got used to them and went to their ends for the most part quietly chewing their cud.

Toward the end of the summer the men were informed that a special job was scheduled for the next day. One of the suppliers of steers had raised a bull that had turned out to be too mean to be of use. The big animal had gored several cows, and the farmer who owned him had decided to cut his losses and have the brute butchered.

The next morning the animal arrived in a large cattle truck, and the men at the slaughter house pursed their lips and nodded admiringly as the bull was unloaded. It was more than twice the size of a typical steer and, as was the usual practice with bulls, had a ring in its nose. The farmer led it onto a large floor scale using a stout pole that clamped onto the ring. A bull's nose is of course very tender, and rings have been used since ancient times to control these big animals.

Once on the scale the bull was found to weigh in at over a ton. The farmer had been instructed to precede the bull through one of the stanchions, and then to pull the bull's head through. As the farmer led the big animal from the scale toward the designated stanchion Sean couldn't help but marvel at the animal's strength. One could see enormous muscles ripple in its shoulders, and no sane person could doubt that this was a creature not to be trifled with.

The bull's eyes were red and he snorted as he was led toward the stanchion. He would clearly have wreaked havoc if not restrained. And then the unthinkable happened. The owner slipped on a wet spot and fell hard on his back, releasing his grip on the ring pole. The pole came unclamped from the ring in the bull's nose and rattled across the concrete floor.

For a moment the big animal stood blinking, evidently unaware of its sudden freedom. Everyone on the slaughtering floor stood riveted in place. The huge beast looked to the left and right and then with astonishing nimbleness was on the farmer, sinking a horn into the hapless man's abdomen.

"Agh-h-h!" the man half screamed as the bull twisted its massive head, driving the horn in deeper. The slaughtering room men watched in horror.

"Stun him!" one of them shouted. But the man holding the stunner froze when the bull lifted its head, one horn dripping with blood. The bull looked around and then continued to gore its owner.

Without thinking, Sean sprinted across the floor and landed the bull a prodigious blow behind its ear. No one had ever seen anything remotely like it. With a low rumble the great beast staggered back, its eyes glazed. In a flash Sean was around in front of it and rendered another sledgehammer punch between the animal's eyes. Without further sound the bull flopped to its stomach.

The man with the stunner regained his composure and rushed across the floor. With a bang he administered the usual coup de grace to the animal's head. But many doubted the necessity. Some likened Sean's blows to that of a grizzly bear.

"There's nothin' smaller than a grown elephant that wouldn't o' fallen dead from such mighty blows," one older worker repeated for weeks to come.

An ambulance was summoned and the hapless farmer was whisked away to the hospital. Miraculously, he survived his wounds. But it took over two hundred stitches to repair his ravaged abdomen, and massive doses of antibiotics to ward off infection. When interviewed by the regional media the attending surgeon said that it was the farmer's fat that saved him.

"I don't think a leaner man could o' survived a gorin' like he took," the doctor stated.

Of course the same media carried a full account of how Sean had saved the man's life. Images of Sean cropped up in papers and television throughout Ireland and England. People far and wide marveled at the mighty arm that had dropped a 2000-pound bull with a pair of punches. Overnight Sean became famous. It was a fame that in time would prove to shape his future.

Chapter 11

Shamus O'Roarke was the general manager and major shareholder of the processing plant. Emma reported directly to him. When he got word of the accident in the steer slaughtering area he immediately went down to the processing floor. The farmer who had been gored was already being loaded into an ambulance. The bull still lay on the slaughter room floor, knocked cold by Sean and finished off by the stunner. The operations foreman hastened over to greet Shamus.

"That's the one that did the damage?" Shamus asked, nodding at the huge bull.

"Aye, that's him all right," the foreman confirmed. "We're not sure what to do with him. Should we hoist and butcher him, or is he evidence?"

"Go ahead and process him," Shamus directed. "I'm sure that's what the farmer would want."

The foreman shouted some orders and the bull was hauled up. The hoist groaned but didn't buckle under the unusually great weight.

"And where's young Sean? Shamus asked.

"Where's Sean," the foreman repeated, scanning the slaughter room. "Ah! There he is."

Shamus motioned for the foreman to tag along and walked over to the small group of men who were talking excitedly with Sean. They all quieted and watched nervously as Shamus and the foreman approached. When Shamus asked Sean how he was, the other men drifted away.

"Oh, I'm fine enough, sir," Sean smiled.

"No injuries?" Shamus asked, taking Sean's left wrist and feeling his enormous arm.

"No, I don't think so," Sean answered, flushing slightly.

"What's this, then?" Shamus asked, examining Sean's knuckles. They were barked and red. Evidently the skin on his left half didn't grow any thicker than that on his right side.

"Ah!   I hadn't even noticed that," Sean mumbled.   "It's nothin'."

"Go up to the medical office and have the nurse look at it," Shamus ordered. "Do you know where it is?"

"Aye, I do," Sean answered.

"Good boy," Shamus smiled, patting Sean on the shoulder. "We'll talk some more in a bit."

Shamus O'Roarke went back to his office and called a glove maker in Dublin. He asked the owner if it would be possible to make a glove that would protect a man's hand when he repeatedly punched a brick wall very hard.

"Aye, it can be done," the glove maker answered. "It's a custom job. I'd have to measure the man's hand."

"That can be arranged," Shamus said. "How long would it take to make such a glove? By the way, this is a very large hand."

"Is it now?   Well, no matter that.   Once I've gotten the measurements, I'm thinkin' maybe two or three days."

"That will be fine," Shamus answered. "I'll be in touch."

Now Shamus O'Roarke had had an entrepreneurial streak since the days of his first paper route. It was he that had initiated Wednesday afternoon tours of the plant. He personally found the slaughtering business to be immensely interesting, and expected the tours to be a big hit with the public. But, despite the fact that plenty of tourists passed through the village each year, the tours had never really caught on. To Shamus it was one of the mysteries of the ages … how a carnivorous race like the Irish and English could pass up an opportunity to see where the meat they devoured came from. In any case, Shamus thought now that he had a foolproof way to turn the situation around.

After ringing off with the glove maker, Shamus called the slaughtering floor and asked the foreman to come up to his office.

"How many steers are we processin' weekly?" he asked.

"Oh, I think we're averagin' maybe 300 a week," the foreman estimated.

"And how much do the stun gun cartridges cost us?" Shamus continued.

"Well, we order 'em from America. The last time I looked I believe they was runnin' us 96 cents apiece, American."

"And what are we payin' Sean Crabbe?" Shamus went on.

"I believe we're payin' him $150 a week, American," the foreman answered, starting to sense where the conversation was headed.

"Let me run an idea past you," Shamus mused, leaning back in his chair and lacing his fingers behind his head. "What would you say to havin' Sean stun the steers with that mighty left o' his?"

"Aye, I guessed you were thinkin' that," the foreman grinned. "I think he could do it. I don't know if he'd *want* to do it, but I'm confident he *could* do it."

"Amazin', isn't it … what transpired down there today?" Shamus murmured.

"Aye. Like nothin' I've seen in me entire life. But I'm thinkin' he might need protection to do it over and over again. You saw his knuckles."

"Already taken care of," Shamus said. "I just got off the phone with a Dublin glove maker. Protection for the skin of his hand should be no problem."

"Well, then…" the foreman grinned. "Should I feel him out on the subject?"

"No, say nothin' for now," Shamus replied. "I'll ask him meself."

After the foreman left his office, Shamus asked Emma to step in. He told her what he was thinking and that he wanted her thoughts.

"It would mean a substantial raise for the lad," Shamus added as a tickler.

Emma said that she had no objection. The decision was Sean's to make. He was a man now, making his own way.

Shamus thanked Emma and called the slaughtering room floor again.

"Send Sean up to me office," he told the foreman. Minutes later Shamus' secretary waved Sean into her boss's office.

Sean carefully opened the polished door and stepped nervously into the paneled office. Shamus rose and shook Sean's hand across his desk.

"Sit down, sit down," Shamus invited, gesturing toward a chair. After Sean had settled carefully into the overstuffed chair, Shamus continued.

"So! How d' you feel about droppin' that bull?"

"Fine enough, sir," Sean answered, shrugging uneasily.

"Think you could do it to a steer?"

"Oh, I should think so," Sean said.

"Is it somethin' you'd like to do day in and day out? Wearin' a protective glove o' course," Shamus asked.

Sean seemed to be confused.

"It'd mean a nice increase in your pay," Shamus pressed.

"D' you mean stun steers with a punch, instead o' usin' the stunner?" Sean asked.

"Aye. That's exactly what I'm thinkin'," Shamus verified. "Would you like doin' that?"

Sean shrugged again.

"Well, sure … I guess … that might be interestin'," he murmured.

"Good!" Shamus grinned. "I'll be sendin' you down to Dublin. There's a glove maker there who needs to measure your … your business hand. It'll be a fun day for you. All your expenses will be paid o' course!"

Sean nodded agreement, and Shamus picked up his phone.

"Annie," he said, "get a round trip ticket to Dublin for day after tomorrow. For young Mr. Crabbe. And we'll be givin' him fifty pounds for expenses."

Shamus rose and again extended his hand across his desk. Sean jumped up and shook the hand awkwardly.

"Annie will call you with the details," he smiled at Sean. "She'll give you the glove maker's address. You can take a cab from the train station to his shop. We'll talk again when you get back."

Sean thanked the plant manager in a slightly choked voice. Two days later Emma drove Sean to the train station. Sean was dressed up in his Sunday best.

"So you've got your ticket then," she asked for the fifth time that morning.

"Aye, right here," Sean answered good naturedly, patting his jacket pocket.

"And the expense money they gave you?"

"Aye," Sean said again.

"Well, then, I'll be off to the plant," she said, kissing Sean on the cheek. "Enjoy Dublin. And be careful."

"I will, I will that," Sean smiled.

With a thumping heart he entered the small station. This was all such an adventure! Never before had anyone outside his own family paid such attention to him. He felt important. He patted the reassuring bulge of his wallet in his pants pocket.

"Fifty quid," he thought. "I should be able to buy a fair lunch with that!"

A half hour later Sean watched the Irish countryside slide by through the window of a train bound for the great city he had heard about all his life, but had never until now had occasion to visit.

Chapter 12

Sean was bowled over by Dublin City. It was his first real trip away from the village where he was born, and certainly his first time spent in a major metropolitan area. The huge buildings, the countless restaurants, the cinemas, everything about the place enthralled him. People on the street occasionally gave him a curious glance, but mostly they seemed intent on their own business. In a small corner of his mind he began toying with the idea that one-day he might move away from the village and out into the world at large.

The glove maker greeted him warmly when he entered his shop. Sean could sense some surprise in the old man's eyes when he took off his jacket. But this lasted for only an instant and he treated Sean like anyone who came in to be measured for custom gloves. The whole business took less than half an hour and Sean had a full eight hours to burn before his train back home departed.

He treated himself to a fancy lunch and then gravitated to the so-called combat zone … an area of honkytonk bars, populated by women who hustled expensive drinks from anyone fool enough to accommodate them. After quaffing a pint of stout, trying to act like a big-city denizen as he did so, Sean was easy pickings. In three hours he had been parted with half his spending money. It finally occurred to him that he hadn't even gotten a peck on the cheek for his largesse.

Again those little warning flags went up in his mind and he went for a walk out in the fresh air. With a bit more than three hours to go, he wandered into a movie and, despite himself, nodded off for a full hour. He awoke with a start and looked at his watch. There was still plenty of time, so he took a cab back to the train station and had some fish and chips before departing.

Sean turned in the unspent expense money the next day when he returned to work at the plant. Then it was back to scrubbing the slaughter room floors. He waited for some of the other men to broach the subject of his new assignment, but none did. Evidently the whole concept was being kept under wraps.

A week after his return he was again summoned up to the plant manager's office.

"How was Dublin?" Shamus O'Roarke boomed when he entered the office.

"Very fine, sir," Sean smiled back.

"The expense money was adequate?" Shamus asked innocently. (He of course knew that Sean had turned in several pounds after his trip.)

"Oh, yes, more than enough," Sean replied.

"Well, then, let's try this on, shall we?" Shamus said, taking a large, black leather glove from a box.

Sean examined the glove. It looked somewhat like a boxing glove, but with fingers. The area over the knuckles was padded with extra layers of leather. Gingerly he slipped the fingers of his great club of a left fist into the glove, pulling and tugging on it with his right hand.

"Fit OK?" Shamus asked.

"Yes, sir, it's a very good fit," Sean answered, still making small adjustments.

"Good!" Shamus boomed. "D' you think you could stun steers with it then?"

Sean made a few punching motions in the air. His arm moved in a blur, and the air made low, roaring sounds as he did so. Shamus felt his mouth go dry.

"Aye, I think I can," Sean said, obviously fascinated at the prospect.

"All right, then. We're goin' to have you try it in private for a few days. The next plant tour isn't until Wednesday next. After that some of the public might drop by and watch you at work.. Will that be OK?"

"Not a problem with me," Sean answered.

"Jolly good! I'll tell the foreman and we'll give things a trial run tomorrow mornin'," Shamus said, moving to the office door and opening it.

"Give them proper whacks," he chuckled, patting Sean on the shoulder as he departed.

"Aye, I'll do my best," Sean answered. Shamus's secretary watched with wide eyes as Sean moved to the elevator, swinging his gloved hand through the air.

The next morning the foreman assembled all the men in the steer slaughtering area and told them what was going to be tried. He called Sean up next to himself and had Sean show everyone his new glove. The men looked at one another in silent wonder, mutely nodding their heads. To a man jack their expressions seemed to say, "If anyone can bring a steer to its knees with one blow, Sean Crabbe is that person."

And so the whole bizarre process got underway. Fourteen steers were brought in from the stockyard and placed in the row of stanchions. Their hind hocks were shackled.

"Well, are you ready?" the foreman asked Sean.

Sean pursed his lips and looked at the row of heads.

"Aye, I guess so," he said a little hesitantly. He stepped up to the first steer.

"It's goin' to die one way or another," he told himself. "What does it matter if I do the deed?"

And so Sean punched the beast between the eyes. To all there it seemed like a mighty blow. But Sean knew he had held back. The steer bellowed and lurched in the stanchion, but it didn't go down. The foreman hastened to Sean's side with a concerned look on his face.

"It's OK," Sean muttered, slightly mortified. "I didn't really let him have it."

"Are you sure, lad?" the foreman asked. "We don't have to do this, you know."

"No, no, I want to," Sean answered. "I'm just goin' to have to land him a good one."

The foreman nodded gravely, stepping back to give Sean room to operate. Sean braced his tree trunk of a left leg on the concrete floor and swung again, this time giving it his all. It was a prodigious, stunning blow and the steer flopped to its belly without a sound.

"Hoist him!" the foreman shouted, leaping forward and unlatching the stanchion.

"It looks good," he said to Sean, his face flushed with excitement. "Shall we keep it goin'? "

"Aye," Sean answered.

"All right, then. You drop 'em and I'll do the stanchions."

And so Sean began working his way down the line. Whack! went his great fist time and again. Ker-flop went the steers. Up they went, hoisted by their hind legs, and from there on it was business as usual. After Sean had dropped the last one in the row, the foreman paused and looked at him.

"Feelin' all right?" he asked, panting with excitement.

"Oh, yes, I'm feelin' fine," Sean answered calmly. "The glove works like a charm!"

"Shall we do another lot, then?" he asked.

"Absolutely!" Sean answered.

The foreman shouted to the men who brought the steers in from the stockyard.

"Bring in another fourteen, boys. We're in business!"

Over where the steer hides were stripped off the carcasses, an older worker quietly crossed himself.

"Saints preserve us," he murmured. "Never in the history of our storied race have such blows been landed."

Sean continued with his new assignment for the remainder of the week. On the second day Shamus O'Roarke slipped quietly through the slaughtering room door and watched for a few moments. The foreman, who knew he was coming down to the floor, met him at the door.

"No problems?" Shamus asked.

"None!" the foreman answered.

Shamus watched Sean drop a few steers.

"Quite a show, isn't it?" he mused at length.

The foreman nodded without smiling.

"To tell the truth, I'm *still* gettin' used to it," he answered.

"Pity the poor bloke who crosses him in a pub," Shamus grunted.

"It won't be me, I can tell you that," the foreman muttered.

"Well, stay at it," Shamus directed, vanishing back into the office areas.

Shamus wasted no time. Within the hour he was on the phone with media types. He told them there was a story of great human interest for them if they could be at the plant by 3 PM that afternoon. A few pressed him for details. But Shamus would only tell them that it involved the lad who had saved the farmer's life by dropping a great bull with two punches. It was enough for them.

At 3 PM Shamus came out of his office and greeted more than twenty reporters and camera people milling about impatiently in the reception area. He still refused to tell them what they were going to see, but asked them to mention the weekly plant tours in any articles they saw fit to print. Having done this, and in view of the number of people attending, he bypassed the elevator and led them down the stairwell, out onto the slaughtering room floor.

"Don't mind us!" he shouted to the men on the floor. "We're only here to observe!"

The timing was such that a new bunch of steers was being brought in and lined up in the stanchions. All of the reporters wondered where the story was.

"As you all may know, we have to stun the steers before hoistin' them up for butcherin'," Shamus shouted above the din. "Well, the reason I called you here today is to demonstrate a new way we have of doin' the stunnin'."

A few of the reporters guessed what was in the works and whispered to their camera people to get over by the stanchions. When the steers had been secured, Sean stepped out of the background, smiling at the assembled press corps. He raised his left arm in greeting. The huge glove on his hand was like nothing any of them had ever seen before. Flashbulbs began to pop, and floodlights on the large, shoulder-held video cameras flicked on.

With gasps bordering on disbelief the reporters watched as Sean methodically worked his way down the row. The event was carried on all the TV news networks that night. By the next morning it was in all the Irish and English newspapers. Protests over the cruelty of it were staged in London. But for the most part the public … a devoted beef-eating public … saw nothing wrong with it.

The weekly afternoon tours picked up significantly the very next Wednesday. So great was the number of curious visitors who showed up that Shamus ordered the tours to be broken up into multiple groups. He was pleased as punch at all the free publicity.

Sean, meanwhile, began getting fan mail at the plant, with a few letters even finding their way to his parents' cottage. They were all from young women, telling him in countless different ways how they'd like to meet him. The other men badgered Sean to share the letters' contents, and when there was no chance of the writer's identity being compromised, he passed them around during breaks. Some of the letters included fetching photographs, carefully posed to conceal the girls' faces.

The men hooted and howled as the letters went from hand to hand. Morale on the slaughtering floor had never been higher. Sean got several requests for interviews from London tabloids. The thought that had begun as a whisper in his mind in Dublin … the thought that one day he might find a way to make a living out in the world at large … changed from a whisper to an insistent roar. Only the details of how he would do it remained a mystery.

Part 2

Out Into The World

Chapter 13

By the time Sean was born, Manuel Liebowitz was in the fifth grade of an elementary school in Brooklyn. From his birth he had been called "Manny." His parents were Jewish immigrants from Ireland, and his father made a modest living as the proprietor of a small shoe repair shop.

Unlike many of his peers, Manny did not excel in scholastics. By the time he was attending high school it was clear that higher education was not in the cards for him. When his classmates discussed their plans for college, Manny would use his family's modest economic means as a feeble excuse for why he didn't plan to continue beyond high school. But none of the others were fooled. It was common knowledge that Manny just wasn't very bright ... at least not in mathematics and the sciences. As a result, virtually all of the Jewish girls gave him the cold shoulder. By the end of his sophomore year he had developed a healthy inferiority complex.

It was a fluke that Manny wandered into an athletic club early in the summer before his junior year. He asked the manager if there was anything he could do to help out, and the manager hired him (at sub-minimum wage) to sweep and do other odd jobs. Manny worked "off the books," which meant that none of his pay was withheld for taxes. And that was fine with him. It just meant more money in his own pocket, and he had never seen anything wrong with breaking the law (other than getting caught).

The so-called athletic club was in actuality a training facility for boxers. Manny quickly developed an affection for the place. No one there had any education beyond high school. Many of the aspiring fighters had not even graduated, and some of the foreigners were barely literate.

In his junior year Manny continued working at the club after school and on Saturdays. His father and mother were not religiously active, and no one objected to him earning a little money on the Jewish Sabbath. While his peers in high school were busy making plans to attend college, Manny wormed his way deeper into the fight world.

The one high school friendship he did cultivate in his senior year was with a Polish boy whose nickname was Rocky. The name was apt. Rocky feared nothing. He had a crushing punch, and had used it more than once on hapless young men who rubbed him the wrong way. Manny mentally toyed with how he and Rocky might have a future in the fight game.

Many of the aspiring fighters at the club were "owned" by Mafia figures. The fighters' expenses were partially or fully paid by these sponsors (depending on how promising the fighter was), and in return the Mafiosi would get all of the fighters' winnings when they went professional. How much of those winnings got channeled back to the fighters was strictly up to the sponsor.

In his senior year, Manny approached one of the more prominent sponsors. His name was Tony Skopelli. Skopelli had grown fat from years of overindulgence on rich Italian cuisine. He knew who Manny was, but acted like he'd never seen him before.

"Whadda yuh want? Do I know you? Get lost! Can't you see I'm busy watchin' dis sparrin' session?"

"I know, I know, Mr. Skopelli. But I got somebody you might wanna have a look at," Manny suggested. What Manny might have lacked in scholastic prowess he more than made up for with chutzpah.

"You got nothin'! Gedoudda here!"

"No, I do, Mr. Skopelli. Really! Why would I lie?"

Skopelli glanced sidelong at this nervy punk. He took the stub of a well-chewed cigar out of his mouth and heaved a bored sigh.

"Where is dis wonder?" he grunted.

"I can have him here tomorrow!" Manny answered excitedly. "You gotta see this kid in action, Mr. Skopelli. He can punch like a … like a …"

"Yeah, yeah," Skopelli answered. "Have Super Boy here in the ring at 4 tomorrow."

"Yes, sir, Mr. Skopelli! You won't be sorry!"

"Your boy might be," Skopelli smirked, waving Manny away.

Manny wangled a short-term locker rental and a pair of gloves, trunks and shoes from the equipment room manager. He promised all of his next week's earnings to pay for the gear. When he left the club that night his head was swimming with ideas. He was a manager! He called Rocky and told him what he'd set up. It was all news to Rocky, and Manny had to sell his friend on the idea. But eventually Rocky agreed.

The next afternoon Manny and Rocky slipped out of school early and hurried to the club.

"This is your locker, champ," Manny said expansively, once they were in the locker room. "Here, here's your key. Suit up and we'll have you do some warmin' up."

Rocky looked at Manny incredulously. Nobody but Manny could even come close to ordering him around that way. But somehow he found himself always deferring to Manny. He unlocked the locker. Inside were gloves, trunks and shoes.

"You get a towel from the equipment room for showerin', after you're done for the day," Manny said, acting like this was all old hat stuff to himself.

Rocky nodded compliantly and changed into the boxing togs.

"We won't tape your hands," Manny explained. "This is just gonna be a short sparrin' session I set up for yuh."

Manny had Rocky run in place and do some pushups. He laced Rocky into the gloves and had Rocky punch him in his open palms. Even with gloves on, Rocky could make Manny's hands tingle.

"Feel good?" Manny asked, pulling on Rocky's gloves.

"Yeah, man, they feel real good," Rocky answered. He was starting to get into the spirit of the thing. He suspected he was a natural!

The big clock on the wall clicked to 3:55.

"It's time. Let's do it!" Manny said. As they walked out of the locker room, Manny gave Rocky a pep talk. He told Rocky to just think of the pug they'd put him in with as one more high school mama's boy. Hit him hard! Take charge!

Rocky listened intently and nodded. So this was the fight game! Already he found himself dreaming about fat purses and his name in the papers.

"Well, here he is, Mr. Skopelli," Manny said as they approached fat Tony. Skopelli eyed Rocky.

"Just a kid," he thought. "But what a jaw! He looks like he can take a punch."

"Ever fought in a ring before?" Skopelli grunted at Rocky.

"No," Rocky answered, slightly mortified by his lack of experience.

"You're steppin' in with somebody's had a lotta fights. You sure you wanna do this?"

"Sure, I think so," Rocky answered, trying to sound casual.

Skopelli motioned to some men across the room, and one in his forties approached. He was dressed in sweats and boxing gloves. He looked like he weighed at least 100 pounds more than Rocky. Manny noticed that one of his ears was cauliflowered.

"Let's see what yuh got," Skopelli said in a throwaway tone. Manny helped Rocky into the ring.

"How long will they spar?" Manny asked Skopelli, feeling he should establish some sort of proprietorship.

"As long as I want," Skopelli snarled. "Now gedoudda there."

Manny stepped through the ropes and gingerly sat down a couple of seats away from Skopelli. Rocky looked down at them, uncertain of what to do. Skopelli looked up at Rocky with amused eyes.

"Ding!" he said, placing his cigar stub into his mouth.

The other fighter walked out toward the center of the ring, holding his gloves out for the customary "hand shake."

"How old're you, kid?" he asked quietly.

"Twenty … one," Rocky lied. The older man shook his head somberly.

"Well, let's see what you got. Don't hold back. Give me everything you got. You ain't gonna hurt me."

The two men backed away from each other.

Bam, Bam! The older man snapped Rocky's head back with two fast jabs.

Wham! He slammed a left hook into Rocky's jaw. The force of the blow sent Rocky back pedaling across the ring. But he didn't go down!

"I knew it … he can take a punch," Skopelli thought. He'd seen plenty of men knocked flat by a shot like that.

"See? Didn't I tell yuh, Mr. Skopelli? Can't he take a punch?" Manny yammered excitedly.

"Shaddup!" Skopelli snarled.

In the ring Rocky's face took on a set look. He wasn't used to being hit like that. In fact he had *never* been hit like that. Most sane people would have started having second thoughts after being stunned so. But Rocky seemed to be rallied by the realization that, for the first time, he had some real competition!

He came back toward the center of the ring in a crouch. The older fighter debated for an instant whether to finish him off. He was only a kid! It was a mistake.

Rocky feinted high and drove a fist deep into the older man's abdomen. With a grunt and a look of surprise the older fighter dropped his gloves slightly.

Boom, Boom, Boom! Rocky hit the older man with a crunching right, left and right to the jaw. The older fighter went down hard on his back, nearly doing a backward somersault.

"Dat's enough!" Skopelli barked.

Manny looked at him with shining eyes. Skopelli looked back, waiting for Manny to shoot his mouth off again. But Manny instinctively kept quiet.

"Be here with your boy tomorrow at 3," Skopelli said in a slightly more friendly tone. He rose to leave.

"You OK, Pete?" he called to the older fighter as an afterthought. Pete rose up on one knee and nodded. As Skopelli left by a side door, Pete smiled up at Rocky.

"You punch pretty good, kid," he grinned. Rocky noticed that one of Pete's front teeth was missing, no doubt from one of his many professional bouts.

"Thanks," Rocky answered. He reached out a gloved hand to help the older man to his feet. Pete's first impulse was to wave him off. But then he thought better of it and took hold of Rocky's forearm.

"I'm gettin' too old for this," he muttered.

Down at ringside Manny was glowing. He flashed Rocky the OK victory sigh. They were on their way! Fame and fortune awaited!

Chapter 14

The next day, at ten minutes 'til three, Manny and Rocky nervously took seats in the back of the club's sparring room. At five after 3 Skopelli waddled into the room and motioned for Manny and Rocky to join him at ringside.

"So you think you wanna be a fighter, huh?" Skopelli asked Rocky. His tone was much friendlier than it had been the day before. Rocky nodded.

"You think maybe you got the right stuff, huh?" Skopelli continued, his fat face even smiling!

"Maybe I do," Rocky retorted.

"Maybe I do, maybe I do," Skopelli mocked, still grinning. "You know somethin', kid? You might be right."

Manny wriggled in the next seat, beside himself with glee. Skopelli glanced his way. Again his face looked more friendly. It seemed to say that he'd be getting around to him after he was finished with Rocky.

"I think you should finish high school," Skopelli continued. "You'll train here every afternoon and Saturdays. Bag and rope work. No sparrin' for starters."

Rocky gulped and nodded enthusiastically.

"After high school, we see what develops," Skopelli added. "Fer now, I'll pay your locker and equipment fees. *Kapeeshi*?"

Manny's heart sank. No expense money ... at least not for now. He cleared his throat. Skopelli glanced at him again, but continued talking to Rocky.

"I'm gonna have Louis take you under his wing. He's gonna be your trainer. You do what he tells you, unnerstan?"

Rocky nodded mutely.

"Hey, Louis!" Skopelli yelled. Both boys jumped in their seats. They turned when they heard someone hurrying toward the ring.

"Louis, Rocky. Rocky, Louis," Skopelli grunted. Louis was a gaunt little man. He shook Rocky's hand, pulling Rocky to his feet in the process. Manny estimated he was in his fifties.

"Remember: Louis' word is law. I don't wanna hear no crap about you. Discipline! Discipline! Unnerstood?" Skopelli barked.

"Understood," Rocky promised.

"Let's start right now," Skopelli ordered Louis. "Get him into a locker."

"Ah-h-h, he's already into one," Manny interjected. Skopelli looked at Manny, slightly annoyed.

"I, ah, rented him locker space and gear yesterday," Manny added nervously.

"You did, huh?" Skopelli answered. "Fer how long?"

"Just for a week," Manny answered sheepishly.

"All right, use dat," Skopelli ordered Louis. Louis nodded and motioned for Rocky to follow him into the locker room.

"How much did it cost you?" Skopelli asked Manny. For a fleeting instant Manny considered inflating his expense, but thought better of it.

"Fourteen dollars," he answered.

"Here," Skopelli said, peeling off a twenty dollar bill. Manny took the bill gingerly, looking distressed at not having six dollars change. Skopelli seemed to understand. He liked that and smiled.

"Keep it! Don't worry about it!" he grunted. "Now let's talk about *you*!"

Manny listened raptly as Skopelli laid out his plans. He wanted Manny to become a talent scout. For the remainder of the year Manny would visit other clubs in New York City and in a few burgs north of the city, expenses paid. After he finished high school they'd see where he'd go from there.

Manny was obviously excited, but suggested in a very small voice that there was one small problem.

"Oh? And what's dat?" Skopelli asked.

Manny explained that it sounded like a great opportunity. But it didn't sound like he'd be continuing on with his Saturday job there at the club. He'd be losing fourteen dollars a week.

Skopelli looked at him with surprised eyes. This kid had stones! He liked that!

"Nah, nah, I thought o' dat," he retorted. "You're gettin' twenty five a week, in addition to your expenses. *Kapeeshi*?"

Manny gulped.

"Fair enough!" he answered contritely.

"OK!" Skopelli exclaimed. "Don't say any t'ing to Rocky about dis, unnerstan? Dis is between us."

"Absolutely!" Manny promised.

"OK. Here's fifty expense money." Skopelli peeled off a fifty-dollar bill and handed it to Manny. Manny looked bug-eyed at the bill. It was the first time he'd ever seen one of these, let alone hold one in his hand.

"Saturday I want you to go over to the Bronx. Dere's a club dere where some tough High School kids work out. Check 'em out. See what dey got."

"Yes, sir!" Manny exclaimed.

Skopelli looked at Manny with shrewd eyes.

"Dat fifty should more than cover your expenses. I want the change, unnerstan?"

"Right!" Manny answered in a more subdued tone.

And so Manny's career as a scout officially began. After graduating from high school he would work full time for Skopelli. For the first year he scouted in New York and New Jersey. But a year later Skopelli began to send him out of town, to Chicago, Cleveland, Los Angeles and other big cities.

Skopelli developed a certain trust in Manny ... at least as much trust as is possible for a man like him. Being Jewish, Manny could never aspire to become a made man in the Mafia, and thus he presented no threat. And, Manny had unlimited gall and seemed devoted to Skopelli.

Manny, meanwhile, was making more money than his father did. He moved out of his parents' place and rented his own apartment. At least once a month he went back to their place for dinner, wearing flashy and expensive clothes. In his third year of full time employment he bought a Cadillac and took them on day trips to upstate New York on the weekends. Manny's mother worried about him and the people he associated with. But Papa shooshed her and told her not to look a gift horse in the nose.

Manny introduced several promising young fighters to Skopelli, and some of them were taken into Skopelli's 'stable.' In his fourth year of employ he was sent to Europe for the first time. There were some clubs in Italy that Skopelli wanted him to check out. An Italian sports car was rented ahead of time for him, and he was met at Rome International Airport by one of Skopelli's colleagues. As Manny made the rounds … Rome, Naples, towns in Tuscany … he couldn't help thinking about the saps who had gone on to college from his old high school. He smilingly reveled in the thought that he wouldn't give the Jewish girls who'd shunned him the time of day now. The truth was he didn't want anything to do with Jewish women. He liked blondes … he preferred the kind of women that Jewish American Princesses never became.

In due course Manny was sent to other European countries … Germany, France, and England to name a few. When he flew into London he gravitated to a pub in Soho one evening and struck up a conversation with a limy. He mentioned that his parents had emigrated from Ireland to America. When he told the other bloke what he did for a living, the Englishman became quite amused.

"The fight game, eh?" he mused. "Well, I guess you know there's a lad in Ireland that can deck any heavyweight in the world."

"Come on! Wha' wha' wha' …" Manny grinned.

"I tell you, it's the truth!" the Englishman said soberly. When Manny pressed him for details, he filled Manny in on the legend of Sean Crabbe … how he'd dropped a 2000-pound bull and saved a man's life. Manny was fascinated and begged his drinking companion to tell him more.

"Well, as I understand it, he works in the same meat packin' plant in Ireland today," the Englishman continued. "And do you know what his job is?"

"No, what?" Manny answered, motioning to the barkeeper to set them up with another round.

"He stuns steers by punchin' 'em. By the dozen, he does! Knocks 'em to their knees with a single punch."

"Wha-a-at?   Why?" Manny pressed, wondering if this Englishman was hustling him for a drink.

"Why what?" Why does he stun 'em?"

Manny nodded.

"Well," the Englishman continued, "they're big animals! They've got to be put down … stunned … before the processin' boys have a go at them!"

Manny learned that the processing plant had tours every Wednesday afternoon. That night he placed a transatlantic call to Skopelli. He told him that there was something he needed to check out in Ireland, and that he'd return to New York Thursday afternoon. By now Skopelli had come to trust Manny's judgment and gave him the go-ahead.

Manny visited a couple of clubs in London on Monday, and on Tuesday he caught a flight to Dublin and drove to Sean's hometown in a rental car. He checked into the village inn and had the innkeeper reserve a place for him in the next day's plant tour.

That night he made friends with the inn's bartender. Manny was a personable chap when it was to his advantage, and he was adroit at winning people's confidence quickly. In time he divulged his tour plans for the next day, and probed for information about Sean Crabbe.

"Ah! Sean Crabbe!" the barman exclaimed. "Sure and everything you've heard about *him* is true! I'm surprised you didn't read about him in the Yank papers."

"To tell the truth, so am I," Manny answered.

One wall of the pub was plastered with framed pictures of people who had enjoyed the inn's hospitality. Included were several newspaper clippings.

"Here!" the bartender said, moving from behind the bar and across to the wall. "You can read about his encounter with the great bull right here. Here's where the world first learned of Sean Crabbe's mighty fist."

Manny followed the bartender to the wall and studied the yellowed newspaper clipping. At the top of the story was a picture of Sean. His massive left arm rested against the suspended, skinned carcass of the huge bull.

Manny read the article twice, stealing glances constantly at the picture of Sean. How could they not have heard about this stateside? It seemed a natural for the American tabloids, if nothing else. Maybe they'd carried the story but he, Skopelli and others had missed it.

Manny stared at the picture of Sean. The man was a freak! Manny wondered if any fighter alive could drop a 1-ton bull with one or two punches. He doubted it. He returned to the bar and continued quaffing mugs of stout until closing time. When he retired to his room his head buzzed in the familiar way. He had long since developed the habit of spending the last hours of his days on the road in one bar or another. There was nothing else he'd rather do with his evenings. And, after several drinks, he'd found that sleep came easily in the innumerable strange beds.

But tonight was an exception. Manny tossed and turned for over an hour. He couldn't tear his thoughts away from the picture of Sean Crabbe. The man's arm looked nearly as big around as his waist! At last sleep claimed Manny, but it was a sleep punctuated by disturbing dreams.

Chapter 15

Manny slept in later than usual the next morning. At 9 AM he got up, showered and shaved, and ordered the most American looking breakfast he could find on the inn's menu. He had five hours to burn before the tour at the processing plant, and after cruising by the plant he drove out into the Irish countryside.

"No wonder my old man misses this place when he's had a glass or two of Mogen David," he thought. Everything seemed rain-washed and green. There were stonewalls everywhere. In the fields, cows and sheep grazed. Here and there was a rustic sign advertising hen's eggs.

"Bet they're fresh, too," he mused. He passed through a small hamlet and stopped by a cemetery. In one corner the stones displayed Jewish stars of David. There was no one around, so he pulled over and strolled out among the graves. Some of the stones were too weathered to read.

"So much history!" he marveled. "Some of these people died in the 1600's!"

He wandered until 11:30 and then headed back to the village. Rather than return to the inn, he dropped into a small pub and had a sandwich and a mug of stout for lunch. At 1:30 he pulled into a visitor's spot at the plant and was directed to the tour assembly room.

Manny purposely maintained a low profile. He hadn't mentioned what his interest was to anyone since leaving London. At 1:50 a woman came in and gave a little spiel about the wonders of a big, modern slaughtering operation, charging the squeamish not to faint. A few people smiled, but most didn't understand that this was her one little attempt at humor. At 2 PM the tour began. Manny tagged along dutifully through all of the uninteresting stuff, and at last the guide informed them that they were going out onto the slaughtering floor.

The whole thing seemed to be timed so that a fresh batch of steers were being led in when they arrived. With clangs the stanchions closed.

"Some of you perhaps know what makes our steer slaughtering operation so unique," the tour operator shouted above the noise. She gave a brief account of how the might in Sean Crabbe's fist had been discovered on that fateful day, and how it had been determined that letting him stun the animals would be more economical than doing it the traditional way.

Everyone smiled and nodded their heads, as if believing every word. And of course everyone knew the real reason for this somewhat macabre practice was publicity, pure and simple. But, no one would have changed a thing. Without exception they had all come to see Sean Crabbe in action.

Manny recognized Sean right away. With a smile and a nod, Sean passed the group and went methodically to work. His massive arm moved in a blur, like a great piston. He was deliberately dressed in a sleeveless tunic that showed off his awesome musculature. The whole group watched in silence as animal after animal dropped. Clang! the stanchions would be thrown open, and with a whoosh the big animals would be hoisted up by their hind legs.

Afterward Sean came over to the crowd to answer questions. Manny got into the loose line of autograph seekers. When his turn came, he stepped up to Sean and fixed him with his most amiable gaze. He handed Sean his business card. Sean smiled back at him and glanced at the card. It bore Manny's name, the word "Scout," and the address of the athletic club in Brooklyn. As Sean scanned the card Manny spoke to him in a low voice.

"I'd like to talk with you sometime."

"About this?" Sean answered, flashing the card.

"Exactly," Manny said. "Interested?"

"Aye, maybe," Sean smiled. "How about over dinner?"

"Tonight?" Manny exclaimed, his face lighting up.

"Aye, that would work fine for me," Sean smiled.

"Fabulous! But my treat, OK? How about at the inn, at, say, 6:30?"

Sean nodded agreement and Manny gave him a little wave.

"See you then!" he said quietly, and stepped aside for the next person.

Once back at the inn, Manny inquired about having dinner served in his suite. That could be arranged, for a small extra charge of course. And so a table for two was set up in the 'reading' area of the 2-room suite.

Manny went down to the pub at 6:15 and seated himself where he could spot Sean when he came into the dining room. At 6:30 Sean appeared. He was dressed in a sport jacket that played down the asymmetry of his torso. Manny noticed that the cloth of his slacks was snug on the left leg, but flapped loosely on his right.

He went out into the dining area to greet Sean and asked him if he'd like to have a drink in the pub before dinner. Sean agreed and ordered an Irish Whisky on the rocks.

Manny turned on all his charm, telling Sean that his parents had actually emigrated to America from Ireland. The whisky fanned their camaraderie. Sean couldn't help but like this Yank! After a couple of drinks, Manny informed Sean that they were having dinner in his suite. For an instant Sean's eyes flickered. But he knew that he could handle any unseemly developments, should they arise.

Once they'd settled at the private table and were left alone with their dinners, Manny got down to business.

"So, Sean, have you ever thought about boxin'?" he opened.

Sean pursed his lips and nodded.

"Aye, I suppose I have once or twice."

"But you've never done any?"

"No, I can't say I have," Sean answered. "I've always … gone easy on me mates, don't you know."

"A noble course," Manny nodded gravely. "You've never used your secret weapon in anger…"

"Well … it's not so secret, is it?" Sean laughed. "But you're right, with the possible exception of that bull."

"Well, I'm gonna lay it right on the line for you, Sean. I've been at this for quite a few years now, and I'm convinced … I think that with the right trainin' you could go straight to the top of the fight game."

"Do you, now?" Sean answered, obviously intrigued. "D' yuh mean become a world champion?"

"That's exactly what I mean," Manny answered. "How much do you weigh … 210 … 220?"

"Well, the truth is I weigh 235 pounds," Sean replied.

Manny nodded that that was so much the better.

"Heavyweight," he mumbled. "Heavyweight champion of the world. Do you have any idea what kind of money…"

Manny pushed his dinner plate to the side and leaned over the table. He stared intently into Sean's eyes.

"Sean, if you want to do this thing, then I'll make you richer than you ever dreamed possible. I'm convinced it can happen."

Sean's heart quickened. He knew it! He knew this day would come!

"How would it work?" he asked. "Would I be goin' to the states?"

"Eventually. But not right away," Manny explained. "We'd get you some intensive trainin' in England, and after you're ready we'd line up some bouts in Europe. Build a reputation … a track record."

"I feel ready now," Sean exclaimed.

"In a way you are," Manny nodded. "There's no doubt that you could crumble any opponent in the first few seconds of a fight. But that isn't what we want to do."

"It isn't?" Sean probed.

"No. We want your big punch to be kept under wraps. It's gonna be our secret weapon. That means goin' several rounds with some tough boys. You've got to train. You've got to learn how to box … how to protect yourself."

"But I'll still finish with me left?"

"Yes, but you'll hold back. You'll use just enough power to end the fight. A lot of the bums you fight in the beginnin' will know the score. They'll lie down, either because we tell them to or because they don't want to be hurt bad."

"It sounds … less than honest," Sean said. Manny stared hard at Sean.

"Sean, listen to me," he said earnestly. "Nothin' in this world is honest when millions … tens of millions of dollars are at stake. I'm gonna tell you somethin'. That left of yours is like a nuclear bomb.

If you unleash it too early … if you show it to the world too early, you'll never get a title shot. That's the way things work."

Sean nodded that he understood. He pushed the puritanical corner of his mind back into the shadows. This was his chance at the big time!

"How would I live?" Sean asked.

"You mean money?" Manny clarified.

Sean nodded. Manny explained the system to him. He determined what Sean earned at the plant and said they'd double it. And, once he started fighting, there would be percentages of the gates.

Sean agreed, but told Manny he didn't want to sign anything yet.

"A handshake is good enough for me," Manny beamed. And so they shook on the new relationship. Manny said that he'd get things lined up in England and would give Sean ample time to give the people at the processing plant two weeks notice.

"Shamus O'Roarke isn't goin' to like it," Sean thought to himself. "But, that's the way of it sometimes."

Manny suggested that they return to the pub. Once seated, Sean called to the bartender.

"Two jars of Guinness, Tommy," he said, laying a five-pound note on the bar.

"Jars?" Manny remarked. "Not mugs, but jars?"

"Aye, it's jars in Ireland," Sean smiled.

By now a small group of musicians over in a corner of the pub was playing lively Irish music. An older couple took to the dance floor and moved 'round and 'round with surprising ease. Manny told Sean about his drive out into the countryside earlier in the day.

"I think I'm fallin' in love with Ireland," he remarked, lifting his jar of stout and clicking it against Sean's.

"Perhaps it's simply comin' back to you," Sean smiled. "Your folks came over from the old sod, didn't you say?"

"Aye, I did," Manny answered in a stout-induced brogue. "I am rememberin' the old times, aren't I?"

"*Erin go bragh*," Sean toasted.

"Wha … What's that? Erin go what?"

Sean laughed.

"Manny, the old memories might be there. But we're goin' to have to re-educate you on the particulars."

"The particulars…" Manny mused. "Aye, we both have a good deal to learn from each other. Erin go … faith and who might Erin be?"

Sean laughed raucously.

"You're a droll leprechaun. That's what I'm thinkin'."

Manny jumped off the barstool and did a little makeshift jig.

"Shall we have another jar on that?" he shouted, laying his own money on the bar.

Chapter 16

Manny returned to London early Thursday morning. His flight to New York didn't depart until 7 PM, so he took a cab to a large metropolitan library. By 3 PM he had made copies of a number of newspaper and tabloid articles about Sean. He'd worked right through lunch and was famished.

"I could use a huge steak and some action," he told a cabby.

"Action? You mean the ladies?" the cabby asked.

"Check," Manny confirmed. "Preferably on the way to the airport."

The cabby drove him to a large saloon that was famous for its generous meals and infamous for its shady ladies.

Manny took a seat at the bar and ordered a pint of stout and his steak. In no time an attractive blonde approached him and hustled him for a drink.

"Give her whatever she wants," he told the barkeeper. While pleased at the easy score, somehow she knew that Manny wasn't the standard pigeon who wandered into the joint.

"Ever done any housekeepin'?" he asked her.

"What … cleanin' and makin' beds and the like?" she asked, obviously intrigued at this off-the-wall approach.

"Yeah, exactly."

"Well, yes I have," she said.

"How much you make a week doin' this?" Manny asked.

The blonde looked at him suspiciously.

"Why?" she demanded.

"Because maybe I got a job for yuh," he responded.

The blonde's pretty eyes narrowed. Just what was this bloke up to?

"You're a Yank, aren't you?" she asked.

"What if I am?" Manny answered. "Would you be interested in makin' what you make here and then some, for light housekeepin' chores and takin' care of a man's needs?"

The blonde gave a little snorting laugh.

"Yours?" she smiled.

"No. A boxer in trainin'."

"Maybe," she said. "Where 'bouts?"

"It ain't set yet, but I'm thinkin' not too far from London."

"Well, sure, I guess," she said.

"Good," Manny said. Write your name and phone number down on the back of this and I'll give you a call."

Manny took out one of his business cards and handed it to her with a pen.

The blonde studied the card for a moment. She began to think that this guy was actually legit. She wrote on the back of the card and handed it back to Manny.

"OK," Manny said. "Can I buy you anything to eat?"

"No. No, thanks," she smiled. "I'll leave you to eat your steak in peace. "When d' you think I'll be hearin' from you?"

"If all goes accordin' to plan, in a week or two."

"OK! It was nice meetin' you, Manny."

Manny smiled at her. She remembered his name from the card. It was a good sign. He glanced at what she'd written on the back.

"I'll be talkin' with you, Vicki," he answered as she strolled away.

Manny's flight chased the setting sun across the Atlantic, and he called Tony Skopelli when he landed in New York.

"It's late. You must be tired," Skopelli said. "You comin' in tomorrow?"

"Oh yeah!" Manny exclaimed. "I got hot stuff to show you!"

"I got some hot stuff for you too," Skopelli said. He didn't sound like his old wise guy self.

"What's up?" Manny asked carefully.

"We lost Rocky."

Manny was stunned. In the five years since they'd graduated from high school, Rocky had racked up an undefeated record, with most bouts ending in knockouts. They hadn't seen much of each other, but Manny still felt that Rocky was one of his few real friends.

"How?" he asked weakly. "Accident … sick…"

"Acci… No, No, he ain't dead," Skopelli barked into the phone. "He left our organization."

"Left!?" Manny exclaimed. "Can he do that?"

Again Skopelli's voice lost its wise guy edge.

"Ordinarily not," he mumbled into the phone. "But Carbino hired him away from us."

Manny took a deep breath. Vito Carbino was a mafia capo, and Skopelli was a member of his organization. That much he knew.

"What're we … what're you gonna do?" he asked.

"What're we gonna do?" Skopelli yelled. "We do nothin'!"

"Yeah, I guess I understand," Manny answered. "It's just that I'm a little ignorant about…"

"A little ignorant? You're a lot ignorant," Skopelli barked. Then his voice took on a softer tone. "But dat's OK. Dere's stuff you ain't supposed to know."

"Yeah, for sure."

"When you comin' in? I got stuff tomorrow morning. Come in after lunch. Get a good night's sleep."

Manny agreed and rang off. He slept in late and had breakfast in one of the countless restaurants at street level. At 1 PM he was at the office. Skopelli came in at 2.

"Hey! Look who finally shows up!" Skopelli yelled when he saw Manny. He motioned Manny into his office.

"So, whadda yuh got?" Skopelli asked, settling behind his desk.

Manny excitedly spread the copied news articles out on Skopelli's desk. Skopelli's eyebrows arched as he scanned them.

"Mama Mia!" he finally exploded. "Dis guy's a gorilla! What … a freak?"

"Yeah," Manny agreed. "But think what he could do in the ring!"

Skopelli nodded and seemed to drift away in thought.

"Why not?" he mused at length. "Dere's no rules says he can't…"

"My thoughts exactly!" Manny exclaimed.

"Get him some trainin', some bouts in Europe…"

Skopelli laid out a strategy almost exactly like the one Manny had already worked out and presented to Sean.

"He holds back. We'll never get a title shot if Carbino finds out about dat left."

"My thoughts exactly!" Manny repeated. "Great minds think alike!"

"You tink you're great, huh?" Skopelli asked, skewering Manny with a hard stare.

"Well … no … it's just a figure of…"

Skopelli grinned at Manny.

"Well, you ain't no dope."

Manny breathed a sigh of relief. At times he actually felt affection for that fat, pockmarked face.

"OK!" Skopelli concluded. "I want you should drop everyt'ing. Dis is your sole concentration. Take the weekend and get back to England on Monday."

"Are we goin' all the way?" Manny asked.

Skopelli pursed his lips and bobbed his head.

"Why not?" he grunted. "If dis monkey has da right stuff. You t'ink he can take your old pal?"

"Who, Rocky?"

"Yeah Rocky. Why you t'ink Carbino stole him? He's gonna be heavyweight champ!"

Manny puffed his cheeks out. It made sense. By now he had no illusions about how champions … particularly heavyweight champions … won their crowns.

"You t'ink he can?" Skopelli pressed.

Manny nodded his head gravely.

"Take Rocky? Yeah, I think he can. If he unloads … really unloads, what human could stand up against him?"

Skopelli studied the picture of Sean and the skinned bull carcass.

"A one ton bull! Mama mia, I t'ink you're right," Skopelli agreed. "OK! Get ouda here! Keep me informed."

Manny took his parents for a drive out to Long Island on Saturday, and on Sunday his mother had him over for dinner. Monday morning he was back on a plane to London. He called Sean and told him that everything would be set in two week's time. Sean told him that he could be in England earlier if necessary.

"No, no, two weeks will be good," Manny spoke into the phone. "I got lots to do. I want to find a private place for you to train.

Remember: secrecy. Don't even tell people you're getting' into the fight game."

"I, ah, I already mentioned it to my parents."

Manny blinked into the phone. This kid was so honest!

"Have they told anybody else?"

"No, I don't think so," Sean answered.

"Good! Ask your folks to keep a lid on it. No harm done. You know where to find me, right?"

Sean said that he did, and they rang off with Manny promising to wire $500 expense money.

Manny wasted no time. After some nosing around he rented a small, vacant farm about 30 miles southwest of London. He had the open area of the barn converted into a training gym. All the furniture in the farmhouse was stored in a shed, and new, cushy stuff was brought in. A freezer was moved into the kitchen and stocked with thick steaks. A cook was hired, and he called Vicki and told her the housekeeping job was hers if she wanted it. He invited her to lunch and showed her pictures of Sean.

"I read about this guy!" she exclaimed.

"Yeah, I thought you might have," Manny said. "But listen, the fact that he's goin' into trainin' to fight is top secret, you understand? You keep your mouth shut!"

"Absolutely," Vicki agreed.

"I think you might be his first ... romance," Manny added. "You think you can handle that?"

Vicki smiled. So she'd be his first? Well, she'd be sure he never forgot her!

"Oh, I think I can," she smiled, looking again at the photos of Sean. "My, he's a handsome one, ain't he?"

"OK! You got the job!" Manny grinned. "Three hundred quid a week. Agreed?"

"Done!" the young woman smiled.

Chapter 17

Sean arrived in London on schedule, two weeks after getting Manny's phone call. He had used only a fraction of the $500 expense money that Manny had wired to him, and offered the rest back to Manny when he arrived. Manny looked at him with amused eyes.

"No, no, that's yours! All of it," Manny reassured him. "Use it any way you like."

The two of them made a night of it in the city and the next morning they drove out to the rented farm (newly transformed to a training facility). Manny had retained the services of one Bruno Schuster to be Sean's trainer. Sean got the same pep talk, in somewhat gentler terms, as Rocky had gotten from Skopelli. "Bruno was boss," and so on. Sean nodded that he understood.

After getting a tour of the barn-turned-gym, Sean was introduced to the two women who made up the household staff. Mrs. Gruber, a plump and red-cheeked middle aged woman, was the cook. Sean guessed that her accent was German. Manny was the soul of innocence when he introduced Sean to Vicki. Vicki beamed and made a convincing show of being totally blind to Sean's deformity.

Sean's bedroom was the biggest one in the house, and it had its own private bath. The sheets on the bed were dark blue, and there was room for a comfortable recliner, a desk and several lamps. All in all it was perfect bachelor's quarters

"Colors and everything OK?" Manny asked him.

"Aye, very nice," Sean chuckled a little awkwardly.

That night he found the queen-size bed to be firm but comfortable. It was summertime and he slept like a log with the bedroom window open. The only sounds out in the country were night bugs singing to each other.

In the days that followed, Bruno proved to be a stern taskmaster. Sean really knew nothing about boxing, and he had to start with the fundamentals of defending himself. The sparring partner Manny had retained to work with him was an old pro named Pat. He drove out to the camp on an as-needed basis. It didn't take him long to convince Sean of the importance of a good defense. By the end of the first week Sean had gotten a taste of what it felt like to have another heavyweight land some clean shots to his head. It was different from the punch on the nose that the bully, Michael Lister, had given him when he was a kid. Even with protective headgear on, he found Pat's punches to be real wake-up calls. And he knew that Pat was not even coming close to unloading on him.

Manny stayed around for the first couple of days, but then left to take care of other matters. He promised to be back within a week. From the start, Mrs. Gruber had fixed three square meals a day, with lots of meat and potatoes.

"Take care of this guy. Make sure he gets enough to eat," Manny grinned at her on the morning he left to return to London. Sean was still at the breakfast table, shoveling in fuel for another strenuous day.

"Oh ja, ja," Mrs. Gruber answered in her singsong voice, replenishing the platter of pot-roasted beef on the breakfast table. Manny told everyone he'd be back in a few days, and started the drive into London.

"I could get used to beef for breakfast," Manny mused to himself. Man, could that old girl cook!

Sean wolfed the big meals down with gusto. He had never worked so hard in his life. In addition to boxing lessons, Bruno loaded him up with hours of work on the light and heavy bags, and at least three hours of running every day. Sean slept like a dead man at night. After only a week he could feel his young body beginning to respond and grow stronger.

Vicki was warm and friendly to him from the outset, but Sean thought it was politeness and nothing more. He had become convinced that a relationship with a person of the opposite sex was never going to happen.

After a hard first week, Sean was relieved on Saturday afternoon when Bruno told him they were knocking off for the weekend. Up until then he hadn't been sure whether or not it would be business as usual through the weekend. When he went into the house and told the women that they were through for the day, Vicki asked him if he'd like to drive into a town on the way to London and take in a movie that night. Sean was more than a little surprised, but said yes.

He still had over $200 of the expense money Manny had given him, and he asked Vicki if she'd like to have dinner with him before the show.

"I'd love to," she answered, smiling prettily. It occurred to Sean that this might upset Mrs. Gruber's plans, and he asked her if she'd prepared anything for their dinner.

"Ach, no, I haven't started anything. You young folks have a good time."

"Would you like to join us, then?" Sean asked, catching Vicki a little off guard.

Mrs. Gruber smiled impishly at Vicki, but then told Sean that she'd be leaving within the hour to spend the weekend with her sister in London.

"I wonder if Bruno is doing anything tonight," he asked himself aloud.

"I know for a fact that Bruno will also be leaving soon, to spend the weekend with his family."

"Well, it looks like just you and me," Sean grinned sheepishly at Vicki.

"So much the better," she smiled. "When should we leave? I think the first show is at 7."

Sean suggested that they leave at 4:30, and went up to his room for a nap. By 4:15 he had showered and changed into slacks, an open collar shirt and a sports jacket. He settled down in front of the living room TV to watch the news and wait for his date.

When he heard her heels clicking down the farmhouse stairs he rose to greet her. He gasped when she walked into the living room. She literally took his breath away. Her blonde hair was swept up in a very attractive way, and it was the first time he had seen her in makeup. She wore a very flattering mini-dress, and a black ribbon was wrapped around her slender neck and held in place by a small rhinestone clasp.

"You ... you look g-g-great," he stammered, feeling his face flush hot.

"Why thank you, Sean. You look nice too," she smiled. "Shall we go?" Sean could only nod stupidly. The plain truth was that she was beautiful. She slipped her arm into his as they walked out the door.

When they got into the car she slid across the seat and snuggled up against him. During the short drive to town she chattered, and Sean strove mightily to think of intelligent responses.

"Oh, look at the ruins," or "Look at the rose garden," she'd exclaim, leaning forward to look across in front of his face. Every time she did so, her soft and fragrant hair brushed his cheek. It made his head swim!

When they walked into a seafood restaurant for dinner, she took Sean's left arm and felt the mammoth muscles through his jacket.

"O-o-o," she cooed approvingly, "you make a girl feel so safe."

Dinner was the best time Sean had ever had in his life. He and Vicki shared a bottle of wine, and his tongue finally loosened up. Vicki laughed at all of his attempts at humor. After dinner, in the movie theater, she put her hand in his and laid her head on his shoulder. By the time they were driving back to the farmhouse, Sean was hopelessly in love.

In the living room Vicki kissed him on the cheek.

"Well, goodnight, then," she smiled. "It was a lovely evenin'."

"Yes, it was," he mumbled thickly. It was all he could do to restrain from begging her not to retire … to spend more time with him. But, she turned and headed for the bedroom. His whole body ached as he watched her shapely form walk out of the room.

Sean sighed and debated whether or not to watch some TV. He decided that that would be anticlimactic to the most fabulous evening of his life. Morosely he climbed the stairs, hung his clothes in the closet and crawled into bed. Despite the wine he'd had with dinner, and despite the morning's rigorous workout, he suspected that sleep was not going to come easily that night.

Outside a full moon hung in the sky, visible through his bedroom's open window. His whole body seemed to be tense and awash with strange, new feelings. He resolved to ask Vicki out again next Saturday night. And what about tomorrow? Everybody was gone but the two of them! What should they do?

Sean's fears about a sleepless night turned out to be unfounded. His young body, vigorously stressed to the limit all that week, quickly surrendered to sleep. Sometime after midnight he awoke with a start. Something had shaken his bed. He rolled over in time to see Vicki slipping in beside him in the moonlight.

"Hi!" he whispered, wondering if he was dreaming.

"D' you mind?" she whispered back. "There's just the two of us…"

Sean rose on his left elbow and pulled her in next to himself. She lifted her face in the moonlight and he kissed her tenderly on the mouth. It was, in fact, the first time he'd ever kissed a girl. His head reeled and his young body quivered. Vicki ran her fingers through his hair and pulled his body against hers more tightly.

The house was silent except for their breathing. Outside, down by the farm's pond, peeper frogs lofted their nighttime songs of love onto the summer wind. With her soft hand Vicki explored Sean's left shoulder and mighty arm. Her eyes shone with obvious admiration. Softly the bedroom curtains rose and fell … rose and fell in the evening breeze.

Chapter 18

Manny returned when everyone was gathered around the kitchen table enjoying supper.

"How's it goin'?" he grinned, shaking Sean's hand vigorously while shrewdly studying his face. He thought he detected a subtle change there … a certain guardedness.

"Well, well," Manny thought to himself, "a boy when I left, a man when I return."

"Vicki!" he greeted with a little wave. His eyebrows arched questioningly when he glanced at her. Almost imperceptibly, she gave a little nod and returned his greeting.

Manny joined the others for dinner. Sean told him that he was feeling great, but that Bruno was working him hard hard hard.

"Is he learnin' anything?" Manny asked Bruno.

"Oh yeah, he's doin' good," Bruno smiled. Later, in private, Manny asked Bruno how long he estimated it would be before Sean was ready for his first professional fight.

"I take it you got plans for him … some real fights," Bruno probed.

"Yeah, you could say that," Manny answered.

"Well then, I think 11 … 12 more weeks. He's plenty strong but he needs lots more coachin' and sparrin' practice."

"That's what I thought too," Manny agreed.

Later Manny sought the team members out individually and handed them their pay envelopes. He caught up with Vicki in the laundry room and decided to verbally verify his initial impression.

"Well?" he asked.

"You were right," she answered in a voice that was all business. "I'm his first."

Manny smiled and pressed an extra 50-pound note into her hand.

"Thanks!" she smiled back.

"You know, in half a year or so we'll be takin' him to the states. You're gonna have to end things when that happens. You think there's gonna be any problem?"

"Maybe," Vicki answered. "But not a big one."

"How you gonna cut him loose when the time comes?" Manny pressed.

Vicki thought about it.

"Probably tell him I've got involved with someone else," she murmured. "That usually does it."

Manny pursed his lips and nodded soberly.

"OK! Good work!" He gave her a pat on the shoulder and left to find Mrs. Gruber.

Sean seemed embarrassed to take the pay that Manny handed to him.

"I don't feel like I've done anything to earn this," he muttered.

"But you have, you have!" Manny rejoined. "You have to realize that you're an *investment* for us. We're gonna make a lotta money off you! *You're* gonna make a lotta money off you!"

Sean nodded, smiling weakly.

"Siddown. I wanna run somethin' by you," Manny said.

"You know," he began, "when I was a kid my father took us on a summer vacation once down to the seashore in North Carolina. We had a nice little cabin right on a harbor where shrimp boats used to come in. Anyway, when the tide was out there used to be millions of these little crabs runnin' around. They came out o' holes in the sand when the tide ran out. You got those little suckers here in England?"

"I think we might," Sean answered.

"Well, you know what they're … no, wait a minute. Lemme describe them first. The thing about these little crabs … about the male ones anyway … is that one of their claws is really huge. I'd bet it's a third of their body weight."

Sean nodded, guessing where Manny was headed.

"I don't know … maybe they use those big claws to plug up their holes when the tide's in. But nah, I don't think the females have them. So I think the males must use them … the big claws … for fightin'. Anyway, you know what they call them?"

"Fiddler crabs," Sean replied.

"Right!" Manny exclaimed. "You've heard about 'em!"

Sean nodded.

"Well, I was thinkin'," Manny continued. "It ain't a bad idea for a boxer to have some sorta ring name … 'Killer,' 'The Jersey Mauler,' like that, you know?"

"Fiddler Crabbe," Sean mused.

"Bingo!" Manny cried. "Whadda yuh think?"

Sean nodded.

"I like it," he murmured. "It's clever. We'd use the proper spellin' o' me last name?"

"Absolutely!" Manny confirmed. "Just imagine the ring announcer. 'And in this corner, from County Louth in Ireland, Fiddler Cra-a-a-be!"

Sean giggled. He pictured his image on posters with the name "Fiddler Crabbe" beneath it.

"OK! We go with that, then," Manny said. And thus was Sean's ring name born.

Manny made himself scarcer during the remainder of Sean's training period. But he talked with each member of the team at least once a week by phone. When he couldn't be there in person, he mailed them their paychecks.

Vicki joined Sean in his bedroom every Saturday night after the others had left for the weekend. She and Sean spent virtually all of their weekends together. Sean had more money than he knew what to do with and they took some trips, spending Saturday nights in hotels and country inns. Sean tried tapping on her own bedroom door one week night. She opened the door but stopped him from coming into her room with an upraised hand.

"No?" he whispered in a puzzled voice.

"Not durin' the week. You need your strength!" she whispered, giving him a little peck on the cheek. "And anyway, I like your room better. It's got that fine, queen-sized bed."

"*Fit* for a queen," he whispered.

"Cheek!" she smiled, closing the door. With a sigh Sean padded down the hall to his own room. It turned out that she was right. He was dead to the world three minutes after his head hit the pillow.

It seemed that Bruno never let up during the week. After the third week Sean began to feel that he was actually earning the money Manny handed or mailed to him. He could feel himself growing stronger, especially in his right side.

Manny instructed Bruno to experiment with Sean's left.

"We don't want him killin' anybody," he remarked. "But we want him to K.O. just about everybody. You know what I'm sayin'?"

"I do," Bruno replied. "And Pat's been around long enough to know a knockout punch when he feels one."

And so Sean was schooled in how hard to use his left, which of course boiled down to how much he should hold back with his left. Every now and then he would unload one on Pat, always on his shoulder so as not to hurt him. On such occasions the blow would knock Pat off his feet and drive him across the ring. Pat would good naturedly get up, rubbing his right shoulder.

"Good one," he'd grunt with a smile.

Bruno related the first such incident to Manny.

"I tell you, I never seen anything like it," he marveled. "One heavyweight knockin' another down with a shoulder punch."

Manny nodded soberly.

"You know he once dropped a one-ton bull with two shots," Manny reminisced.

"Oh yeah, it was in all the papers," Bruno said. "And after that he was droppin' 30 … 40 steers a day, wasn't he?"

"That he was," Manny answered. "I watched him in action one day. That was the day I first met him."

"You know, if he ever really unloads on somebody's head, he's gonna kill them," Bruno mused.

"I know, I know," Manny agreed. "That's why it's important to train him how to hold back. Use enough for a convincin' knockout, but no killin' shots. At least not until we tell him. You know what I'm sayin'?"

Bruno nodded. He knew exactly what Manny was saying, and why.

"Fiddler Crabbe, undisputed heavyweight champion of the world," Bruno thought to himself. "Wow! I wonder if they're gonna take me with him to the top." Sadly that would turn out not to be the case.

<u>Part 3</u>

<u>The Fight Game</u>

Chapter 19

Sean completed his training during the ensuing weeks. Throughout it all Manny feigned total ignorance of Sean's involvement with Vicki. Eight weeks into the training period Manny informed Sean and Bruno that Sean's premiere bout had been scheduled in Wales. The main event would be a relatively small affair, and Sean's bout would be preliminary to that. But it would be a chance for Sean to experience the arena crowd and all that went with it.

Manny arranged for Rufus, the brother of the equipment room manager back at the athletic club in Brooklyn, to be flown over. Back stateside Rufus had the reputation of being one of the best cut-men in the business. Rufus and Bruno would act as Sean's seconds.

Sean and Rufus immediately hit it off. Rufus seemed to be as blind to Sean's deformity as Sean was to Rufus' dark skin. As Sean's prowess grew, Pat poured it on more and more intensely. As the end of the training period approached, Bruno told Manny that he was confident Sean would be able to protect himself in the ring.

"And of course there's no better trainin' ground than some real fights," Bruno added.

"Exactly," Manny concurred. "From here on out let's have him spar without any head protection. Tell Pat to give him some good shots. Let's see if he can take a punch, and let's give him a taste of what's in store for him."

Bruno nodded and the instructions were passed along. After a few sparring sessions without protective headgear, Sean had amply demonstrated that he could take a punch. When Pat gave him the first stiff headshot he saw stars. In instinctive retaliation he dropped

Pat with a left hook. Even holding back, it was enough to send Pat tumbling across the ring.

"Hey! Hey!" Manny shouted from ringside. "What're you tryin' to do, kill your sparrin' partner? He's givin' you a taste of what you can expect in a real fight. You don't use a punch like that 'til I tell you to, understand?"

"Sorry," Sean apologized, crossing the ring and helping Pat up. "You OK?" he asked solicitously.

"I think so," Pat answered, moving his lower jaw back and forth. Sean felt truly bad. For the first time he began to fully appreciate what power lay in his left hand.

"If I'd o' given him a steer-stunnin' shot, I'd o' killed him!" he thought to himself with a worried frown.

Manny privately instructed Vicki to stay away from Sean two weeks before the bout in Wales.

"I want him restless and mean when he climbs into that ring," he told her.

Vicki nodded that she understood The weekend before the Wales fight she told Sean that it was her time of the month and that she'd be going to London to visit her mother over the weekend. Sean accepted the red light as gentlemen have down through the ages.

Sean, Manny, Bruno and Rufus took a plane to Wales and Sean got his first taste of a pre-fight dressing room. Even though it was only a preliminary bout Manny was agitated and hyper. He babbled pep talks to Sean while Bruno wrapped Sean's hands in tape. It was contagious and Sean could feel the bloodlust rising within himself. Bruno remained silent throughout, and Rufus busied himself with towels and with Sean's robe.

Outside the arena Sean's name was listed as Fiddler Crabbe. There was no picture of him, since his bout was only a prelim. Nonetheless the poster had excited him when they arrived at the arena.

AT 7 PM there was a knock at the dressing room door and a stranger told Manny it was show time.

"OK! OK! Here we go! How you feelin'?" he asked excitedly, tugging at the boxing gloves that Bruno had laced onto Sean's hands. The left glove had been custom made to fit Sean's mammoth left fist.

"I feel good!" Sean grinned. Rufus was holding his robe up. On its back was the embroidered image of a fiddler crab, and emblazoned beneath the picture was the name Fiddler Crabbe.

"Let's do it!" Manny cried. "Remember … you box for seven rounds and drop him in the eighth."

"And if I get into trouble before then?" Sean asked.

"Don't worry, you won't," Manny cryptically replied. Sean thought he understood, but he felt slightly embarrassed and looked at Bruno and Rufus. Both men avoided eye contact. Bruno checked the tape around the top of his gloves and Rufus adjusted the collar of his robe.

Sean expected the crowd to roar when they entered the arena. But he was disappointed. For the most part the four in his group were ignored as they made their way to the ring. In fact people were still filing in, and the arena was only half full.

Manny sensed Sean's disappointment.

"Relax!" he admonished. "This is only a prelim. Your day will come. First you gotta show the world who you are."

The four men climbed up into the ring. The crowd audibly quieted when Rufus helped Sean out of his robe. Few if any had ever seen a physique quite like Sean's. He did the usual shadow boxing warm up in his corner, and people stared bug-eyed at his massive left arm and fist.

The ring announcer did his thing and the bell rang. Sean advanced as a southpaw, leading with his right. The other fighter was a good boxer and Sean began to enjoy himself. It was refreshing to be up against someone who wasn't wearing protective headgear.

The other fighter was considerably more experienced than Sean, and tied him up regularly. When the referee told them to break, Sean would push him away with his left hand. The force he exerted was enough to make his opponent run backward to keep from falling over. It had an interesting effect. After a few such pushes Sean began to detect a trace of fear in his opponent's eyes. The other fighter began to circle to the right, staying away from Sean's left punches.

Occasionally Sean would throw a left, always being careful to land it on the other fighter's shoulder or upper arm. Even though he held back, the force was enough to send his opponent reeling. Twice in the first five rounds it resulted in a knockdown. The crowd had never seen anything like it … one heavyweight knocking another down with shots to his arm and shoulder. They began to become rowdy. By round six a big, blue bruise began to emerge on his opponent's right upper arm.

In round seven the other fighter came on strong toward the end. With eight seconds to go, he surprised Sean with a crunching right to the forehead. Sean dropped to the canvas, stunned. The crowd, now nearly filling the auditorium, hooted and jeered. As Sean picked himself up, ears ringing, he looked with dazed eyes out over the sea of humanity. Many of the men's faces were red, and some looked inebriated. Most were sweating almost as hard as Sean was. Female faces, intermingled with those of the men, bore looks ranging from admiration for Sean's strength to twisted cries for blood and mayhem.

Sean was not saved by the bell, although he might as well have been. His legs felt wobbly when he plopped down on the stool in his corner. Rufus' face was grave, and he wafted smelling salts under Sean's nose. They cleared his head immediately.

"You all right, lad?" Bruno asked with a worried frown.

Sean nodded and smiled weakly.

"He got to me!" he exclaimed.

"Welcome to the fight game," Bruno grinned. "Are you ready to take him out?"

"Aye," Sean nodded.

"Remember: knockout power, not killin' power!" Bruno whispered hoarsely into Sean's ear. Sean nodded as Rufus shoved a mouthpiece between his teeth. He stood up, pounding his fists together and the bell rang. The crowd was now at fever pitch. They seemed to sense that something new and major was imminent.

With the bell's gong, the other fighter ran toward Sean. Sean's knockdown had given him newfound courage. Although Sean couldn't have known it, an agreement had been reached between both camps that neither fighter would go for a knockout in the first seven rounds. Such arrangements were routine. They gave insiders an edge in pre-bout betting. Starting with round eight it would be go-for-broke, may the best man win.

Sean's opponent clearly thought the advantage was his. This kid he was up against had a dangerous left, but he himself had the greater boxing skills. He had murder in his eye as he approached Sean in a crouch.

Sean clinched with him and pushed him hard into a corner of the ring.

Wham! Sean landed a sledgehammer blow on his opponent's upper right arm. The arm didn't snap, but it was a paralyzing shot. The other fighter's right dropped helplessly.

Crunch! Sean followed with a left to his opponent's unguarded head. The other man crumbled to the canvas, out like a light. The crowd went wild. Flashbulbs went off like fireworks. The referee directed Sean to a neutral corner. He began counting. By the count of ten the other fighter hadn't moved.

Manny and Sean's seconds flooded into the ring. In seconds many strangers joined them.

"Is he all right? Is he all right?" Sean kept asking frantically. Then he saw the other fighter, on his feet but groggy.

"Thank God," Sean thought gratefully. Manny was mussing his hair and holding his right arm in the air. The ring emptied somewhat when a microphone dropped down on a long cord. The ring announcer grabbed hold of it.

"Ladies and gentlemen," he intoned in the classic ring announcer voice. "The winner by knockout in fourteen seconds of the eighth round: the bright new heavyweight from Ireland, Fiddler Cra-a-a-a-be!"

Chapter 20

The story of Sean's win in Wales was carried in the Welsh sports pages, and it received mention in several English papers as well. The gist of the news wasn't so much Sean's victory, but rather that the bull-killing steer-stunner from Ireland had put on boxing gloves and had done to a heavyweight boxer what he'd been doing to cattle.

Manny already had other preliminary bouts lined up in Hamburg, Paris and Rome. Sean won all of these by knockouts too, dutifully dropping his opponents in the rounds designated by Manny. Manny was making more money from pre-bout bets than they were getting for the bouts themselves. That was the rationale for prearranging the round that would end the fight.

With each win, Sean's fame spread. By the time Manny made a move to set up a fight in London, the promoters were clamoring to make it a main event. For it was clear to all by then that Sean would be the evening's major draw.

The gates had steadily increased with each fight, and Sean's cut correspondingly grew. As the main event in London loomed, he already had more money in three London banks than he'd ever dreamed possible.

Back stateside Tony Skopelli watched Sean's climb through the ranks with mounting excitement.

"Keep dat left under wraps," he warned Manny during one of Manny's trips back to New York.

"Oh yeah," Manny promised, "he seems to have a good feel for doin' that … for holdin' back just the right amount."

"Dose bums in Europe … dey layin' down for him or what?"

"Actually, we ain't had to play that card," Manny answered. "All we been doin' is agreein' on six, seven … maybe eight rounds, and then it's open season, best man win."

"You layin' off any personal bets?" Skopelli asked innocently.

"No, No," Manny exclaimed. "You know I never do that."

"Uh huh," Skopelli grunted. "I t'ink we get him five ... six more matches in Europe ... Get him to contender rank. Den we bring him over."

"How many fights over here, you figure, before he gets a title shot?" Manny asked.

"Maybe none," Skopelli shrugged. "Carbino might want to arrange somethin' right off."

Manny nodded, unable to conceal his excitement. In the year or so that he'd been working with Sean in Europe, Rocky, had won the heavyweight crown. Of course he did this as a member of Vito Carbino's stable, and Skopelli and his people got nothing out of it.

"We teach your punk friend, Rocky, a lesson, huh?" Skopelli grinned wickedly.

"Oh yeah," Manny nodded somberly. "If I tell our boy to do it, he'll definitely ice the Rock."

"But not kill him!" Skopelli added nervously. It was clear that, while one part of Tony wanted vengeance for Carbino's seduction of Rocky, another part of him didn't want to arouse Carbino's wrath.

"No, no way!" Manny remarked. "But it'll definitely be payback time for Rocky leavin' us, if that's what you want."

"I want," Skopelli growled, obviously relishing the prospect of Rocky getting his lights punched out.

Sean's main event in London was a sellout. Many of the old photos from his pre-boxing days were dusted off and run by the media in the weeks before the fight. Manny's very tentative feelers for any kind of pre-bout arrangement fell on deaf ears. For reasons unknown, the opposition camp was having none of it. Perhaps Sean's apparent lack of true killing power in his left, up until then, had convinced them that their boy could take him.

The night of the bout Manny was particularly hyper in the dressing room.

"What round?" Sean finally asked him.

"No round," Manny murmured. "We got no understandin'. This guy is comin' after you from the openin' bell. Understand?"

Sean, sitting on the dressing table's edge, nodded agreeably. The prospect didn't seem to alarm him. Anxiety about Sean's confidence started alarms ringing in Manny's head.

"Listen! Listen!" he urged, pulling on Sean's gloves. "This guy can hurt you! He outweighs you by thirty pounds! I think you should go for a quick knockout!"

"Is that an order?" Sean answered, looking Manny steadily in the eye. Manny felt wariness course through his body. What a difference a few professional bouts had made! Sean's innocence had disappeared. He had changed into a dangerous animal … a promoter's dream!

"Eye of the killer," Manny thought, returning Sean's gaze.

"No, not an order," he answered, slapping Sean on the shoulder. "Follow your instincts. I ain't worried. Bruno trained you good. You know how to take care of yourself. But don't get caught, OK? This is a must win, understand?"

"Aye, understood," Sean answered, punching his gloves together savagely.

When they filed into the arena Sean couldn't help contrasting the present scene with his first preliminary bout in Wales. The London arena was filled to capacity and the noise was deafening. It was blood stirring! Sean's opponent was a brute of a German heavyweight. Sean was clearly the favorite with the British crowd. The noise in the arena doubled when they entered.

"Knock his bloody block off, Fiddler," men screamed at him. Women clapped wildly. One exceptionally well endowed one jumped out of her aisle seat and rushed back toward them. A police officer headed her off, but not before she made eye contact with Sean and smiled seductively.

"Welcome to the big time," Manny shouted in Sean's ear. "I can probably get her for after the fight if you want her!"

Sean looked at Manny with amused eyes. Manny was grinning from ear to ear and sweating. He obviously reveled in moments like this.

"You want?" Manny shouted again in Sean's ear.

Sean shook his head no. Manny nodded agreeably, understanding why but revealing nothing.

Once both fighters and their handlers had entered the ring, Rufus helped Sean out of his robe. The crowd reacted more wildly than ever at Sean's extraordinary physique. When he shadowboxed and threw his left in looping hooks the crowd roared. Sean and the German met at mid-ring and the referee gave his usual instructions. When Sean held out his gloves for the customary 'shake,' the German arrogantly slapped them aside.

"Touchy, touchy," Sean smiled to himself as he returned to his corner.

It was clear from the opening bell that the German had been schooled to avoid Sean's left. He circled nimbly to Sean's right, firing savage shots at Sean's face. Some of them got through. Two minutes into the first round Sean could taste blood in his mouth. The German's eyes brightened malevolently at the sight of the cut opened in Sean's upper lip.

At round's end Rufus went to work on Sean's lip while Bruno squirted water into Sean's mouth and sponged his face.

"How we doin'?" Bruno shouted. "You know you're cut?"

"Aye, I can taste me blood," Sean answered.

"I think you better end this!" Bruno yelled into Sean's ear. "Next round this bum's gonna go to work on that cut big time."

Sean nodded. It was the first time he'd actually shed blood in the ring. The thought of his face being transformed into a lump of scar tissue horrified him.

At the bell for the second round he moved quickly past the ring's center and landed a pile-driving left hook on the German's shoulder. The crowd roared as the German staggered from the crushing force of the blow. Although it didn't seriously damage the big man, the sheer force of it was enough to strike fear in his mind. His worried eyes reflected the certain knowledge that he couldn't survive a shot like that to the head. Instinctively he raised his right hand, dropping his left. Sean sensed the opening and swung his right with everything he had. It felt wonderful not to hold back! The shot caught the German square on the tip of his jaw and the big man crumbled to the canvas. He tried to get up at the count of six, but his legs collapsed like spaghetti beneath his massive body. It was all over in Round 2!

Manny swarmed into the ring with dozens of others. He and Bruno hoisted Sean onto their shoulders. Sean grinned, spitting the mouthpiece out into Rufus' upstretched hand. He raised his right glove in victory, grinning out over the sea of screaming faces. He felt great! It was as if this was the first real fight he'd ever had … the first one he'd won legitimately! No pre-arrangements, no freak of nature stuff. He'd dropped a major European heavyweight with his right! The normal half of him was a fighter that could slug it out with the best of them!

The media throughout the United Kingdom had a field day with Sean's victory.

"Fiddler Crabbe's Right A Killer Too!" the London Times blared. Back in the states several ring magazines carried spreads on Sean's rapid ascent. The tide had definitely shifted, and Manny's job got a whole lot easier. Other camps now began contacting him, seeking bouts. It was clear that Fiddler Crabbe had become a major draw, and anyone who fought him would walk away with his share of a very handsome gate.

Back in New York, Tony Skopelli put a call through to Vito Carbino.

"Whadda yuh t'ink?" Tony asked respectfully. "We make some money?"

"Absolutely," Vito answered quietly. "Come to dinner tomorrow night at my place. Six o'clock. We discuss."

"At your restaurant?" Tony asked nervously. Carbino looked into the mouthpiece of his phone. What … this fat slob thought he was getting invited to his house?

"Yeah … at the restaurant," Vito answered in a friendly tone.

"OK!" Tony exclaimed in a voice unmistakably eager to please. "See you den, boss."

That night Tony tossed and turned in his bed. How was it going to play out? Would they have Crabbe take the crown from Rocky, and then have Rocky recapture it in a rematch? Would they make the first match a draw, and have Sean win match 2, with Rocky winning in match 3?

"Whatever makes duh most bucks," Tony mused, rolling over and punching his pillow. The money thrilled him. Finally, one of his boys was getting a title shot!

Suddenly the unsettling thought that Vito might try to steal Sean away from him, as he'd stolen Rocky, coursed through Skopelli's mind. He started to sweat. His breathing became labored.

"I swear I'll whack Vito personally if he tries dat again," Skopelli railed in his mind. "Fair is fair!"

Tony couldn't help curling his toes as he thought about what they stood to make. Twenty million easy by the time the whole thing played out! Manny did good work. This was the best fighter he'd ever brought into the stable. Tony decided that he'd have to reward his ace talent scout with a bonus. Maybe a new Lincoln. Why not? He knew where he could get a loaded one for next to nothing!

Chapter 21

At Skopelli's order, Manny scheduled six more bouts in Europe, the last to occur in Dublin. Six more wins, coupled with Sean's international acclaim, would legitimize a shot at the heavyweight crown in America. All of the bouts were booked in big European cities, and Sean's fame grew with each victory.

After the fourth bout, Manny quietly told Vicki that he wanted her to break off with Sean and to disappear.

"I don't want him nursin' a broken heart when we go to America," he told her. Vicki nodded that she understood.

"Whadda yuh think? Is he gonna be tore up?"

"I don't know," Vicki answered pensively. "I think maybe not."

Manny grinned at her impishly.

"I thought he was totally smitten by your charms."

Vicki smiled back.

"At first, I think he was," she continued. "But lately … I don't know. He might be tougher than we give him credit for."

Manny pursed his lips and nodded agreeably. The last thing he wanted was for Sean to sink into a deep funk.

"How you gonna break it off?" he asked.

"Oh, I thought maybe a letter," Vicki answered.

Manny nodded his agreement with that.

"Let's do it this Saturday morning," he told her. "Pack up and I'll drive you into London Friday night."

"Shall I slip the letter under his door or …?"

"No. We'll let Mrs. Gruber hand it to him at breakfast Saturday mornin'. I want we should all be there to lend him moral support."

And so the whole thing was done. Saturday morning Sean joined the others at the breakfast table. Just as he began to wonder where Vicki was, Mrs. Gruber quietly handed him an envelope.

"What's this?" he asked, but then noticed the writing on the envelope. 'To Sean, From Vicki.'

"Excuse me," he told the others, rising and walking over by the door. Manny candidly watched his face while he tore the envelope open and read its contents. He was relieved when Sean smiled and gave a little snort.

"Well, that's that," Sean muttered, returning to the table.

"Wha Wha What that's that?" Manny asked with innocent eyes.

Sean seemed to be lost in thought for a moment, but then handed the letter to Manny.

'Dear Sean,' it began. 'We never really got to know much about one another, and maybe I should have told you about Jack. Before meeting you, I was divorced from him. He went to Australia and returned a couple of weeks ago. We saw each other again, and the old feelings were still there. We've decided to get married again, and I'm going back to Australia with him. I'll always have fond memories of the good times you and I shared. I know you'll be a great success. My best wishes are with you always. Vicki.'

Manny carefully folded the letter and handed it back to Sean.

"Well I'll be," he murmured with sad eyes. "I didn't know ..."

Sean nodded back at him.

"I kind o' gathered," he answered. "My hunch is you're the only one who didn't."

Sean looked at Bruno and Rufus.

"Both o' you knew, didn't you?"

Bruno and Rufus both nodded gravely. Sean held the letter out to Bruno, but Bruno declined reading it with an upraised hand.

"She's gone then?" he asked.

"Aye," Sean answered, "gone for good, I'd say."

"Well then. No trainin' today," Bruno said. "Let's all take the day off!"

"What are you gonna do?" Manny asked Sean.

Sean thought about it, and at length said that he might go into London and get snookered.

"Now you talkin'!" Rufus exclaimed. "Mind if this nig ... if this African American tags along?"

"No ... no I'd like the company!" Sean smiled. "Have you seen London?"

"Man, I ain't seen squat since comin' over here," Rufus complained.

"Well then, let's get cleaned up and make a day of it!"

Sean looked at Manny and Bruno.

"Any other takers?" he asked.

Bruno shook his head.

"Son's birthday party this afternoon," he smiled. "But thanks!"

"Not me," Manny stated. "I'm flyin' back to New York this afternoon.

So Sean and Rufus drove into London. Sean showed Rufus some of the sights … Big Ben, Parliament, Buckingham Palace. By dinnertime they had landed in a large pub in the East End. Rufus was enjoying himself immensely. The attitude in England was decidedly different than in America. From the first time he had met Sean, Sean had been completely color blind to Rufus' heritage. They had been mates from the get go.

"That little gal don't seem to have hurt your feelin's much," Rufus allowed, taking a long pull on his mug of stout.

"She didn't at that," Sean answered. "Our relationship had been coolin' down of late."

Rufus nodded.

"Shoot, Irish, you gonna have your pick of the bunch once we gits to America."

"You think so?" Sean smiled.

"I knows so! And dat's a good thing. A man fightin' in the ring needs a liddle company now an' den."

Sean nodded, sparking a mischievous idea in Rufus' head. Why not get Sean set up with some pretty little thing tonight? Rufus scanned the room for prospects but saw none. He did spot a well-dressed black man at the bar. One might think that someone with Rufus' background would not be quick to prejudge, but the truth was that he immediately assumed the man at the bar was a pimp.

As soon as Sean excused himself to visit the head, Rufus ambled over to the bar.'

"How you doin'?" he asked casually. The other man looked at him a little surprised.

"Pretty good," he answered.

"Say, man, I'm from America, and I ain't too hip about dis London scene. You know what I'm sayin'? But I got dis friend who could use some female company tonight. Can you help him out?"

The other man studied Rufus with amused eyes. It was clear what Rufus thought his profession must be. He nodded back at their table.

"Your friend is Fiddler Crabbe?" he asked. Rufus gave a little start.

"Yeah, dat's it!" he exclaimed. "You know him!"

"Well, I'd wager everybody in England knows him."

"Yeah, o' course, o' course!" Rufus babbled.

"I'd like to meet him. By the way, my name is Malcolm," the stranger smiled, holding his hand out palm up. Rufus slapped the hand and grinned toothily.

"Right on!" he said. "Come on over. Dey call me Rufus."

Sean returned to the table and Rufus introduced him to Malcolm.

"Actually, my full name is Malcolm Boyd," the stranger said. "I'm a sportswriter for The Times."

Rufus, who was drinking from his mug, gave a little choke.

"Of course!" Sean smiled. "I've read your column many times."

The three men drifted comfortably into sports talk, and after a couple more stouts Sean suggested that they order some dinner.

"So, what brings you two into London?" Malcolm asked. (The location of Sean's training camp, out in the countryside, was by now common knowledge.)

"He's showin' me the sights!" Rufus exclaimed.

"Good for you!" Malcolm said. "But it's getting dark now. Did you have anything in mind for this evening? Perhaps I can be of help."

Sean grew pensive and Rufus shifted nervously in his seat.

"You know what I'd really like to do?" Sean murmured. "I'd like to visit The Fighters' Home. I've wanted to do that ever since readin' an article you wrote about it."

Malcolm beamed.

"Perfect!" he cried. "I can introduce you to some of the old boys there. I know most of them."

The three men took a cab, and on the way Malcolm mentioned that 'The Home' had fallen on hard times. Sean pressed him for details.

"It seems they've fallen behind in their mortgage payments," Malcolm sighed.

"How far behind?" Sean asked.

Malcolm rubbed his lips.

"Six months, I think," he answered. "Truth is I've been putting together another article these last few days. Scare up some contributions, don't you know?"

The cab delivered them to their destination, and Malcolm introduced Sean and Rufus to many of the retired fighters who were assembled in the home's large common room watching TV. Everyone knew who Sean was, of course, and they were all thrilled to meet him. In due course the resident manager sauntered in and was introduced. At an opportune moment Sean quietly asked the manager if they could have a word in private. The manager nodded and led Sean out into the kitchen.

Sean related what Malcolm had mentioned about the mortgage situation.

"It's true, sad to say," the manager mumbled. "Actually we're now seven months in arrears. I got the first eviction notification in Monday's post."

"How … much are your monthly payments?" Sean asked.

The manager looked at Sean cautiously but engagingly.

"Twelve hundred pounds," he answered.

Sean reached into the inside pocket of his sports jacket and took out a checkbook.

"I'd like to help out," he murmured, scribbling in the book.

The manager nodded gratefully.

"It would be greatly appreciated," he said. "Much of our help comes from fighters still active in the ring."

Sean tore the check out of the book and handed it to the manager.

"Fifteen thou …" the manager stammered, staring bug-eyed at the check. "Bless you, Fiddler. We thank you from the bottoms of our hearts!"

"Glad we could help out," Sean smiled, squeezing the other man's forearm.

They rejoined the others in the TV room and chatted some more. After a while Sean told the others that it was getting close to his bedtime and that they'd have to be going. The old fighters nodded their understanding to a man. All of them knew the rigors of training, and remembered the bliss of a good night's sleep.

Sean and Rufus took their leave of Malcolm once they were outside.

"Thanks so much," Sean said, shaking the sportswriter's hand. "That was a real treat."

"It's been my pleasure. I'm so glad you liked it," Malcolm answered.

Sean and Rufus took a cab back to where they'd parked their car, and returned to the farm.

When Malcolm arrived back at his flat, there was a request on his answering machine that he call the manager at The Fighters' Home. It was late, but he decided to chance catching the manager still awake.

In breathless tones the manager told Malcolm of Sean's contribution.

"Fifteen thousand pounds?" Malcolm repeated in disbelief.

"Believe it or not," the manager answered.

Malcolm rang off and sat down at his PC. Twenty minutes later he transferred a file to the newsroom at The London Times.

"Did I make the Sunday edition?" he asked the editor on the phone.

The editor studied Malcolm's article on his computer screen.

"Oh sure," he reassured Malcolm. "Even if you didn't, we'd hold the presses for this one. Good article!"

Malcolm thanked his boss and crawled into bed.

"What a world," he mused happily as his head sank into the pillow. The next morning the lead article on The Times sports pages carried the headline, 'A Heart As Big As His Punch.'

Back at the farm, Sean sat reading the Sunday paper.

"How do you suppose Malcolm knew?" he asked Rufus. "Did you say anything to him?"

"Did I … Irish, I ain't know 'til this minute that you do such a thing! Fifteen thousand pounds? Man, how many dollars is that?"

Sean smiled across the table.

"Who knows," he thought aloud, "someday I might end up there."

"Say what?" Rufus laughed. "No way! You gonna be the champ, man! And dis boy gone be your cut man!"

"That you are," Sean smiled over his coffee cup.

Rufus grinned hugely at his friend.

"Oh man, Irish, wait 'til you sees New York! We gonna live high!"

"First there's Madrid and Dublin," Sean reminded.

"Oh yeah," Rufus answered, his face turning serious. Then he brightened again. "But we ain't sweatin' that, is we? You the *Man*, Irish, you the ***Man***!"

Chapter 22

The London Times story about Sean's generosity went out on the wire services and was in newspapers worldwide by Monday. When Manny met with Skopelli on Monday morning, Skopelli was reading the story.

"What's wid dis guy?" Skopelli barked. "Is dis our money he's givin' away?"

Manny, who had already read the story, winced uncomfortably.

"No, it's from his earnin's," he answered. "He's had four main events so far. And as far as I know, he spends next to nothin'."

"Fifteen t'ousand pounds! It says here dat's over thirty large," Skopelli challenged. "I t'ink maybe we're payin' Mr. Manhattan Gandhi too much."

"Well," Manny answered cautiously, "we've been givin' him the standard cut. And you know, he's pullin' in record gates over in Europe."

Skopelli nodded shrewdly.

"And dis kind of publicity can't hurt," he grumbled.

"Exactly!" Manny confirmed.

"OK," Skopelli said. "So what's next?"

"Two more main events in Europe, and then we come stateside, right?"

"Right. I had a preliminary meet with Carbino. It looks like we're gonna get a title shot. Crabbe KO's Rocky in the first match, and Rocky recaptures the crown in the second."

"Wow!" Manny exclaimed. "Wow Wow Wow! Major bucks!"

"Big time major," Skopelli grinned back. "Stick around. I'm takin' you to lunch."

Manny was slightly stunned. This was a first for him!

"We get outta here at noon," Skopelli continued. "You like Italian?"

"I *love* Italian!" Manny beamed.

"OK. Scram for now. I got calls to make."

Manny retreated to his desk and tried to think of something to do. At length he began rummaging around on the Internet, looking for boxing regulations. He couldn't find anything that precluded Sean's eligibility to fight in America. The time passed quickly and he was jolted from his reverie by the sound of Skopelli's voice.

"You ready?" Skopelli barked.

Manny jumped. "Wow! Twelve o'clock already?"

Skopelli smiled and Manny followed him out to the elevator. Once down in the building's garage, Skopelli waddled over to a new Lincoln Town Car. It was a gorgeous machine. Manny thought wistfully that one-day maybe he'd be able to afford one like it.

Skopelli took a set of keys out of his pocket and handed them to Manny.

"Here," he said, "we take your car."

Manny looked at Skopelli with confused eyes.

"Your car, Dumb Dumb," Skopelli grinned, nodding at the Lincoln.

"I don't get it," Manny answered weakly, looking at the keys.

"Dis is yours … a bonus!" Skopelli said. "Press dat right button on duh remote. It unlocks the doors."

Manny stared bug-eyed at the Lincoln.

"I … I don't know what to say, Tony," he murmured.

"So you say nothin'! Let's go! I'm starvin'! You know where La Trattoria is?"

"Yeah! Yeah, I do!" Manny answered. He opened the doors and slid in behind the wheel. The seats were soft leather. The car smelled new. He started the engine. The odometer read 34 miles. The big car floated like a dream, up the garage ramp and out into the street.

"You like opera?" Skopelli asked as a formality, punching the CD button without waiting for Manny's answer.

"I love opera," Manny answered.

"You sure you ain't Italian?" Skopelli grinned.

Manny smiled back and blushed.

"I'm feelin' more and more like it," he answered humbly.

"Dat's good," Skopelli said. "You know, us Italians are very big on loyalty. And we take care of our own."

Manny nodded but couldn't think of anything to say. Skopelli began to hum along with the music. By the time they pulled up in front of La Trattoria, he was singing along in Italian.

"I shoulda took lessons," he grunted as he opened the passenger door. "People say I got a good voice."

"Oh yeah, you do!" Manny answered enthusiastically. He slid out of the driver's seat and handed the keys to a carhop.

"Brand new! Be careful, right?" he glowered at the young man.

"Yes, sir!" the carhop smiled. "She's a beauty!"

Skopelli pushed Manny ahead of him toward the restaurant's entrance. Manny walked into the elegant establishment feeling grandiose. The Maitre 'D smiled up from his lectern, obviously recognizing Skopelli.

"Right this way, gentlemen."

Tony bought the two of them the most sumptuous lunch Manny had ever had. It was 3 PM by the time they finished with a round of cordials. Manny's head was swimming from the two bottles of Chianti they'd split. Back in the garage Skopelli had Manny drive him around to his car.

"Dat's all for me for today," Skopelli said. "I need a nap." He looked at Manny.

"You look like you could use one too," he added. "I see you tomorrow."

Manny felt a rush of affection for Skopelli as he pulled his new car away. He still couldn't believe it! What should he do with his Cadillac? Sell it? His mother was having him over for dinner Wednesday night. Maybe he'd give it to his old man. Wouldn't that bowl them over though? Yeah. That's what he'd do.

Chapter 23

Now Vito Carbino had no intention of letting fat Tony Skopelli get his hands on the kind of money a couple of matches between Sean and Rocky would bring in. The truth was that, although Skopelli was part of his organization, Carbino despised him. The night he'd had Skopelli over to his restaurant for dinner, it was a stretch for him to maintain a cordial and friendly face while Skopelli wolfed down the Italian food. Skopelli, on the other hand, had been feeling as elated as Manny did at their luncheon. He took Carbino's dinner invitation as a signal that Vito wanted a more intimate relationship. It seemed obvious to him that he was moving up in the organization!

Carbino decided that the solution lay in wooing Sean away from Skopelli's camp, much as he had wooed Rocky away. However, he knew that doing that twice in a row would be politically unwise. His peers were all willing to cut one another some slack for an occasional go at larceny, but no one condoned greediness. And of course no capo wanted another one getting too much richer than himself. Money was power.

Vito decided that the best course of action would be to have his representatives approach Sean anonymously at first. If Sean were interested, then he'd work out a deal with a capo in Chicago. Technically, Sean would join the Chicago camp, but off the books Vito would retain half ownership. Everything would of course be handled discreetly, and the New York mob would be none the wiser.

Although Skopelli had been careful to conceal Sean's true power from the world, Carbino knew the facts. When a title shot had been tentatively arranged with Rocky, Vito had instructed his legal staff to do a full background check on Sean. After reading their report, he had no doubt that Sean could take any heavyweight out with one devastating punch. Indeed in his own mind he decided that, once Sean had been wooed away from Skopelli, Rocky would not win the title back in the rematch. Rocky was only one heavyweight champ among many. But Sean had worldwide appeal.

Rocky would never approach the earning potential of Fiddler Crabbe.

Vito arranged for a threesome of his most diplomatic legal people to travel to Madrid for Sean's scheduled bout. They were all astute and polished men.

"Remember … a fishing expedition only," he instructed them in his conference room. "Strictly anonymous for openers. If he's interested, we seal the deal in Dublin."

Everyone nodded that he understood.

While Carbino was busy with these machinations, Manny flew back to England and shared the possibility of a heavyweight title shot with Sean and the rest of the team. He felt it was important to motivate them. After all, everything hinged on Sean winning the bouts in Madrid and Dublin. And Manny wanted no slip-ups at this stage of the game.

The strategy seemed to work. Bruno became even more focused on polishing Sean's skills, and Sean trained like there was no tomorrow. Manny had offered Mrs. Gruber a generous increase in salary if she could save him the trouble of hiring another housekeeper. She gladly accepted. Indeed the extra work was, in her mind, more than offset by getting that other female out of the house.

The Madrid bout was scheduled for November. Manny, Sean, Bruno and Rufus flew to Spain a week before the fight. By now Sean rated a private suite in one of Madrid's best hotels. Three days before the fight Manny called a halt to all training and took Sean down to the Costa Brava for some rest and relaxation. He wanted to keep close tabs on his boy, steering him clear of booze and females and making sure that he ate well. They returned to Madrid the afternoon before the bout.

After dinner, Manny personally escorted Sean back to his suite.

"Get a good night's sleep," he smiled. "Two more wins and we fly to New York."

Sean assured him that he'd turn in after winding down watching an English language movie. At 7:30 he was roused by a knock on the door. Three well-dressed men greeted him from the hallway.

"Good evening, Mr. Crabbe. We wondered if we might speak with you for a few minutes."

"What about?" Sean asked, wondering if these three were from the media or what.

"Frankly, about money," the spokesman answered. "About how to maximize your earnings in the next few years."

"Well … OK, come in then," Sean invited. He was skeptical and not particularly money-oriented, but he figured it couldn't hurt to listen to their pitch.

"I should probably ask my manager to join us," he said, motioning for them to take seats.

"Ah-h-h, we'd like to talk with you alone for a few moments if you don't mind," one of the others suggested.

Sean shrugged and told them to go ahead. Within minutes it became clear to him what their agenda was.

"You mean bail out on Manny?" he asked. All three lawyers sensed Sean's loyalty and began to backwater immediately.

"Not necessarily," one of them said. "I'm sure our … clients would be happy to have someone with Mr. Liebowitz's abilities also join their organization."

"Just who do you represent?" Sean queried.

"Well, we'd like you to think about this privately for a while, and talk with you again before getting into details," another one answered. "Of course you have to do what you feel is best. But we recommend that you not discuss anything with Mr. Liebowitz, or with anyone else, until we have an opportunity to talk again. If it's convenient for you, we'd like to get back to you in two weeks. If you want to look into this further after we talk again, then we'll be more than happy to get Mr. Liebowitz involved. Is that agreeable with you?"

Sean nodded.

"Aye, I suppose it is," he murmured. "Roughly speakin', how much better d' you estimate we'd do in your organization?"

"Roughly speaking, we estimate your share of future gates would be double what you'll get in your present arrangement."

Sean pursed his lips and nodded appreciatively. He had never met anyone in Manny's organization, and didn't feel any loyalties beyond those for Manny. If Manny came along as part of the deal, and also realized a lot more money, where was the harm?

"I'll give it some thought," Sean promised, rising to signal the end of their conversation. "I have to be turning in. Big day tomorrow."

"Oh, yes, we'll be watching!" the men agreed, smiling and shaking Sean's hand.

"Let's see," one of them continued. "You'll be back training outside of London in a couple of weeks. How would you like us to contact you?"

"Ah! I have a private line in me room there," Sean exclaimed. He jotted the number down on a piece of hotel stationery and handed it to the men. "You can reach me there weeknights after 7 PM."

The three men told Sean what an honor it was to have met him and took their leave. After they left, Sean decided to forego the rest of the movie, and turned out the suite's lights. He settled into an easy chair with a view of the city. The suite was on the hotel's fourteenth floor, and the lights of nighttime Madrid stretched out to the horizon. Sean sighed happily. Madrid, or any city on earth, could be his place of retirement. In a few months he'd be a millionaire. He resolved that he wouldn't let the money slip through his fingers like so many chumps had done down through the years. He'd get some expert financial advice. Maybe the three from this evening would be able to steer him toward a good firm. They were obviously successful in their fields.

"Should I tell Manny?" he mused. He decided that he wouldn't, at least not right away. Best, perhaps, to wait and see what the strangers had to say next. But then he'd insist that Manny be included.

His thoughts drifted back over the past three days. The south of Spain was truly beautiful out on the coast. Maybe he should think about retiring there on the Costa Brava. Or why not a villa here in Madrid, and another one there? He'd be able to afford it.

Did a pair of Spanish eyes lie in his future? Would this turn out to be *his* island? With a sigh he rose and got a soft drink from the wet bar's refrigerator. Ordinarily there would also have been wine and beer, and several bottles of liquor on the shelf behind the bar. But he knew that Manny had had all but the soft drinks removed.

"No strong drink for you tonight, Fiddler," he chuckled. And of course no feminine company. He personally thought that the age old fight world axiom ... that a woman robs a fighter of his aggressiveness and weakens his legs ... was the purest form of malarkey. But, Manny was calling the shots. There'd be time aplenty for partying after he gained the crown.

Chapter 24

Sean's bout in Madrid took a bizarre turn. His opponent was a big, swarthy Spaniard with hair like a poodle's. It had been prearranged that he and Sean would go six rounds, and starting with the seventh it would be best man win.

For some reason the big Spaniard began to tie Sean up constantly from the opening bell. By the end of Round 4 Sean could hear the crowd booing. Partly because of that, and partly because he wanted to box, Sean decided more aggressively to break out of the incessant clinches without waiting for the referee to intervene.

At the start of Round 5 the other man tied Sean up with Sean's left arm pinned between them. Sean swept his arm out, away from his body, thinking to push the other fighter away. But somehow the Spaniard ended up hanging onto Sean's outstretched arm, completely out of contact with the mat. When Sean looked into his eyes they were wild with terror and disbelief.

Sean literally waved his massive arm up and down in an attempt to shake the other man loose. This man weighed 223 pounds, and Sean was shaking him up and down like he was a rag doll! The crowd audibly grew silent with wonder.

"Diablo!" the Spaniard yelled, and bit Sean's massive forearm. Sean could scarcely believe it. He gave his arm a mighty swing toward the ring's center, and the Spaniard lost his grip. He sailed through the air, completely upside down. The small of his back hit the top rope and he flipped over it. For a moment his feet caught on the ring apron outside of the ropes, but then he pitched forward and crashed into the photographers and spectators at ringside.

The referee ran to the ropes and stared at the tangle of bodies. Then he seemed to regain his composure and began to count. Technically it was a knockdown.

Down on the arena floor the big Spaniard's handlers pulled him to his feet and pushed him toward the ring apron, screaming in Spanish.

"No mas, No mas!" he screamed back at them, pushing them off and staring bug-eyed up at Sean. He was counted out and Sean won the match by TKO.

Back in the dressing room everyone was howling with laughter as Rufus applied ointment to the bite marks on Sean's forearm.

"You had that crazy Spaniard scared nine ways inside out!" Manny roared.

"Did you see the poor devil's eyes?" Bruno laughed.

"Dat boy didn't want nothin' more to do wid duh Fiddler," Rufus yelled.

Sean laughed so hard that tears squeezed out of his eyes.

"I'm not gonna get AIDS, am I?" he asked Rufus. Rufus' eyes lost some of their merriment and he bent over and looked closely at Sean's forearm.

"Nah, I think you gonna be OK," he said. "He give you a good nip, but he not break the skin."

The next day one of Spain's leading matadors dispatched a particularly aggressive bull. When he was awarded one of the dead bull's ears, he held it up to the crowd and then bit it.

"Ole! Ole!" the crowd chanted hysterically, rocked with waves of laughter.

Sean and the rest of the team returned to England and, after a few days of rest, got back into the routine of training.

"One more to go, back on the old sod," Manny grinned at breakfast. "Will any of your old crowd be there do yuh think?"

"Aye," Sean answered. "I know for a fact that me Da' and a few of his friends will be there."

"Maybe after the fight, you take a few days and visit back home before we leave for the states," Manny suggested.

"Good idea," Sean agreed, buttering one of Mrs. Gruber's incomparable cheese biscuits.

Two weeks after the Madrid fight Sean made a point of returning to his room every evening by 6:30. But his phone never rang. After ten nights with no call from the three strangers, he wondered whether he should tell Manny about the strange visit in Madrid. Sheepishly he realized that he hadn't even gotten the men's names. And, Manny would probably be peeved and want to know why he hadn't been filled in from the start.

"Best to say nothing," Sean thought to himself. Evidently they, or the organization they represented, had changed their minds. Sean wasn't unduly upset. He was still going to earn a ton of money.

Back in New York, Vito Carbino had indeed rethought his strategy after listening to his three lawyers.

"We don't think he's going to make any change unless his manager, Liebowitz, is included in the deal," they told Vito.

But by then Vito had heard about the hot car that Skopelli had given to Manny. His instincts told him that Manny wouldn't consider jumping ship, particularly since it would mean a move to Chicago. And in any case no capo in Chicago would trust Liebowitz.

"OK," Vito said. "No further action on this. I'll figure out something else."

Vito slept on it for a couple of nights. The existing plan … to have Crabbe win the crown and then to lose it back to Rocky … would be a big money maker, no doubt about that. But could he trust Skopelli to keep his end of the bargain? And did he want him getting his hands on that kind of money? He rightly sensed how his theft of Rocky had stung Tony. After they had the championship, what was to prevent Fiddler from punching Rocky's lights out in the rematch, and go on from there to rake in hundreds of millions?

Vito knew that the public's image of the mafia, as a monolithic and disciplined army, was a myth. At best the mob was a network of warlords, with money largely determining its hierarchy. The more money a boss or capo had, the more soldiers he could afford to retain on his payroll. He knew how quickly Skopelli's allegiance could evaporate if he got his hands on some really big money.

On the Friday following the weekend in Madrid, Vito summoned Rocky to his office.

"How you doin', Champ?" he greeted. "You gettin' everything you need?"

"Oh yeah!" Rocky grinned. "Life's never been better!"

Vito told Rocky about the tentative arrangement with Fiddler Crabbe's people. He noted Rocky's dismay at the prospect of lying down for another fighter, even though he'd recapture the crown a few months later.

"You don't like that, do you?" Vito asked.

"Well … " Rocky shrugged morosely. By now he had no illusions about how the fight racket worked. "Frankly, no. But if that's how it's gotta be."

"But it isn't," Vito said quietly.

"No?"

"Uh uh. I don't trust them to play it straight on the rematch."

Rocky shook his head up and down vigorously, obviously relieved.

"So how do we really play it?" he asked.

"You think you can take him?" Vito answered.

Rocky nodded.

"His head ain't no different from anybody else's," he said. "If I get in a clean shot … scramble him … I can definitely take him out for the count."

"I don't care if you take him out for good," Vito said. "I want his boxin' career to end permanent in that first match."

Rocky nodded soberly. He had often thought that he could disable another fighter, if not actually kill him, under the right circumstances.

"They expect it to go ten rounds, and then for you to lie down in the eleventh," Vito continued. "Crabbe won't be expectin' anything before then. I think you should ice him in the ninth."

"It's done!" Rocky nodded. "If he's not expectin' anything, I'll nail him, no sweat. The power in his left ain't even gonna be a factor. If I don't kill him, he'll be sellin' pencils for the rest of his life."

Chapter 25

In the time remaining before the bout in Dublin, Sean mailed four tickets and dressing room passes to his father. He also reserved two double rooms, for Lester and his friends, in the same Dublin hotel that Manny had booked him and the other team members into.

One week before the fight, Manny told Rufus and Bruno that he'd like a private word with Sean. Rufus and Bruno beat a hasty retreat from the breakfast table, and Manny freshened Sean's cup of coffee.

"Whadda you know about this guy Smythe?" Manny asked.

Sean arched his eyebrows.

"Well, I know he's English and he's tough. And I know he's a contender."

"More than that. Did you know that the winner in Dublin gets the next title shot at Rocky?"

"No … no, I didn't know that," Sean answered.

"Well, I just found it out myself," Manny continued. "So you see what the stakes are. And we got no deal with his camp … nothin'! It's gonna be best man win from the openin' bell."

"Aye, a crack at the crown does up the ante, doesn't it?"

"Big time!" Manny muttered. "And lemme tell you somethin'. They don't call this guy 'The Compactor' for nothin'!"

"What's his record?" Sean asked.

"Thirty two main events. Twenty-seven knockouts. No losses."

Sean was silent. He didn't look scared. But Manny was relieved to note that he didn't look cocky either.

"We're takin' the wraps off o' your left," he said in a low voice. "Assumin' we win Dublin, the fight with Rocky is already a done deal, so we don't need to hide anything from here on in."

Sean's face relaxed visibly.

"So I can unload on him if I have to," he mused.

"You *will* have to. *Count* on it!" Manny snapped. "I want you to take him out in the first round, understand?"

"Aye," Sean nodded. "The first round it is."

The team traveled to Dublin two mornings before the fight. On arriving at the hotel, Sean found that his father's group had already checked in and were all waiting for him down in the hotel pub. Sean unpacked and went down to join them.

Lester and the three other men greeted Sean raucously. They had already been quaffing stouts for about two hours and were in high spirits. Everyone nodded understandingly when Sean declined Lester's offer to buy him a pint, and ordered iced tea instead.

"No Irish sorrow until after the fight, right?" one of them teased.

"Aye," Sean smiled. "But I promise we'll lift some jars back home after the bout."

"You're comin' home then?" another asked.

"Didn't I tell yuh?" Lester interjected. "Seanie's gonna spend some time with us before leavin' for America!"

"Jolly good," the other men chorused, promising to do some proper partying back home.

By 6 PM everyone was hungry. Sean ordered the biggest steak on the pub's menu, medium rare. When he offered to pick up the tab after the meal the others would have none of it. To a man they insisted on buying him dinner.

All of them were twenty or more years older than Sean, and by 8 PM it was clear they were running out of steam. Everyone looked relieved when Sean rose and announced that he had to get a good night's rest.

Sean didn't see them again until he was in his assigned dressing room at the big Dublin arena. When Lester and the others came in, Sean introduced them to the other team members, and then they lined up against the wall, out of the team's way. It was a new experience for them, and they remained quite subdued and even reverent as Rufus wrapped Sean's hands and laced on his gloves. When Bruno held up his hands and Sean banged away at them with a few shots, they puffed their cheeks out and looked at one another in awe. At fight time Manny turned to the four and suggested they return to the dressing room after the bout.

"Oh yes," they chorused, hurrying toward the door. At the last moment Lester turned back toward Sean.

"Good luck, son," he said, giving Sean a hug. Sean was shocked at how small his father seemed to have become. And Lester, in turn, stepped back and looked with shining eyes at Sean's torso.

"They've made quite a man outa yuh, haven't they?" he marveled.

"Aye, they've worked me hard enough, they have," Sean smiled, glancing at Bruno.

"You'll do well … I know you will," Lester said with a worried look, and hurried out the door behind the others.

"OK," Manny said, rubbing his hands together, "here we go. You remember our little discussion?"

"Aye," Sean answered as Rufus helped him into his robe.

"No need to hold back, that's the main thing," Manny repeated. "You do whatever it takes. This is a must win!"

"But not kill him," Sean grinned.

"Well …" Manny shrugged, "whatever! Just win! Don't mess with this guy. He's a mauler!"

The arena erupted into pandemonium when they entered it. It was an all-Irish crowd, and Sean was the clear favorite. He scanned the sea of faces once he'd entered the ring. At length he saw four hands waving at him frantically from a dozen rows back, and he could even hear one of his father's friends yelling.

"Do him proper, Fiddler!"

The bell for Round 1 sounded and Sean met 'The Compactor' in midring. Smythe was being very cautious, and somehow Sean couldn't bring himself to unleash the power of his left and end things as Manny had instructed. They boxed one another, and Sean began to enjoy himself. The Irish crowd was the noisiest he had ever heard, and to a man it seemed that they were rooting for him.

Two and a half minutes into Round 1 he heard Manny screaming at him from ringside.

"What'd I tell yuh? What'd I tell yuh?"

Reluctantly Sean decided that he'd have to end things as he and Manny had agreed, and he launched a roundhouse left at Smythe's head. As it turned out, Smythe was backpedaling at that moment, and the shot roared by a fraction of an inch from his chin. He looked startled, and before Sean could pull his left fist back, Smythe caught him with a vicious left hook to the cheek. It knocked Sean flat. At the referee's count of four, he heard the bell ring.

"Get up! Get up!" he heard Manny screaming, as if from a far distance. Then it hit him: the bell wouldn't save him! With all the will he could muster, he pulled himself to his feet on the count of eight. He looked around in a daze for his corner. Finally he saw Rufus, waving a towel up and down to attract his attention.

He made his way to the corner on spaghetti legs and collapsed onto the stool. Rufus pressed the white towel against his cheek below his right eye. When he pulled it away it was soaked crimson.

"I'm cut?" Sean slurred thickly, looking with bleary eyes at Rufus.

"Yeah, he caught you good," Rufus mumbled, going to work on the torn flesh.

Manny rushed into the ring and knelt at Sean's side.

"Stupid! I was stupid, wasn't I?" Sean cried, tears squirting from his eyes.

"No you weren't," Manny scolded. "You went for him like we planned."

"But too late! Stupid!"

"It's never too late," Manny shouted into his ear. Bruno waved smelling salts under Sean's nose and the acrid fumes began to clear his head.

"Can you go on?" Manny asked anxiously.

"Aye," Sean answered, his vision clearing and his voice settling down.

"Finish this thing, then! Finish it *now*!" Manny urged.

Rufus had stemmed the flow of blood and the ring doctor approached, motioning for Sean to stand up.

"How are you feelin', lad?" the doctor asked.

"Good!" Sean exclaimed. The doctor studied Sean's eyes carefully, and pulled on his wrists.

"Want to continue?"

"Yes! Yes I do!" Sean answered.

The doctor pursed his lips and shook his head up and down. The warning whistle sounded and Rufus scooped up the stool, stepping through the ropes.

"Make us proud, Irish," he grinned.

"Now or never!" Manny shouted into his ear. And then the bell for Round 2 rang.

Smythe charged out of his corner with homicide in his eyes. He had both gloves to the sides of his head, and immediately unloaded a vicious right at Sean's head. Sean easily picked it off with his left, and then clinched. He felt Smythe struggle to break free. But propelling himself forward with his massive left leg, he managed to stay tied up with Smythe long enough to raise his left and land a devastating blow to the back of Smythe's ribcage. Sean put everything into the blow, and he could feel something give when it landed. Although he couldn't know it at the time, his sledgehammer fist broke three of Smythe's ribs.

With a terrible animal sound, Smythe lurched forward. Sean backed away with upraised hands as Smythe sank to one knee.

"Neutral corner! Neutral corner!" Manny yelled from ringside.

Sean retreated and the ref began counting. At the count of four, Smythe's face blanched white and he coughed. Pink, frothy blood bubbled from his lips. From the corner his handlers threw in a towel. The bout was over!

The Irish crowd went ballistic and flashbulbs were going off everywhere. It was one of the few times a heavyweight bout had been ended with a body shot.

Sean fought his way through the mass of bodies that flooded into the ring.

"Are yuh OK?" he asked Smythe, who sat gasping in his corner.

Smythe looked up and forced a wan smile.

"It looks like you cracked a few o' me ribs, Fiddler," he wheezed.

Sean's eyes went limp with remorse. He couldn't answer. Smythe seemed to understand.

"A tough game we're in, eh what?" he grinned.

"Aye," Sean answered softly.

"Good luck in New York," Smythe added "Give Rocky more o' the same."

"Thanks," Sean said hoarsely, and then he was pulled away by a jubilant Manny.

The microphone descended from on high, and once again Sean heard the magical words.

"Ladeez and gentlemen-n-n. The winner and top contender for the heavyweight champeenship of the world: Fiddler Cra-a-a-be."

Out in the crowd, ruddy-faced Irishmen were pounding each other on the back. Sean couldn't find his father in the seething mass of humanity. Nine rows back a fight broke out. Bare knuckles were flying and beefy men were going down. Women were screaming and squirming out of the way.

"*Erin go bragh*!" Manny yelled in Sean's ear. His eyes were as bright as a fox's and filled with exultation. Behind Sean, Rufus struggled to get him into his robe.

"So, we're learnin' a bit o' the Gaelic, are we," Sean teased back.

"Aye, me boyo, that we are," Manny trumpeted, hoisting Sean's right arm aloft and signaling 'Number 1' to the TV cameras.

Chapter 26

Sean and his entourage were nearly mobbed on the way out of the arena. Although Manny and the other team members were jubilant, it was only with an effort that Sean managed to smile at the throngs of well-wishers. He could not shake the specter of Smythe coughing up pink froth.

Lester and his friends bulldozed their way through the mass of humanity and followed Sean and the others into the restricted dressing room area. When they arrived at the dressing room door, Manny waved Sean, Bruno and Rufus inside, but motioned for Lester and the others to wait in the hallway.

"How is he?" Lester whispered hoarsely.

Manny quietly pulled the dressing room door shut.

"I think he's fine," he said to Lester. "The fight doctor should be along any minute. My hunch is that they're gonna want to take Sean to the arena infirmary and put in a few stitches."

Manny sensed that Lester seemed anxious and unsure of what to do next.

"Why don't you wait here until the doc's had a look at him," he suggested gently. "Then you can see him."

Lester and the others nodded vigorously, eager to do the right thing.

"Ah! Here he comes now," Manny exclaimed, giving the fight doctor a little wave and opening the dressing room door for him. The doctor smiled at Lester and the others as he entered the dressing room with Manny.

"Friends o' yours?" he asked Sean, nodding at the door.

"Aye," Sean replied. "It's me Da' and some o' his cronies."

The doctor gave a little laugh.

"Well, let's have a look at that cut," he exclaimed, bending over and staring intently at Sean's cheek.

The doctor put on a pair of disposable gloves and gingerly pressed the swollen flesh around Sean's gash. Sean couldn't help but wince.

"Good job," the doctor grunted to Rufus. Sean smiled at Rufus, and Rufus broke out into a toothy grin.

"OK," the doctor said. "We need to clean this up a bit and pull it closed while the wound is fresh. Shall we do it right here?"

Sean nodded and the doc looked at Manny and the others.

"D' you know where the arena infirmary is?"

"Sure do," Manny affirmed. "I checked it out before the fight."

"OK, I'll be waiting for you there," the doctor said. "Feeling all right?" he asked Sean.

"Aye, I'm feelin' fine," Sean smiled. "How's Smythe?"

The doctor shook his head up and down, pleased by Sean's concern.

"He's going to be fine," he said gently. "He's on the way to the best care possible, even as we speak."

"Cracked ribs?" Sean asked timidly.

"Aye," the doctor answered. "But he's in no danger. There's no need to worry about him. Let's concentrate on getting *you* fixed up."

Sean nodded lamely, and the doc left. Manny poked his head out the door and suggested to the men in the hallway that Lester step inside.

"Oh, absolutely!" the other men chorused, stepping back while Lester followed Manny back into the dressing room.

Once inside, Manny retreated to a corner and made a call on his cell phone. Bruno and Rufus were similarly occupied, and Lester seized the opportunity to talk privately with Sean.

"How are you, son?" he asked softly, squeezing Sean's forearm. Sean looked at Lester and tears welled up in his eyes.

"What is it?" Lester whispered, leaning close to Sean. "Are you in pain, boy?"

"No, it's no that," Sean whispered back. "I just can't get past the sight o' Smythe coughin' up his own blood."

Lester nodded soberly, guessing at what Sean must have witnessed in the ring.

"I could o' killed him, Da'," Sean whispered in distress.

Lester searched his mind frantically for the right words.

"I'm beginnin' to see what a terrible business this is," he murmured carefully. "Frankly I'm thinkin' you should quit it right now, and come home with me. You could continue your education."

Sean looked at Lester gratefully. Trust his Da' to place his welfare above all else.

"It's basically over," he muttered softly.

"You mean you'll not be goin' to America?" Lester asked brightly.

"No, no, I'll be goin' there all right. But…" Sean glanced at Manny and the others.

"We'll talk about it in a few days," he whispered, clearly not wanting anyone else to overhear. Lester nodded understandingly.

"Will we be seein' you again while we're here in Dublin?" Lester asked.

Sean thought about that for a moment.

"No, I think it'd be best if you all went back home," he answered. "I'm bone weary and will be sleepin' in tomorrow. I'll rest better if I know you're not waitin' on me."

Lester looked at Sean with sad eyes. He stole furtive glances at the gash in his son's cheek. The whole side of Sean's face was puffy and swollen. He was thankful that Emma wasn't here to see her boy in this kind of shape. Sean seemed to guess what was on Lester's mind.

"I'll be fine, Da'," he reassured his father. "Tell Ma I'll see her in a couple o' days."

"Aye, I'll do that, son. You get some rest."

On an impulse Lester hugged Sean.

"Love you, boy," he whispered.

"Love you too," Sean whispered back.

Lester walked stiffly out of the room and rejoined his friends. Sean could hear them asking about him as his father walked out the door.

"OK!" Manny exclaimed, once Lester had left the room. "Let's get you over to the infirmary!"

"You need us?" Bruno asked.

"No," Manny replied. "Let's pack it all up. Bring his clothes over to the infirmary when you're through. I think we've done all the damage we can do here for one night."

Chapter 27

It took nine stitches to pull the wound on Sean's cheek closed.

"This will knit nicely," the doctor said after finishing up. He was clearly pleased with his work. "I expect nothing more than a hairline scar."

Sean nodded gratefully.

"The stitches should come out in six or seven days," the doctor continued. "If you're here in Dublin, I can do it at my office. Or, if you're out of town, another doctor can do it."

The doctor handed Sean his card and applied a bandage.

"That's it. We're done here," he smiled. "Still feeling OK?"

"Aye, I'm feelin' fine!" Sean smiled. "I'm just a wee bit tired."

The doctor nodded knowingly.

"To be expected," he said softly. "It's been a rough night for you, both physically and emotionally."

He looked into Sean's eyes and pulled on his wrists.

"Listen," he added, "I don't want you to worry about Smythe, understand? He's going to be all right."

Sean frowned but didn't answer. His eyes were full of contrition. The doctor placed his fingers under Sean's chin and raised his face, forcing him to make eye contact.

"Not to worry!" he repeated. "He's going to be *fine*. It wasn't your fault. This is a hard game you men chose to play. No worrying! Deal?"

"Deal," Sean smiled weakly. The doctor gave Sean's shoulder a little squeeze and turned to Manny.

"Good night's sleep," he ordered. "Big breakfast when he awakes."

Manny, who had been through all this before, nodded agreeably.

"Thanks for everything, Doc," he smiled.

"OK!" he said to Sean, once they'd exited the infirmary. "Let's get you to bed!"

The ride back to the hotel was a quiet one. Everyone sensed that Sean wasn't in a talkative mood. Back at his suite, Sean left his clothes in a heap on the floor and sank gratefully into the large and comfortable bed.

"Thank You, God," he murmured after turning out the bedside lamp. He wasn't quite sure what he was thanking His Maker for. The novocain that the doctor had administered was beginning to wear off, and the right side of his face was starting to throb. With a sigh he rolled over and laid the left side of his face on one of the bed's downy pillows.

"Two more bouts," he thought. "And both of them rigged. It'll be a walk in the park."

But Sean felt both guilt and relief about the bouts' pre-arranged outcomes. Part of him despised the dishonesty of it all. Yet another part of him was grateful that he'd not, in fact, actually have to do battle with the current champ. It wasn't that he feared for himself. What he dreaded was getting into another situation where he might instinctively do more damage than he'd done to Smythe.

"Only two more to go," he repeated to himself. For he'd decided weeks ago that he'd retire after 'losing' the crown back to Rocky. Manny wasn't going to like it. But he and his partners would really have nothing to beef about. They stood to make millions on the two fights.

"No mas," Sean thought, remembering the bout in Madrid. He drifted off wondering what he was going to do with his share of the gates. He decided not to mention his retirement to Manny until he'd been paid for the second bout.

Sometime during the night Sean had a terrible nightmare. He dreamed that his punch to Smythe's back had literally driven several broken ribs through Smythe's heart and completely out through his chest. Smythe fell to the canvas, blood gushing in spurts from his rended chest.

"It looks like you've killed me, Fiddler," the fallen gladiator gasped.

"Uh-h-h!" Sean screamed in a guttural cry, sitting bolt upright in bed. For a moment he didn't know where he was. He sat in the darkness, heart thudding in his chest. His body was soaked in sweat. Then he remembered that he was in a Dublin hotel, and became aware of his throbbing face.

He gingerly felt his swollen cheek. It was hot and puffy. He pressed gently through the bandage, on the wound, but thankfully there was no pain there. With a sigh he turned on the bedside lamp and made his way into the bathroom. Sean opened the small container of painkillers that the doc had given him and took one with a glass of water. His watch indicated that it was 2 AM. Guessing that he wouldn't sleep anymore, he shuffled back to bed and turned out the light.

"Thank you, God," he whispered again into the darkness. This time he understood why he was thankful. He was grateful that he hadn't actually taken another human's life.

"It was only a dream," he repeated to himself over and over. His worries that he'd not sleep again proved to be without basis. Within twenty minutes the pill he'd taken not only dimmed the throbbing in his cheek, but caused waves of relaxation to sweep over his body. He slept soundly until 10 AM, and this time it was happily a sleep free of unsettling dreams.

When he awoke he dialed Manny's extension.

"Well! That was a good sleep!" Manny boomed over the phone line. "How are you feelin' this mornin'?"

"Not bad," Sean answered groggily. "What's the plan?"

"Big breakfast for everybody, my treat," Manny replied. "Then I'm sendin' you home and we're flyin' back to London."

"I need to get cleaned up. See you in the restaurant in half an hour?"

"We'll be there," Manny promised.

Bruno and Rufus were both unabashedly happy to see Sean when he entered the hotel's dining room. They all made small talk through breakfast. Oddly enough, no one seemed interested in discussing the previous evening's fight.

"Any word on Smythe?" Sean asked at length.

"He's fine," Manny answered. "I read about him in this mornin's paper. Three cracked ribs, but they expect a full recovery. That was some kind o' punch you gave him!"

Sean shook his head and looked down at the table.

"All I can see is him coughin' up pink bubbles," he murmured.

"No sweat," Manny answered. "I read that the broken ribs lacerated his lung a little. There was some minor, localized bleedin' in there, but no big deal."

"You the man, Irish," Rufus murmured, pressing Sean's forearm. Sean looked at his friend gratefully.

"I'm just happy that it wasn't more serious," he said.

"Oh yeah," Rufus agreed with round eyes. "If you tagged him dat hard in de head, you'd killed him for sure."

"Now, now," Manny chided, "let's not blow things out o' proportion."

Rufus ducked his head submissively.

"He's right," Sean said. "Thank God I only broke his ribs."

"Well, no worries with the two bouts in America," Manny continued. "The only thing there is for you and Rocky to put on a convincin' show."

Sean nodded, privately noting for the first time that Bruno and Rufus knew about the arranged bouts. It made sense that they *would* know … particularly Bruno. Yet it embarrassed Sean a little bit that they did. He gave Rufus a mortified glance, but Rufus avoided eye contact, only pursing his lips and nodding his head up and down almost imperceptibly.

After breakfast, Manny jotted his cellular phone number down on the back of one of his business cards.

"Call me as soon as you know what flight you'll be arrivin' in New York on," he told Sean. "I'll meet you at the airport."

"I'll do that," Sean promised. "Are you stayin' around for a bit, or…"

"No, we're headin' back to the farm this afternoon," Manny answered. "But I've booked you here at the hotel through tomorrow. Get some more rest, and give my best to your folks, OK?"

"Aye, I certainly will," Sean promised.

"How long you figure before comin' over to the states?" Manny asked tentatively.

"Oh, I expect I'll be spendin' no more than a week with the folks."

"Great!" Manny grinned, holding out his hand. "We'll be seein' you after that."

Sean shook Manny's hand and turned to Bruno and Rufus.

"Be seein' you, Bruno," he smiled, shaking Bruno's hand.

"Enjoy your vacation, champ," Bruno smiled back.

Sean held his hand out, palm up, to Rufus. Rufus grinned and slapped it.

"Stay out o' trouble," Sean grinned.

"You too, Irish," Rufus grinned back at him. "Don't forget dem stitches."

Sean went back to his room and stared at his face in the mirror. The swelling had already lessened considerably. The angry redness was turning purplish. He carefully lifted the bandage and studied the stitches in his cheek. He marveled at how a rip in the human body could be sewn up quite like a torn jacket.

Sean carefully pressed the bandage back into place and stretched out on the bed. Surprisingly, despite having slept nearly around the clock, he dozed off again. He awoke at 2 PM, hungry as a bear, and went back down to the dining room. The place was all but deserted. He ordered a big hamburger and a milkshake. The cold, rich drink felt unbelievably delightful sliding down his throat.

That afternoon he took in a late matinee and then had a light supper in one of Dublin's better pubs. The other patrons recognized him and greeted him, but for the most part respected his privacy.

After finishing dinner, he joined the crowd at the pub's bar. In no time at all a pretty woman approached and wiggled in between him and another drinker. She struck up a conversation and Sean bought her a couple of drinks. It was clear what her evening's agenda was. But even as he enjoyed her company, Sean knew that they'd be parting there in the bar.

After a while he kissed her lightly on the cheek, and whispered into her ear.

"I'm goin' to get a night's rest. It takes a while for us pugs to come back from a fight."

She nodded that she understood.

"Are you sure?" she smiled. "I can help you relax."

"I know. Here!" he said, taking a fifty pound note from his wallet and laying it before her on the bar. "I'd like you to buy yourself somethin' pretty."

The woman looked at the note with disappointment tugging at her eyes. But, she accepted Sean's decision gratefully enough.

"Good luck in America, Fiddler," she murmured, pulling Sean's head down and bussing him on the cheek. With a smile, she put the note in her purse and walked away toward the powder room.

Sean watched her shapely form withdraw, and wondered if he'd made the right call. It had been quite a while since Vicki and he…

Part 4

America!

Chapter 28

Once back at the training camp, Manny told Bruno that he'd be training a promising young welterweight from Liverpool. Bruno couldn't conceal his disappointment.

"You're not missin' anything," Manny half apologized. "The next two fights in the states are a done deal. There won't be any real trainin' to speak of."

"I know. I just thought…"

"Nah, we need you here!" Manny insisted. "I think this new kid has real possibilities."

Bruno nodded.

"You're the boss," he smiled half-heartedly.

Manny clapped him on the shoulder.

"I'm givin' you and Mrs. Gruber both a couple weeks off," he said. "We could all use a rest."

After Bruno and Mrs. Gruber had departed, Manny and Rufus drove to the airport and caught a flight to New York.

"There she is," Rufus murmured as the jumbo jet glided down over Long Island in its final approach. He and Manny both stared at the lights that stretched to the horizon.

"Just like we left her," Rufus mused.

"Greatest little town on earth," Manny added.

"Where we gonna train our boy?" Rufus asked.

"Well," Manny answered, "there ain't really much trainin' to be done. We're gonna have him work out at the club in Brooklyn."

"Awright!" Rufus exclaimed. "I still be on the team?"

"Oh yeah," Manny assured him. "I don't think Sean would have it any other way."

Rufus grinned. He was clearly pleased.

"Yeah, we be brothers," he murmured. "Who gonna train him?"

"You know Louis?" Manny asked.

"I know Louis? What, Rocky's old trainer? O' course I knows him! He gonna train de Fiddler?"

"Yeah, we thought that might be a good match," Manny said.

"Oh yeah, I hear tell Louis ain't no friend o' Rocky's since he jump ship."

"Is that right?" Manny mused. "Ver-r-ry interesting."

Rufus was glad to be back on his old turf. His brother, Seth, was the club's equipment room manager. When Seth's wife learned that Rufus was back in town, she insisted that he come over for Sunday dinner. Rufus loved his niece and nephew like they were his own and eagerly accepted. When he arrived, he got down on the living room floor and the two youngsters wrestled with him.

Manny went to work at Skopelli's office the following Monday morning. Skopelli of course knew about the Dublin win.

"A close one, huh?" he grunted, after Manny had settled into a chair.

"Very close," Manny agreed. "Our boy learned a hard lesson."

"He cuts easy, huh?" Skopelli continued.

"Wel-l-l," Manny answered carefully, "maybe … maybe not. He took a very hard left hook."

"What is he, some kind o' stupid?" Skopelli growled. "Why'd he hold back and let dat bum get to him? He could o' blown everyt'ing."

"I know, I know," Manny conceded. "He'd be the first one to agree with you."

"So what happened?" Skopelli pressed.

"Well, he boxed for a couple minutes. I think he wanted to give the hometown crowd their money's worth. After I got his attention from ringside, he went for the kill. But he missed."

"And Smythe nails him."

"To the wall!" Manny confirmed. "I thought it was over! But, he made it up and then the bell saved his butt."

"And the next round … Wham!" Skopelli mused.

"Like nothin' you ever saw. He ties Smythe up and goes in over the top. I tell yuh, for a moment I thought he killed him."

"How many ribs?" Skopelli queried.

"Three, I read. Pushed right into his lung."

Skopelli grimaced. It was like nothing he'd ever heard about in the boxing world.

"I bet dat stung," he joked.

Manny grinned.

"He was pukin' up blood."

"No kiddin'! Dat must o' been a sight," Skopelli said, leaning back in his big leather chair. "Oh, well. All's well dat ends well. The important t'ing is, we get the title shot."

"And …" Manny murmured.

"No change. Rocky lays down in the eleventh. Our boy just has to make it look good. But o' course he really only gives Rocky a love tap."

"And after?" Manny asked.

"Rematch, like we discussed. Rocky takes his crown back."

"Interesting. I'm surprised Car … Mr. Carbino is so trustin'," Manny mused.

"What, trustin'?" Skopelli barked. "You mean he might t'ink we don't keep our agreement in the rematch?"

"Well, somethin' like that," Manny answered.

"Are you nuts?" Skopelli stormed. "You don't unnerstan' how dese t'ings work! Me cross Carbino? Sure, when pigs fly."

"You're right," Manny admitted. "I'm not suggestin' you ever would. I'm just … it's nice to know that Mr. Carbino knows that."

"Yeah, well, Vito and me are gettin' on real good dese days. We worked all dese details out over dinner one night, his invite."

Manny arched his eyebrows.

"Wow!" he remarked. "Pretty soon you make capo, no?"

"Who knows?" Skopelli smiled. "Stranger t'ings have happened."

Back across the Atlantic Sean rented a car in Dublin and drove home. The Irish countryside was as beautiful as ever. Emma fell on his neck in tears when he knocked on the cottage door. She pulled the bandage on his cheek back and examined the stitches.

"If I'd known it'd come to this, I'd o' never let you get into it," she scolded.

Sean nodded humbly. He didn't even try to downplay the cut, knowing it would be futile.

They had a quiet supper that night, and Lester and Emma pumped Sean for every detail of his time away. When he told them that he'd had a friendship with the housekeeper, Emma took particular interest. She was properly incensed when Sean related how Vicki had eventually hooked up with her ex again.

"Why the little tramp!" Emma seethed. "Playin' with you when it fit her purposes."

Sean laughed and Emma was relieved to see that his heart hadn't been broken.

"All o' the girls you used to know are fascinated by your success," she said breezily.

"Are they now? And how would you be knowin' that?"

"Oh, I talk with their mothers," Emma smiled demurely. "You've become quite a catch, you know."

Sean snorted.

"It's the unvarnished truth!" Emma insisted.

"Aye," Lester agreed, tamping tobacco into his pipe. "I expect it is at that. You know, Sean, nothin' stirs a woman's heart like a handsome bank account."

"Not all women," Emma complained.

Lester looked at her with twinkling eyes.

"Aye, not all," he agreed. "There are always one or two pearls among the dross."

Before they turned in for the night, Emma told Sean to keep the next night open. She was having her father and Lester's parents over for dinner. The prospect pleased Sean. The only down side in his mind was that Grandma Mary wouldn't be there.

"I think I'll visit Grandma's grave tomorrow mornin'," Sean murmured.

Emma's eyes softened.

"She'd like that, Sean. She'd like that a lot."

"Is Peck's flower shop still in business?" he asked.

"Oh yes," Lester answered, smoke swirling around his head. "They've still got the prettiest roses in all o' Ireland."

Chapter 29

When Sean awoke he could hear Emma and Lester already having breakfast in the kitchen. He put on a robe and went out to join them.

"How's our boy this mornin'?" Lester boomed.

"Oh, fine enough," Sean smiled.

"Can I fix you some breakfast?" Emma offered brightly.

"No, no thanks, Ma, I think I'll just fix meself some toast."

Lester and Emma made small talk with Sean until it was time for them to leave for work.

"There's cold cuts in the 'fridge if you're home for lunch," Emma said, kissing Sean on the head.

Sean rose and hugged her.

"Have yuh got money in your pocket?" Lester asked sheepishly. Sean laughed and gave Lester a hug too.

"Aye, money's one thing I'm not lackin' these days," he smiled.

After Lester and Emma were gone, Sean wandered into the bathroom. He removed his bandage, showered, and carefully shaved around the stitched wound. It occurred to him that things had changed … that he was a grown man now, and only a guest in his father's house. He decided to cut his visit short. The length of his stay had never been discussed, and Lester and Emma would be none the wiser.

After getting dressed, Sean sat down at the phone and made reservations for a flight to New York. It was Monday and he reserved a seat on a Wednesday afternoon flight.

"Plenty o' time for the get-together tonight, and maybe treat the folks to dinner tomorrow night," he thought.

At Peck's flower shop he bought a dozen roses in a pretty vase. Old man Peck was delighted to see him, but sensed Sean's reason for buying the flowers and refrained from being too jovial.

"Good luck in America, lad," the old man said as Sean headed out the door.

"Thanks, Mr. Peck. Thanks a million," Sean smiled back. "And give my best to Mrs. Peck."

Once in the cemetery, Sean had to search for Grandma Mary's grave. Like Manny had done so many months before, he marveled at how old some of the stones were. Some of the names on newer stones he recognized … people who'd been alive when he was a boy. He passed a freshly covered grave and stared with eyes of disbelief at the inscription. It was Pee Wee, one of his old school chums. Dead at 20. What could have happened? He'd have to ask Emma or Lester when they got home from work.

At last he found Grandma Mary's stone. Grandpa Shamus' name and birthdate were inscribed next to hers, but the date of his death remained uncarved in the smooth granite. Sean did the math. Grandpa was now 74 years old. How long before he'd take his place next to Grandma?

With a sigh Sean propped the roses against the marker and bowed his head. He thought he ought to say something, but no sound came out. No matter, he thought. If Grandma Mary's spirit was there, she'd know his thoughts. It was a beautiful, peaceful spring day.

The old song, "Danny Boy," drifted up from memory. How many times had they sung that in primary school? He knew it by heart and silently began to sing the words. The last few lines brought him up short.

And I shall hear, tho' soft you tread above me
And all my dreams will warm and sweeter be
If you'll not fail to tell me that you love me …

Sean's breath caught in his throat and tears welled up in his eyes. He knelt and pushed the vase of roses more firmly into the turf.

"I love you, Grandma," he whispered. "I miss you."

Two rows away the song of a bird drew his attention away from the roses. Tiny and full of life, the singer's feathers were as blue as Grandma Mary's eyes had been. For a moment the little bundle of fluff returned his gaze, and then it flew away. Sean watched to see where it would enter the trees. But it never did. As it receded into the distance it climbed higher and higher, and finally vanished from sight.

"Grandma?" Sean whispered. He crossed himself and walked slowly back to the rental car.

"So many here in this one graveyard," he mused as he walked through the rows of headstones. People who had loved and hated, succeeded and failed. Here and there a special marker identifying a fallen soldier or sailor. Had they left young sweethearts behind when they marched off to war? Had the young women married someone else in time, keeping the memory of their first love forever locked in a secret corner of their hearts?

War was such madness. And was it not the same with the business he'd gotten into? Two men, each trying to pound the other senseless. And the crowd screaming the while for blood.

Almost without thinking, Sean steered the car through the village and pulled up in front of Grandpa Joe's little shop. When he entered, a little bell over the door tinkled and Grandpa stepped out of the back room. Neither of them could speak for a moment. Grandpa came through the shop and embraced his grandson.

"What a stout mountain of a man you've become," he cried at length, stepping back and squeezing Sean's arms. "Sit down, sit down, Bubby, and tell me of your travels."

Sean talked with Grandpa Joe at length about his time away. Thankfully, business was slow and they weren't interrupted. When the conversation turned toward the upcoming events in America, Sean's face grew dark.

"What is it, Bubby? What's troublin' you, boy?"

Sean shook his head morosely.

"I don't know what I'm gettin' into, Grandpa. You see, the whole thing is fixed."

"Fixed? You mean faked?" the old man pressed.

"Aye. I'm to gain the crown in the first fight, and then lose it back in a rematch."

"But why ..." Grandpa Joe murmured.

"Oh, a variety of reasons, I reckon. It makes for a record gate in the rematch. And I'm thinkin' there are great sums wagered ..."

"So them in the know make a killin'."

"Aye, that's their game all right."

Grandpa Joe and Sean both grew silent. At length Sean spoke again.

"I'm ashamed for bein' part of it," he confessed.

"What happens if you choose not to be?" Grandpa Joe wanted to know.

"Yuh mean, like, play the second fight honest ... hold onto the crown if I can?"

"Aye, somethin' along those lines," the old man mused.

"I don't know," Sean answered. "The problem is, I don't know what sort of a crowd I've fallen in with. The only contact I've had over here is a chap called 'Manny'."

"And what about him?" Grandpa Joe queried.

"Oh, I like him well enough. His folks actually came from Ireland. But ... the others in his organization ... the higher ups ... I don't know. They might be criminals."

"Sure and they are, aren't they?" Grandpa muttered indignantly. "Riggin' the boxin' and all."

"I'm not exactly playin' the game of life straight, am I?" Sean muttered, recalling one of their old talks. Grandpa Joe seemed to remember it too.

"Well, now, let's have a careful look at that, shall we," he answered. "If it isn't your idea ... if you're only followin' orders ..."

Sean looked at his grandfather.

"But the point seems to be, I don't have to play along."

"I don't know about that!" Grandpa exclaimed. "From all you've observed, I don't like the possible consequences of crossin' them up ... not a bit."

"I suppose I could just quit now ..."

"And if you did, d' you think they'd let you go?"

Sean gave that some thought.

"I don't know," he murmured at length. "They've already made some money off me. But then again they've also spent a lot. And o' course nothin' approaches what they stand to make in the next two bouts."

"And you?" Grandpa pressed.

"Me? If I go along with the plan, I'll be a rich man. I'll be a millionaire easy."

Grandpa Joe puffed his cheeks out. Whoever would have thought …

"So if you drop out now, you might get your legs broke or worse. And if you play it straight in America, the same," he muttered.

Sean shook his head ruefully.

"Well, you know, Bubby," the old man continued, "a man could do a lot of good with money like that. We all read about your generosity with the Old Fighters' Home. Think o' the good you done there."

"Aye," Sean nodded, "it's a point, it's a good point. Who's to be hurt if I play along? I hardly feel obligated to uphold the honor o' the fight game. I'm beginnin' to think the whole business is crazy."

"Are yuh now?" the old man answered. "I must confess I've always enjoyed watchin' the fights."

"Aye, and so did I," Sean agreed. "But havin' been in the ring … it changes a man's views."

Grandpa Joe nodded, beginning to appreciate what Sean had been through.

"Well, what do you think you'll do?" he asked.

"I think I'm gonna take the bloody money and run," Sean replied.

"You mean quit after losin' the title back to the Yank?"

"Aye. By then my … sponsors will have recouped their investment many times over. There shouldn't be nearly the problem."

"I think it's a wise course," the old man approved.

"O' course all this is a family secret," Sean murmured. "Like I say, I don't know much about the people I'm dealin' with."

"Understood," Grandpa agreed. "Mum's the word."

Just then a customer entered the shop and Sean decided to leave.

"We'll be seein' you and Grandma tonight at supper, then," he said.

"Aye, we'll be there, Bubby. We'll talk some more then."

Chapter 30

Dinner with the grandparents was a relaxing time for all. Grandpa Joe kept a low profile, giving Sean's other grandparents ample opportunity to talk with their grandson.

After dinner Emma and her mother-in-law cleaned up, and the men went out into the backyard and relaxed in the wicker chairs there. Lester sought clarification on what Sean had hinted at in the Dublin arena dressing room, and they pretty much went over the same ground that Sean and Grandpa Joe had covered earlier in the day. Again, Sean admonished all to keep his plans secret, and everyone saw the wisdom of that.

After a while Emma and her mother-in-law joined them. Emma set out a pot of coffee and cups on the backyard's picnic table, and the six of them had a fine time of it. Lester asked Sean if he could still do the one-armed pull-ups, and Sean did several using a fruit tree limb. Grandma Rose called Sean over to her chair. She felt his left arm when he knelt beside her. Her hands flew away like they'd touched a hot stove, and as quickly returned. Everyone laughed.

"Pity the blighter on the receivin' end o' that!" Grandpa Shamus crowed.

"Aye," Sean answered, "a few have already had a taste."

The family revelry went on into the night, and by the time the grandparents took their leave everyone was ready for bed.

"Good luck, Bubby," Grandpa Joe whispered when he gave Sean a farewell hug. "Play the game *smart*!"

"Aye, that I will," Sean answered, meeting the old man's eyes fondly.

Tuesday morning was much the same as Monday. After Lester and Emma left for the day, Sean wondered what he should do. On an impulse he drove to the processing plant and walked down to the stockyards. The men there immediately recognized him and raised such an uproar that the steers in the pens grew restless. His old friends encircled Sean and marched him into the processing rooms. Everyone stopped what they were doing and mobbed him. For a while it was like old times. One of the men wanted Sean to drop a few steers. But the foreman intervened.

"Are yuh daft?" he scolded. "Them fists are worth a million quid now. Do yuh think he's gonna risk them on the noggin o' one o' these bloody cows?"

The foreman thought about calling Shamus O'Roarke. But he thought better of it. If Sean wanted to see Shamus, he'd go up to his office. As it turned out Sean never did. After ten minutes he knew the men should be getting back to work, and he told them he'd have to be going.

"Busy day, busy day," he fibbed. "It's great to see you hard workin' blokes again."

"Good luck, Sean," they shouted. "Give the Yank double what you gave Smythe!"

Sean smiled and waved goodbye. As he drove away he realized that no one but he had really changed. Men who had never fought in the ring were as pumped up as ever at the prospect of a good match. He mused that practically every man is at heart a warrior. The only thing that changes that is a taste of life in the trenches.

Sean returned to the cottage and fixed some lunch. He snoozed and watched some TV in the afternoon. The soap operas were a new experience for him, and he marveled at the rancor and steamy intimacies. It occurred to him that women, in their fashion, were as war-like as men.

Sean had invited Lester and Emma to join him for dinner at the inn. When everyone returned from work, they got cleaned up and walked outside.

"Let's walk," Lester suggested. "It's a fine evenin'." And so it was. The air was like an angel's kiss, and fragrant with the smell of the sea. Sean and Emma readily agreed, and off they set. Unbeknown to Sean, some of his old pals had suggested to Lester that they throw a surprise bash for Sean at the inn's pub. Lester promised to deliver him there after they'd finished dinner.

Sean and his parents had a sumptuous meal. For a change, Sean had the fisherman's platter and it was as delicious as anything that ever crossed his lips. Several other couples in Lester's and Emma's peer group were in the dining room. They greeted Sean and wished him well. Emma positively glowed with pride.

After dessert Emma excused herself and headed toward the powder room. Lester took Sean by the arm and walked him toward the adjoining pub. Sean assumed that his father wanted to buy him a drop of stout.

"What about Ma?" he objected.

"Tush, tush, not to worry," Lester grinned. As they entered the pub the whole room erupted into a rowdy rendition of 'For He's a Jolly Good Fellow.' Sean stood frozen inside the entrance, round-eyed and grinning like a fool. All of his old pals were there.

"Have fun!" Lester shouted. "We'll leave a light on for yuh."

While Sean watched his father walk back out into the dining room, the pub crowd surrounded him and practically carried him to the bar.

"A fine, frosty jar of stout for the next heavyweight champion of the world," one of them shouted to the bartender. It would be the first of many. Pint after pint slid down Sean's throat. Along the way he asked, in a somber moment, what had happened to his old friend, Pee Wee.

"Killed in a car accident," several responded in a moment of temporary sobriety. "All alone he was."

"This one's to Pee Wee," Sean said with a red but sad face.

"To Pee Wee," the others chorused, lifting their ales. For a while they reminisced about their fallen comrade. But nothing could dampen their spirits for long.

Sometime between 8 and 9 a group of young women came into the pub.

"Well, look who's come to see the champ," one of the guys shouted. Sean looked over at the group and recognized several girls he'd grown up with.

"Go on, go on," several of his friends prodded him. "Say hello to them. Do yuh think they came into this den of iniquity to see us?"

"No, no," Sean demurred shyly. But his pals would have none of it, and pushed him toward the table of young women. All of the girls beamed as he approached, and one of them pulled a chair up to the table and asked him to join them for a bit. Sean blushed, but gallantly took the seat. At the bar his cronies howled with laughter.

The girls insisted on buying him a stout, and he soon warmed to their affectionate attention. That little voice whispered to him that it was his fame that excited them. But what the hey, he thought, who's to blame if he enjoyed himself?

"Did you hear about Lillian and Pete?" one of the girls eventually asked him.

"Lillian and … Peter Connolly?" Sean asked carefully.

"Aye," another answered. "Pete met a girl at university. From a fine Dublin family, she is. They've got engaged to be married!"

"How about that," Sean murmured, arching his eyebrows.

"Aye, and little Miss Lillian took it hard," another exclaimed. Sean looked at her, his eyes encouraging her to continue.

"Off to Belfast she went. We hear she's workin' in a textile mill there."

"And what about you, Sean Crabbe," another girl asked. "Any romantic involvements to tell us about?"

Sean was slightly taken aback that they'd even consider such a thing were possible in his case. What a change since his high school days! The girls at the table seemed once again to be totally oblivious to his deformity. He sensed that any of them would gladly accept a date if he asked them out.

With a blushing face he ducked the question, but the girls continued to flirt with him. By the time he'd finished his pint of stout, the boys at the bar had grown quiet. He felt he should rejoin them. Thanking the girls for the drink, he told them how good it was to see them all again. They seemed to understand, and all smiled up at him with bright, admiring eyes.

"Good luck in America, Sean," one of them said. The others chorused the same. As he walked back toward the bar, one of them called after him.

"Come back to us one fine day, Sean."

Things got noisier once again as soon as Sean rejoined his mates at the bar. There were more rounds of stout, and some time later he looked over and saw that the girls had left. Someone began singing 'My Wild Irish Rose,' and by the third line the lot of them were raising the roof off the pub with their singing.

By midnight Sean found himself stumbling through the streets on his way back to the cottage. His head was swimming, but he was in high spirits. What a night it had been! He entered the cottage as quietly as he could, shed his outer clothes and slipped into bed.

"Good night, son," Lester's voice called from the master bedroom. Sean grinned in the darkness. Trust them to hear him, no matter how quiet he was.

"Should we wake you in the mornin'?" Emma called.

"Aye, for sure," Sean slurred. "It's a good two hour drive into Dublin.

"Of course, wake me in the mornin'," he groused to himself. "You'll be goin' off to work and it's the only chance we'll have to say goodbye."

Chapter 31

By the time he had quaffed two cups of coffee on Wednesday morning, Sean was sufficiently clearheaded to bid Lester and Emma a proper goodbye.

"Let us know how you like America," Lester said, hugging his son tightly.

"Aye, I'll write often, Da'," Sean promised.

When it was Emma's turn, her countenance grew dark. After hugging Sean she stepped back and gazed into his eyes.

"Promise me you'll always let us know where you are," she murmured.

Sean was puzzled. Of course they'd always know that.

"What…" he began.

"Promise me!" Emma admonished.

"O' course, Ma. I promise," Sean answered.

"God be with you, son," she whispered, giving him a kiss on the cheek. And then they were gone.

With a sigh Sean went back into the cottage and packed his things. Less than an hour later he was out of the village and on the road to Dublin. After turning in his rental car he dialed the cell phone number Manny had given him. He told Manny what time he'd be arriving in New York that night.

"Tonight?" Manny exclaimed. "Man, I thought you were gonna spend a week with your folks."

"Well, you know how it is," Sean apologized. "I'm no longer a kid … I'm a guest in me parents' house now. And there's an old Irish sayin': company is like fish. After two days it begins to stink."

"Yeah, I've heard that one. Are you sure it ain't Jewish?" Manny chuckled. "Anyway, I'm in Cleveland. Have you got somethin' to write on?"

Sean fumbled in his jacket pocket and told Manny to fire away. Manny gave him the name and address of a hotel close to the fight club in Brooklyn.

"I'll call right now and reserve a room for you. I'll see you at the fight club on Friday mornin', say 10 o'clock. You got its address, right?"

Sean assured him that he did.

"Don't rent a car for now, OK?" Manny suggested, fretting privately over New York's expressways. "Take a cab to the hotel."

Sean agreed to that and they rang off. Dinner was served on the flight to New York, and not long after finishing his meal Sean watched the sun dip slowly below the western horizon.

"Amazin' how long it's takin'," he mused. "We're chasin' it almost as fast as the earth turns."

The customs people in America recognized Sean, and he was accorded VIP treatment. By 10:30 that night he fell into his hotel room bed. He slept soundly and enjoyed an American breakfast in the hotel dining room the next morning.

It was a full day before he'd be meeting Manny, and lacking anything better to do Sean decided to check out the fight club. It was only blocks from the hotel and an easy walk.

"So this is America," he thought as he strolled along the sidewalks, taking in the sights and sounds. It was a fine spring morning and all the trees were blushing green. Here and there a dogwood was in bloom, and it seemed that tulips were pushing up out of the soil in practically every yard he passed.

Rufus was one of the first to spy Sean when he entered the club.

"Hey! Looky here! Look who's arrived!" Rufus shouted. He held his hand out, palm up, and Sean slapped it with a broad grin.

"How you doin', man. It's good to see you!" Rufus cried. "Hey, Seth! Come out here and meet The Man!"

Rufus' brother came out from behind the equipment room counter and shook Sean's hand.

"We already got your special gloves in stock," Seth smiled. "We gonna take good care o' you."

"How's dat cut?" Rufus asked solicitously, touching the bandage on Sean's face.

"Good!" Sean reassured him. "I guess the stitches should be comin' out tomorrow."

"Yeah, it's near time, ain't it?" Rufus said. "Manny'll get you hooked up wid a doctor. He gonna be back tomorrow."

"Aye, I'm supposed to meet him here at 10," Sean exclaimed.

"Well what you doin' tonight?" Rufus asked. "I kind o' owes you, Irish, showin' me the sights o' London and all."

"No plans," Sean shrugged. "Have you got any suggestions?"

"Shoot, man, I knows where dey plays some sweet jazz over in Harlem. You want to have dinner and go listen?"

"Sounds great," Sean answered. "When do we leave?"

"I meet you here at 4," Rufus suggested. "We take the train into Harlem."

Sean agreed, and Rufus and Seth gave him a tour of the club. Seth had already set Sean up with a locker, and handed him the key.

"Well, I see you at 4," Rufus told him after they'd finished up.

"Aye, here at 4," Sean smiled. "It was a pleasure meetin' you, Seth."

"Same here, Fiddler. The pleasure was all mine," Seth smiled.

Once outside, Sean wondered what to do. Here he was in America's Big Apple. Rufus had said they'd take the trains into Harlem. Sean decided that New York's transit system was as good a place as any to start his exploration of the New World.

Chapter 32

Sean figured out which train went into downtown Manhattan, and climbed aboard. He watched wide-eyed as they penetrated into New York's famous skyline. He got off the train at Canal Street. Everyone but he seemed to know where they were going.

Once back up at street level Sean found a magazine stand and asked the vendor if he had any maps of the city. The operator looked at Sean with round eyes.

"Hey! Ain't you Fiddler Crabbe?" he asked.

"Aye, that I am," Sean smiled.

"Holy Toledo! How long you been in America, Champ?"

Sean glanced at his watch.

"About half a day," he grinned.

"Half a … well I'll be!" the operator cried, extending his hand. "Can I help you out … give you a steer?"

Sean smiled gratefully. He'd heard horror stories about how tough New York could be. But so far he found it to be as friendly as Ireland.

"Well, it's gettin' close to me lunch time," he answered. "Is Chinatown far from here?"

"Not far at all, Champ."

The vendor pulled a map out of one of the stand's magazine racks.

"We're right here," he explained, unfolding the map and marking it with an X. "If you follow this route, you'll be right in the center o' Chinatown. You like Chinese food?"

"Aye, I love it," Sean answered.

"You ain't never gonna taste better," the operator smiled. "It's the real McCoy. If you feel like stretchin' your legs, it's an easy walk from here."

"Aye, I think I'll do that," Sean said. "How much do I owe yuh?"

"For you, two bucks," the operator grinned.

"Two … dollars?" Sean clarified, pulling out his wallet.

"Right. Two smackers," the newsman grinned.

Sean paid and thanked him, starting off on foot. He rubbernecked up in wonder at the tall buildings.

"Real McCoy," he thought. Bucks … Smackers … he liked America! Twenty minutes later he was in the center of Chinatown, scrutinizing the oriental signs and trying to decide which restaurant to eat in.

"One's as good as another," he finally decided, entering a street level establishment.

"One?" the proprietor asked, not seeming to recognize who he was.

"Aye," Sean smiled, following the proprietor to a table.

"What do you suggest?" Sean asked the waiter, once he was seated.

"What you like? Po'k? ChickEN? Fish?" the waiter asked.

"Seafood's fine," Sean answered.

"This pretty good," the Chinaman said, pointing to an item on Sean's menu.

"Right enough. I'll have that," Sean smiled.

"What you want drink?" the Chinaman asked.

"Just tea, if yuh have it."

"Oh yeah, we got tea," the waiter smiled. "You relax. Enjoy pictures," he added, waving to the delicate murals on the restaurant's walls. "Food be ready pretty quick."

Sean poured himself a cup of tea, and minutes later the waiter placed a plate in front of Sean. He took the cover off a bowl of steaming seafood on a bed of crispy, fried rice noodles.

"Faith," Sean thought as he spooned some of the delicacies onto his plate. "This is a bit of a change from fish 'n chips!"

He leaned forward and examined the wonderful smelling stuff. There were shrimp and scallops, and a whole lot of other things he didn't recognize. With a happy sigh he pushed the chopsticks aside and picked up a fork. He shoveled some of the saucy fare into his mouth and nearly swooned. The newsstand guy was so right! This was the Real McCoy!

"New York, New York, it's a wonderful town," he hummed to himself, munching away in ecstasy.

After lunch Sean wandered over to Wall Street, and on an impulse entered The New York Stock Exchange.

"This is the hub," he thought as he watched the action from the visitors' gallery. "This is what makes America, and Ireland for that matter, and all the free world go 'round. Money!"

Afterward, again out on the street, Sean kicked himself for not having gotten the names of the mysterious visitors in Madrid. Soon he'd be coming into a prince's ransom. How to invest it? Surely, if there was expert help to be had, this was the town to find it in!

Chapter 33

Sean arrived back at the club by 3:45. Rufus was waiting for him.

"Hey, man," Rufus greeted, "it's party time! You take a nap and get all rested up?"

"No, I've just come back from Manhattan," Sean grinned. "I went to Chinatown for lunch."

Rufus stared at him with wide eyes.

"Say what?" he cried. "You already ridin' the trains?"

"Aye, it was easy," Sean smiled.

"Irish, you too much!" Rufus exclaimed. "I gonna have to keep my eye on you."

Sean returned to the station with Rufus, and they took the trains into Harlem. Both were hungry by the time they got up to street level.

"What you like, man?" Rufus asked.

"To eat?" Sean queried back.

"Yeah. Ain't you hungry?"

"I'm starvin'. I like anything."

Rufus scanned the street.

"Dis place down the street got good ribs. You like ribs?"

"Let's do it!" Sean agreed.

Sean was fascinated by the café that Rufus picked out. His was the only white face in the entire establishment. But no one seemed to care. If anything, a few men were interested because they recognized him. Rufus was in seventh heaven, playing the sidekick to the world's next heavyweight champion.

The ribs were delicious and there were lots of them. After dinner Rufus asked Sean if he'd like to walk some of the meal off.

"Absolutely!" Sean exclaimed, slapping his belly with his hands. Dusk was beginning to fall on New York, and the lights were coming on all over Harlem. Sean could hear subway trains roaring by under grates in the street He sucked the oily smelling air that rushed out of them into his nostrils. A pusher approached them and offered to sell them some cocaine.

"We don't use dat stuff, man," Rufus scolded. "Don't you know who dis is?"

The pusher looked at Sean almost sheepishly, and evidently didn't have a clue.

"Dis here is Fiddler Crabbe! He fightin' for de heavyweight crown dis summer."

"Sorry," the dope peddler muttered, fading into the shadows.

By the time Sean and Rufus had walked for half an hour, hookers were working the streets. They seemed mostly interested in passing cars, but every now and then one of them would glance at Sean and Rufus. Rufus would grin and wave them off. Some were dressed so scantily that it stirred Sean's blood up. This didn't escape Rufus' eye.

"Uh Huh," he muttered. "Um Hm-m-m. Oh Oh-h-h."

Eventually they arrived at Dooby's, Rufus' favorite jazz club. A burly bouncer waved them inside. The place was a big room, with a large dance floor and a bar along one side. On the wall opposite the bar stood a bandstand. Five musicians were in the process of setting up their evening's gig. Sean noticed that there was an electronic keyboard, a sax, a trumpet, bass and drums.

"We's early," Rufus explained. "But dat's cool. We gets our pick."

Rufus led the way to a table close to, but a little off to the side of the quintet.

"You sit right in front of dese boys when dey really jammin', dey make you deaf," he grinned.

"What can I get you?" a very pretty waitress asked them.

"Hey, liddle daughter, how you doin'?" Rufus shouted. "You still goin' to school?"

"Every day," she smiled.

"Dis pretty girl gonna be a doctor," Rufus told Sean.

Sean smiled politely at her. The moment she had spoken he'd detected a certain learnedness.

"You know who dis man be?" Rufus continued. The young woman looked at Sean but didn't seem to recognize him.

"Dis be Fiddler Crabbe!" Rufus cried. "We just come over from Ireland. He gonna fight for de heavyweight crown!"

"Well!" the waitress exclaimed. "How do you do? I've heard the name."

Sean jumped to his feet and took her hand in his. Rufus continued.

"What your name be, liddle daughter? Ol' Rufus don't remember squat dese days."

"Jasmine," the pretty woman smiled. "I'm pleased to meet you, Mr. Crabbe."

"Call me Sean," Sean smiled. "Fiddler is just me ring name."

"Uca pugilator," Jasmine murmured.

"Uca what?" Rufus challenged.

Sean smiled at his pal.

"Uca pugilator," he repeated. "I believe it's a species of fiddler crab."

"Very go-o-o-d," Jasmine exclaimed, pleasantly surprised. She looked at Rufus and raised her little order pad.

"What we want … what we want?" Rufus asked rhetorically. "You like champagne, Irish?"

"Well … sure," Sean answered. "But isn't that a mite fancy?"

"Nah, nah," Rufus admonished. "Bring us two champales, Jasmine honey."

Less than a minute later Jasmine set glasses and two bottles on their table.

"Champale," Sean mused, studying the label.

"Taste it, taste it!" Rufus urged, filling his own glass. Sean took a pull right out of the bottle.

"Blimey!" he exclaimed. "This *does* taste like champagne."

Rufus giggled in delight.

Time slid by painlessly, and three rounds of champale later the place was filling up. Here and there in the sea of black faces Sean would spy a white one. More often than not it was a white woman with a black man. Sean noted absently that there were no white men with black women, and wondered why.

By 9 o'clock the place was jammed and the band was in full swing. It was the best live music Sean had ever heard. Here he was, in the country where jazz was born, listening to the people who invented it. The small part of the dance floor not occupied by tables was filled with dancing bodies. Many were spinning around and hitting their hips together.

"Dat's de bump," Rufus explained. "You never seen dat before?"

Sean assured Rufus that he hadn't. It occurred to him that some of the men were outgunned by the derrieres of their partners.

"But then again," he mused, "they ain't exactly fightin', are they?"

Sean guessed that other couples were improvising to the music. He marveled at how uninhibited everyone seemed to be. Black men spun and moon-walked, and their partners smiled and shook their hips.

"It doesn't get any better than this," his young mind exulted.

Chapter 34

At 10:30 a very large, somewhat obese black man lurched up to the table and stood glowering down at Sean.

"You Fiddler Crabbe, ain't you, boy?" he slurred. "You thinks you stronger than Bubba, don't you?"

"Hey, man, chill out!" Rufus cried. "Dis man wid me!"

"Is I talkin' to you, Uncle Thomas?" the big man snarled. "I doin' business wid dis man. Keep yo' black nose out."

"Here, now," Sean said. "We're not lookin' for any trouble."

"Ain't gonna be no trouble," Bubba said in a falsetto. "Not if you fights Bubba."

"I can't do that," Sean began, "I'm a professional…"

"Not dat way, man. I ain't crazy," Bubba interrupted. "Arm rasslin'. You know how to arm rassle?"

"Well, yes," Sean answered.

"Man, what you smokin'?" Rufus shouted. "De Fiddler break your fat arm off!"

"It's OK," Sean said, motioning for Rufus not to get so excited. "It might be fun."

"Oh, man," Rufus moaned, sinking down in his chair and looking up at the ceiling.

"You think it gonna be fun, huh? I hear tell you pretty strong in your left arm," Bubba said, settling his huge form on a chair and wrapping his ankles around it. "What you willin' to bet, Bubba whack yo' knuckles on dis table?"

Men at an adjoining table were all ears and obliged Sean and Bubba by removing empty champale bottles from the table. Bubba swept Sean's and Rufus' glasses aside.

"Well, how about a bottle of champale?" Sean suggested.

"A bottle of champale?" Bubba laughed in a deep voice. "Man, you ain't exackly bustin' with confidence, is you?"

Sean shrugged.

"OK, dat's cool. We rassle for a bottle o' beer. Le's do it."

Bubba pulled the sleeve of his T-shirt up over his shoulder. Sean estimated that he weighed over 400 pounds. His arms were enormous, but they were smooth and fat. Sean's own hardware was well concealed under the jacket he wore. He pursed his lips and nodded his head up and down admiringly.

"I'm impressed," he congratulated Bubba. "You're one big man."

"Yeah, well dere's only one way you gonna get dese knuckles on the table, and dat's by liftin' dis chile off de floor. You ready, sucker?"

Sean smiled and leaned forward. He put his elbow on the table and grasped Bubba's left hand in his own great paw.

"Psychin' me out, are we?" he thought. "Two can play that little game."

Sean squeezed Bubba's hand with his great club of a fist. Bubba felt stabbing pains, and his eyes flickered. Rufus read the signs immediately and sprang to his feet in glee.

"You boys ready?" he crowed, placing his right palm on their interlaced hands.

Sean grinned wickedly at Bubba.

"I reckon we are," he drawled.

"OK. When I lifts my hand ..." Rufus said.

When Rufus raised his hand, Bubba gave a mighty lunge. Sean could see the big man's black face flush red. He was strong ... no doubt about it. But not nearly strong enough. Sean never budged. For a few seconds Bubba's eyes were shut tight and his face was contorted as he poured everything he had into his left arm. When nothing gave, he opened his eyes and they met for an instant with Sean's.

"Ready?" Sean grinned. And then, Wham! He smashed Bubba's knuckles down on the tabletop. The force of it did in fact lift Bubba out of his chair. The big man's ankles came unwrapped from the chair's legs, and the chair shot across the floor like a cannonball, careening into the adjoining table. With a grunt Bubba fell to the floor.

"Are yuh all right, lad?" Sean asked, rising and extending his left hand to help Bubba up. At first Bubba would have none of it. But then, evidently realizing how ridiculous he'd look trying to get up unassisted, he accepted Sean's help. Sean braced his left leg and easily lifted the huge man to his feet. By now a large crowd had gathered around them. Everyone was agog with amazement and disbelief.

Sean put his face up close to Bubba's and smiled.

"I believe you owe me a beer," he grinned.

"Oh … yeah," Bubba said in a chastened tone, taking a five-dollar bill out of his wallet and laying it on the table.

"Don't feel bad," Rufus cried. "Fiddler here in de Guinness Book O' Records for doin' over a hunderd one-arm pull-ups."

Bubba nodded his head.

"I believe it," he admitted. "Guess I'll be goin'. Good luck with Rocky, man."

"Thanks, Bubba. I appreciate that," Sean called as Bubba beat a hasty retreat out of the club.

A chunky but shapely woman approached Sean.

"Show us what you got under dat jacket, Sugar," she smiled.

Rufus looked at her and began to object. But Sean, his head now swimming from more champales than he could remember, said he didn't mind. He shrugged out of his jacket. The crowd hoo'ed and hummed at the enormity of the left half of his torso.

"Make a muscle!" the woman urged him, her eyes all aglow. Again Rufus began to object but Sean waved him off.

"It's OK," he smiled, "I don't mind." He tried to pull the sleeve of his short sleeve shirt up around his shoulder, but it was too tight on his arm. When he flexed his bicep the sleeve split wide open. The black woman shrieked and began stomping around and around in a circle. Sean couldn't take his eyes off her soft flesh, jiggling provocatively under the thin material of her dress.

"OW! OW!" she yelled time and time again. "That be too much! OW!"

She pushed Sean down into his chair and sat on his lap.

"You want to come home with me, big man," she murmured, running her hands over Sean's shoulders. Sean was inclined to say 'Yes' when he heard Rufus calling softly to him.

Sean looked at his pal, and Rufus shook his head 'No' almost imperceptibly.

"What?" Sean objected thickly.

Rufus didn't answer him, but spoke to the woman.

"Girl, what you want to make trouble for? You knows you belongs to dat bartender."

The woman looked over toward the bar. A big man behind the bar was watching as he wiped the bar's polished surface with a towel.

"Yeah," she conceded, "but dis boy so *pretty*!"

"Nah, nah," Rufus said, rising and pulling her to her feet. "We don't want no trouble."

With a sigh, she smiled at Sean.

"'Bye 'Bye, Sugar," she murmured, moving away toward the bar with swaying hips.

"Come on," Rufus said in a low voice. "Time for us to be goin'." He laid a five-dollar bill on top of the one already on the table, and spied Jasmine's face in the crowd.

"Be seein' you, liddle daughter," he called. "Hope dis helps out wid de schoolin'."

Once outside, Sean complained to Rufus.

"Man, I had a good thing goin' in there."

"You think you had a good thing?" Rufus demanded, turning and facing him. "What you think … dem gals in dere is virgins? You know what happens to me if you catches sump'n and can't fight?"

Sean looked at Rufus with surprised eyes.

"I goes in de East River, dat's what," Rufus grumbled. "Come on, Irish, I takin' you *home*."

Chapter 35

The next morning Manny arrived at the club an hour before his appointment with Sean. Rufus was already there, adjusting one of the sparring ring's ropes.

"Got a minute?" Manny called, motioning for Rufus to come down out of the ring. Manny spread one of the morning paper's sports pages out on the ring apron.

"What's this?" he demanded, pointing to a news article.

Rufus stared at the paper uneasily, shifting from foot to foot.

"Could you read it?" he asked meekly. "I don' got my glasses."

Manny looked at him, mildly surprised. Comprehension crept into his eyes.

"It says here that a 400 pound gorilla got his arm nearly twisted off by Fiddler Crabbe last night in Harlem."

"Yeah, dat's de truth," Rufus smiled nervously. "I was dere."

"You were there," Manny repeated. "It says Fiddler almost went home with a B-girl."

"Yes, suh, dat's true too," Rufus mumbled. "She be hittin' on him pretty hard."

Manny looked intently at Rufus. His eyes began to fill with disappointment.

"You know what could happen if we screw up Skopelli's investment?" he more stated than asked. "I could end up in a box, and we don't even want to think what could happen to you!"

"I knows it, I knows it," Rufus mumbled, hanging his head. "Dat's what I tole de Fiddler."

"What … what'd you tell him?" Manny demanded.

"I tole him if he catch sump'n, den I ends up in de East River."

Manny looked at Rufus and confidence began to steal back into his eyes.

"You told him that," he mumbled. "And what'd he say?"

"He don' say nothin'. We come home den."

"OK, you're cool," Manny said in a more relaxed tone. "But listen: I don't want you takin' him into Harlem anymore, understand?"

Rufus shook his head up and down vigorously.

"You the boss, Manny," he answered.

"OK. What're you doin' with the ropes?"

"I's tightenin' 'em up," Rufus said. "Dey works loose."

"Good idea," Manny approved. "We don't want nobody gettin' any rope-a-dope habits."

Rufus climbed back onto the ring apron.

"Dere's jes one thing," he said as Manny moved away.

"What's that?" Manny asked, glancing back at him.

Rufus avoided eye contact, but continued in a low voice.

"Dat boy be needin' company … female company."

Manny nodded in agreement.

"I think you're right," he answered. "But I'll worry about that, you dig?"

Rufus nodded and darted a glance Manny's way.

"You callin' de shots, Manny."

An hour later Sean arrived and he and Manny greeted each other boisterously.

"You want a tour?" Manny asked.

"No, I got one yesterday," Sean grinned. "Rufus and Seth showed me around."

"Oh! Then you got a locker already?"

"Aye. With all me special gear inside."

"Well," Manny said, "then how's about we get you settled into your apartment?"

"Sure!" Sean agreed. "I'm not stayin' at the hotel then?"

"Nah, nah, that was just temporary," Manny explained. "I got you set up in a nice furnished place. Lots more room."

Manny and Sean went out and got into Manny's car.

"Beautiful car," Sean murmured on the way to his new digs.

Manny smiled.

"A gift … from my boss," he answered.

"Blimey!" Sean exploded. "This was a gift?"

"The organization rewards them that makes money for it," he smiled at Sean.

"Does it ever!" Sean murmured.

"You'll be meetin' Tony … Mr. Skopelli tomorrow," Manny added.

"He's your boss?" Sean guessed.

Manny nodded.

"You'll like him," he said enthusiastically.

Sean nodded and smiled back. He wondered if he would.

Manny pulled the Lincoln up in front of an attractive complex of single story apartments.

"Nice and quiet. Nobody makin' noise above you," he mentioned as he led Sean down a sidewalk.

Once inside, Sean was impressed. The place was new and modern … much better equipped than anything he'd seen in Europe.

"Big screen TV," Manny said with a wave as they passed through the living room. "Lots o' chairs for entertainin'."

Sean nodded politely, doubting that he'd be doing much entertaining.

"King size bed," Manny continued, leading the way into the master bedroom.

"Ample room there," Sean murmured.

"This is where the housekeeper/cook will stay," Manny said casually, opening the door to another bedroom.

"Housekeeper/cook?" Sean asked.

"Yeah," Manny answered. "I'm still interviewin' for the position. Mr. Skopelli wants you eatin' nothin' but good food. And you ain't gonna have time to clean house."

Sean nodded appreciatively.

"I thought I'd be eatin' in restaurants," he admitted.

"Nah, that gets old quick. Believe me, I know," Manny said. "She'll be takin' care o' your laundry too. It'll be just like back at the farm."

Sean smiled and wondered just how much like the farm things would actually be.

"She'll probably be an old woman," he thought. Manny, ever the astute and sly one, guessed Sean's thoughts and smiled to himself.

"So, I'll drop you off at our doc's office," he said. "It's just down the street. He's expectin' you."

"For me stitches?" Sean murmured.

"Yeah. After you're done there, take the rest of the day off. Maybe get your stuff moved over here from the hotel. We're meetin' Mr. Skopelli tomorrow at the club, 11 o'clock. Be there early."

"Good enough," Sean agreed.

The doctor was a pleasant man. He told Sean that everything was healing nicely. After the stitches were removed, Sean walked back to his hotel, called a cab and moved his gear over to the new apartment.

By the time he'd finished unpacking it was lunch time. He walked down the street to a chain restaurant and took a seat at the counter. A pretty young waitress took his order. During a lull he struck up a conversation with her.

"I'm new here," he smiled. "Just come over from Ireland two days ago. What's a bloke do in New York to keep out o' trouble?"

The waitress looked at him suspiciously, but then decided he was no threat.

"Well, let's see … you're new …" she thought aloud. "There's no end to what a newcomer can see in New York. Do you like museums … shows …"

"I like a good museum," Sean answered. "I've read o' The Museum O' Natural History …"

"Only a train ride away," the waitress smiled.

"By the way," Sean grinned, "my name's Sean … Sean Crabbe. I guess I'll be comin' in here fairly regular."

"Cra … Wait a minute!" the waitress exclaimed. "I think I saw you on TV the other night. Are you Fiddler Crabbe?"

"Aye," Sean grinned. "That's me ring name. But me friends call me Sean."

"Well … sure!" the waitress blushed. "I'm Julie."

"Good to meet yuh, Julie," Sean said gently, reaching his hand across the counter. Julie placed her hand in his and Sean gazed into her eyes. After a few seconds Julie lowered her eyes and gently pulled her hand back.

"Well!" Sean exclaimed. "I'll be goin' for now. I'll see you again, I hope. D' you work here every day?"

"Pretty nearly," Julie answered shyly.

Once outside, Sean turned toward the train station.

"Another fine day," he thought, strolling along with a bounce in his step. "Julie … Julie … pretty name for a pretty girl."

Chapter 36

After dropping Sean off at the doctor's office, Manny had some lunch and went to work. Eventually Skopelli called him into his office.

Tony had of course read the account of Sean's adventures in Harlem. Like Manny, he was concerned about their investment.

"You know about dis?" Skopelli asked, holding up the news article.

"Oh yeah," Manny answered. "I already had a little talk with Rufus."

"Uh," Skopelli grunted. "What'd you tell him?"

"I told him 'no more trips to Harlem'."

"And?"

"Oh, he agreed," Manny said. "Rufus may not be a rocket scientist, but he's no fool either."

"Yeah, he knows duh ropes, don't he?" Skopelli agreed. "So what about dis kid? What's it gonna take to keep him out o' trouble?"

"Well…" Manny winced, "I'm still gettin' to know him. And he's changed since I first met him. Time in the ring does that to young guys."

"Does he need strong armin' … finessin' …?" Skopelli queried.

"In my opinion, finessin'," Manny thought aloud. "He's like all fighters … you push, their first instinct is to push back."

Skopelli nodded agreement.

"OK," he mumbled, "here's how we set t'ings up. Trainin' from 8:30 to 11:30 every mornin'. Den a long lunch break. More trainin' from 2:30 to 6:30. Den dinner. He should be too bummed out by den to wanna go out and get into trouble."

"That should work, all right," Manny nodded.

"You got him set up in an apartment? I want a cook for him. Three squares of good food every day. No gettin' fat."

"He's in an apartment all right. But I'm still interviewin' for the housekeeper/cook position."

"What's wrong wit' Mrs. Gomez?" Skopelli asked. "I t'ought she was available."

"Yeah, she is," Manny acknowledged. "But I was thinkin' about gettin' somebody younger."

"What? For a little side action?" Skopelli asked.

"Yeah … that's the way it was in England. It worked out pretty good."

"Hm-m-m," Skopelli thought out loud. "Did he know we set him up dat way?"

"Oh no," Manny exclaimed. "I acted like I was real surprised when I found out about their little fling."

"Good," Skopelli approved. "You never know how a pug'll take dat sort o' t'ing. Some don't mind. Others get insulted."

Manny nodded. Skopelli asked when he'd be meeting Sean.

"Well … are we still on for tomorrow mornin' at the club?" Manny asked.

"Oh yeah. 11 tomorra," Tony affirmed. "Let's give him a week off, to get adjusted. A week from Monday we put him to work. Are we usin' Louis for his trainer?"

"That's the plan," Manny affirmed. "Rufus says there's no love lost between Louis and Rocky since Rocky left us."

"No kiddin'," Skopelli laughed. "That's interestin'. No big deal for duh bout in July, but after Rocky recaptures duh crown, who knows?"

"That's what I was thinkin'," Manny said. "Who knows what the future holds? We got some other promisin' heavies comin' along."

Skopelli waved Manny out of his office, saying he'd see him and Sean at the club the next morning. Manny returned to the club that afternoon and told Louis how they wanted to handle Sean.

"How you gonna keep him out o' trouble on the weekends?" Louis grinned.

"I'm workin' on that," Manny answered. "Your job is to work him hard every afternoon. Take the starch out o' him."

"No problemo," Louis answered. "He won't want to do nothin' but fall into bed on weeknights. I guarantee it."

Sean, meanwhile, took the Red Line back into Manhattan and got off at 79th Street. He walked to the American Museum of Natural History. When he arrived he was bowled over by the size of the place. There were 25 buildings and tens of thousands of displays! Obviously he'd be able to take in only a small fraction of the museum in one afternoon. Even at that, he found he wasn't concentrating on things all that well. His mind kept drifting back to what Manny had said about the housekeeping and cooking situation. For the first time it occurred to him that his relationship with Vicki might not have been all that spontaneous. Had Manny set him up with a playmate? And was it about to happen again?

Sean smiled at the idea that Vicki might have been hired to do more than cleaning chores. In hindsight it didn't particularly bother him. On the other hand, things here in America were shaping up differently. The truth was that he harbored secret aspirations for Julie, even though he'd only seen her once. And if that didn't work out, he knew that he wanted to connect on his own in the future. Being supplied with female companionship by another man just wasn't his cup of tea.

Of course he didn't actually *know* that Manny had fixed him up in England. Manny had seemed surprised enough when he learned that he and Vicki had been an item. Still, the more Sean thought about it …

Sean smiled to himself, moving from display case to display case and from hall to hall. Whatever the situation had been in England, he resolved to set Manny straight for future purposes. From here on out he'd find his own girlfriends. Period!

By 4:30 Sean had seen as much of the museum as he felt he could absorb in one visit. He drifted back out onto the streets of New York. What a huge and mighty place it was! Dublin had excited him, but New York was more than his mind could grasp. There were people everywhere … thousands and thousands of people! The streets and boulevards were indeed canyons of concrete and steel. And there were restaurants of every conceivable kind at street level. It was getting to be dinnertime and he decided to eat in Manhattan. Afterward he took a cab to Times Square and made the rounds of a few bars. But, it was lonesome drinking alone, and before 9 PM he was on a train back to Brooklyn.

It was good to gain the sanctity of his new apartment. He watched some TV before turning in. It occurred to him that he didn't really want someone else, of Manny's choosing, sleeping in the apartment with him.

"Yet another thing to talk over with Manny tomorrow mornin'," he thought, rolling the TV channels and exploring the plethora of programs available in America.

Chapter 37

Saturday morning Sean was at the club by 9 AM. Manny came in at 10.

"Well, that was quite a little toot you and Rufus had in Harlem," Manny greeted him.

"Rufus told you?" Sean asked weakly.

"No, I read about it in the papers."

Sean looked at Manny with disbelieving eyes.

"You don't get it, do you?" Manny admonished. "You're fightin' for the heavyweight title in July. Here in America you're big news."

"Aye, I'm beginnin' to see that," Sean admitted. "It's gonna take some getting' used to."

Manny nodded his head and smiled.

"No harm done," he said. "Sit down. I want to go over some things with you."

Manny first told Sean that they'd both have the next week off. He'd already decided to take Sean out of town for five days, for much the same reasons as he'd taken him to the Costa Brava in Spain.

"Monday mornin' we're leavin' for a trip up into New England," he more stated that invited. It didn't even occur to Sean to argue.

"I've heard o' New England," Sean replied. "It's actually several states, isn't it?"

"Yeah, it is," Manny affirmed. "I thought we'd do Connecticut, Rhode Island and Massachusetts ... Mystic Seaport, Newport, Boston ..."

"Sounds like fun!" Sean grinned. "D' you have business there?"

"No ... no, it's gonna be strictly vacation for both of us. We'll take my car and just explore. How'd you sleep in the new bed last night?"

"Fine enough," Sean acknowledged. "By the way, I'd like to discuss the cook and housekeeper thing."

Manny nodded, inwardly becoming all ears.

"Was Vicki hired to be more than a housekeeper?" Sean asked innocently. Manny looked blankly back at Sean.

"Whadda yuh mean?" he asked, putting on a puzzled face.

"You know ..." Sean continued. "Was she ... was our ... friendship less than an accident?"

"What are you askin' me? If I hired her to keep you occupied?" Manny snorted.

Sean pursed his lips and shook his head 'yes'. Manny guffawed.

"Come on, Sean. I'd never do somethin' like that."

Sean nodded sheepishly.

"Whatever gave you that idea?" Manny pressed.

"Well," Sean sighed. "I'd never had much luck with the ladies before then."

"Yeah, man, but you were a nobody before then! You gotta realize, you're a famous guy now. You were already gettin' famous back in England."

"And," Sean thought to himself, "that's the big attraction, isn't it? Not me, but me fame."

Manny's mind was still on high alert. Sean evidently wasn't comfortable with the idea of being supplied with female company. He couldn't blame him.

"I haven't had time to interview anyone for the position here," he murmured tentatively, candidly watching Sean's face.

"Well, I wanted to talk to yuh about that too," Sean said.

"I'm listening," Manny nodded.

"I appreciate all you're doin' for me, settin' me up in such a grand apartment and all," Sean began. "But to tell the truth, I'd rather be alone there."

Manny nodded. "No problem with that," he said. "Anything else?"

"Well," Sean added, "it seems to me that older women are the better cooks. More experience, don't yuh know?"

"Somebody like Mrs. Gruber," Manny murmured.

"Aye, exactly!" Sean exclaimed brightly.

"Well," Manny mused, rubbing his chin, "there *is* an older lady we've used before. She has to spend her evenin's at home and would only be available durin' the day."

"That sounds perfect!" Sean cried excitedly.

"OK. I'll see if she's available," Manny promised. "Whatever you're comfortable with."

It was still over half an hour before Skopelli was due to show up, and Manny showed Sean where the coffee machine was. Each poured himself a cup, and they made small talk until 11 AM.

When Tony Skopelli came into the area where they were waiting, he grinned broadly at Sean. He was so affable when he approached that it caught Manny off balance.

"So you're Fiddler Crabbe," Skopelli smiled, shaking Sean's hand. "I'm Tony Skopelli."

Sean was also blindsided, and secretly chastised himself for having prejudged Skopelli.

"I'm pleased to meet you, Mr. Skopelli," he stammered, shaking Tony's hand.

"Tony … call me Tony," Skopelli smiled warmly.

"Aye, I'm honored," Sean murmured. "And you probably know my real first name is Sean."

"Yeah," Skopelli grunted. "Siddown. Let's chat."

Sean sat down next to Skopelli, and Manny slid into the seat next to Sean. He was speechless and even a little envious at Tony's warm treatment of Sean.

"So! You gettin' everyt'ing you need?" Tony asked.

"Aye!" Sean exclaimed. "Manny's fixed me up with a super nice apartment."

"Good, good," Skopelli approved. "Whadda you t'ink o' New York?"

"I'm bloody overwhelmed," Sean answered. "And I haven't scratched the surface even."

"Yeah, there's plenty to do in this burg," Tony grinned. "Sports, shows, concerts … opera! You like opera?"

"To tell the truth, I've never been," Sean confessed.

"We go sometime … the t'ree of us," Tony said, lighting a cigar and glancing at Manny. "Us Italians, we love opera. I can even translate some o' the Italian songs for you two."

"That sounds great!" Sean said eagerly.

"Let's talk a little business," Skopelli said, blowing smoke up at the ceiling. "You know duh score on duh next two bouts, right?"

"Aye," Sean answered cautiously. "I'm to capture the crown and then lose it back to Rocky."

"Right!" Skopelli confirmed. "Dat's duh way the world turns. But you ain't gonna coast from now to July, *kapeeshi*?"

Sean nodded that he understood.

"We want you to be ripped … nothin' but muscle when you take dat robe off. Duh world's gotta t'ink dat you ripped duh crown off Rocky's head."

Sean kept nodding.

"So Louis is gonna work your butt off dese next t'ree months, unnerstan?" Skopelli continued. "You're gonna be rich, but we're gonna make you earn it."

"I understand," Sean said.

"Dat whole deal … dat you take Rocky by storm … makes for a monster gate in duh rematch. Den it's Rocky's turn to body build. Dere'll be plenty o' prematch publicity. Duh world will see him in great shape. Half duh people on earth are gonna be watchin' to see him get his revenge. You know?"

Sean and Manny both nodded that they understood.

"OK, Manny'll fill yuh in on your trainin' schedule. I take you two to lunch, whadda yuh say?"

Manny's eyes widened in amazement. Sean deferred to Manny with a sidelong glance.

"Hey, we never turn down free food!" Manny exclaimed.

"OK. We go to a big Irish place I heard about," Tony said. "In honor of our boy here."

Tony drove the three of them across to Manhattan Island and pulled up in front of a big restaurant with shamrocks all along its front. Once inside he scanned the menu and spoke to Sean.

"So what's good, Sean. I eat mostly Italian."

"Well," Sean answered, perusing his own menu. "I see they've got Irish beef stew. That's always good. And they've also got one o' me favorites, corned beef and cabbage."

"Cabbage, huh?" Skopelli grunted. "I'll have duh beef stew," he said to the waiter. "And bring us all some big mugs o' dat Guiness stout. Dat's Irish, ain't it?"

"It is," Manny affirmed. "By the way, Tony, in Ireland they call 'em 'jars' and not 'mugs'."

"Jars?" Skopelli barked. "Jars are for pickles! Whoever heard o' drinkin' beer out o' jars?"

Manny and Sean both laughed. By lunch's end Sean was totally won over by Tony. And Manny was awash with newfound admiration for his boss' shrewdness.

Skopelli dropped them off again at the club. Manny told Sean he'd call him the next evening and let him know when he'd pick him up for their New England junket.

"Pack for five days," he told Sean as he took leave.

Sean nodded obediently.

"Connecticut, Rhode Island, Massachusetts…" he thought as he strolled back to his apartment. All places he'd heard about now and then back in Ireland. Now he'd actually be seeing them.

"Whoever would o' thought," he mused, breathing in the spring air. "And all because o' me deformity. What a strange world we live in!"

Chapter 38

Sean and Manny had a fabulous five days in New England. Connecticut was beautiful and, in places, not unlike Ireland in springtime. Mystic Seaport was quaint, and Newport alone was worth the trip. Sean and Manny both stuffed themselves with lobster, which was in plentiful supply on the waterfront. They toured some of the 'Summer Cottages' … fabulous mansions built by scions of old, in spare-nothing attempts to one-up each other. Manny was bowled over by the hundreds of beautiful yachts in the Newport Yacht Basin, and secretly vowed to moor one of his own there one-day.

Sean got a special charge out of that stronghold of the Irish, Boston. He insisted on touring the campuses of Harvard and MIT. Again, they ate too much in some of the downtown oyster bars.

They ended up taking a ferry across Long Island Sound and returning to New York by touring part of Long Island. On the way back Manny informed Sean that he'd hired Mrs. Gomez to clean, do laundry and cook. When they reached the western part of the island he called her on his cell phone and asked her to meet them at Sean's apartment. She had her own key and was waiting for them when they arrived.

Sean liked her from the start. They agreed that she'd start on Monday morning, and would have the weekends off.

"You gonna be OK on your own, tomorrow and Sunday?" Manny asked as he left.

"Aye, for sure. Not to worry," Sean assured him.

"Well, stay out o' trouble," Manny waved.

Sean kicked back and watched TV for the rest of the evening. Saturday morning he walked to the trains and went to the Bronx Zoo. He had always loved wildlife, and had heard since childhood that this was one of the world's great zoological parks. He spent the day, and had dinner at the diner back in Brooklyn. Once again Julie wasn't there.

Sean returned to the diner the next day at noon, and this time he found Julie working behind the counter. After some small talk he screwed up his courage and asked her out. She appeared startled and troubled.

"I'm involved with someone," she said gently.

Sean was mortified and mumbled that he should have known.

"It's OK," she reassured him. "My boyfriend is a big fight fan. When I told him you'd come in, he wished he'd been here to meet you. I'm sure he'd still love to meet you."

"Well, I'm gonna be pretty busy, trainin' you know," Sean objected.

"He's right over there. Why don't you go say 'Hello'? I'll bring your dinner over to you if you like."

It was only with an effort that Sean suppressed a groan. He felt rotten and embarrassed and wanted nothing more than to get out of there. He morosely looked over his shoulder at the booth Julie was nodding toward. In the aisle, in front of the table, sat a young man in a wheelchair, reading the Sunday paper. His back was to the counter and he hadn't noticed Sean.

Sean looked back at Julie, nodded without speaking, and slid off the counter stool.

"Top o' the mornin'," he said, sliding into one of the booth seats so that he wouldn't be looking down on the wheelchair's occupant. He noticed that the young man had no legs.

"Your fiancee said you'd like to meet me. I'm Sean Crabbe."

"Fiddler Crabbe!" the paraplegic cried. "Well, this is an honor!" He extended his hand and Sean was surprised at the strength of his grip.

He told Sean that his name was Sam Steadman. He'd followed Sean's career in Europe, and had already bought tickets for the upcoming title bout in July. He was so enthusiastic that Sean couldn't help liking him from the start. Sean barely noticed Julie when she brought his Sunday dinner to the table.

"Here," Julie said to Sam, setting a hamburger in front of him. "Sean won't have to eat alone."

Sean was curious, but couldn't think of any way to broach the subject of Sam's legs. So the two men talked about boxing and other things. By the time Sean had finished his plate of food, they had become quite relaxed around one another.

It occurred to Sean that Julie probably told Sam everything, so during dessert he mentioned that he'd asked her out before finding out that she had a boyfriend. Sam nodded soberly.

"I can't blame you. She's a lovely girl, isn't she?" Sam murmured.

Sean thought he might have made a gaffe, and munched on a forkful of apple pie in embarrassed silence. Sam sensed his discomfort.

"It must be lonesome for you, being so far from home and all alone," Sam said.

"Well … it looks like they're gonna be keepin' me busy, startin' tomorrow mornin'," Sean answered.

"'They' being your trainers?" Sam clarified.

"Aye. I expect it'll be strenuous goin', to say the least. I'll be too tired to be lonesome durin' the week."

"And what about your weekends?"

Sean shrugged.

"Are you open to suggestions?" Sam asked. Sean looked at him inquisitively and nodded.

"How about the three of us doing some sightseeing between now and July," Sam said. He seemed to be so guileless and eager to help out that Sean was moved and inclined to accept.

"Are yuh sure?" he asked. "Sometimes three's a crowd."

"I don't think that'll be so in our case. We could use a friend … we'd like to be *your* friends."

Sean took a long sip from his cup of coffee. What a sly fellow Sam was, he thought. By extending his hand in friendship, he'd effectively claimed exclusive ownership of Julie. Only an unmitigated cad would hit on her now.

"I'd like that," Sean said at length.

"Great!" Sam exclaimed, fishing a business card out of his pocket. "There's a lot of things to see in New York. If you'd like to do something next Saturday, why don't you give us a call toward the end of the week?"

Sean scanned the card. Sam was evidently an Amway distributor. The card indicated that the phone number was for both his home and business.

"Give *us* a call," Sean thought. So they were living together.

"I will. I'll give you a call," Sean promised, tucking the card into his shirt pocket. "What'll we do?"

"You name it," Sam grinned. "There's no end of the things to see. Maybe you'll have some ideas by the end of the week."

Sean told Sam what a pleasure it was to have met him, and they said 'So Long'. He paid for his dinner at the counter and offered to pay for Sam's hamburger too, but Julie declined.

"Thanks," she said softly when she handed him his change.

"Thank *you*!" Sean smiled. "Sam's a great guy. Did yuh know the three of us are makin' a day of it this comin' Saturday?"

"You're kidding!" Julie exclaimed.

"Aye … I mean 'No', I'm not kiddin'," Sean grinned. "If it's all right with you, that is."

"Sure!" Julie replied. "You two must have really hit it off!"

"Aye, we did," Sean said. "I think we're gonna be mates."

Sean returned to the table and left a tip for Julie.

"Be seein' yuh," he smiled, extending his hand. Sam grasped the hand and gave it a manly squeeze.

"We look forward to it," he smiled. "Until then, Fidd … Sean."

Once outside and walking back to the apartment, Sean couldn't help smiling to himself.

"Life is full o' surprises, isn't it?" he thought. "Who'd have guessed an hour ago that things would take this direction?"

Mrs. Gomez would be cooking three meals a day for him, and he wouldn't be going to the diner very much, if at all.

"Just as well," he muttered. He resolved to read the paper every day, and educate himself on some of New York's attractions. It occurred to him that, with him along, Sam might be comfortable taking Julie to places that he might otherwise be inclined to avoid.

"Sammy, you're a sly one, all right," Sean grinned. "Legs or no legs, you'll fare well in the game o' life."

Chapter 39

Sean was introduced to Louis the next morning at the club.

"I was Rocky's trainer, you know," Louis grinned. Sean was surprised.

"Were you now? I had no idea!" Sean exclaimed. "How long have yuh been in this … organization?"

"Longer'n I can remember," Louis stated. "Rocky used to be here."

"Wha-a-at?" Sean cried. "I didn't know *that*!"

"Yeah. He abandoned us for bigger bucks or somethin'."

"Well I'll be," Sean muttered.

"Well, get into your sweats," Louis said. "It's time to put you to work."

True to the plan, Louis worked Sean mercilessly all morning. Sean dug in willingly and did each exercise until he felt the burn. By 11:30 it was clear to him that the emphasis was now going to be on body building, rather than boxing.

Mrs. Gomez had a healthy lunch fixed for him when he returned to the apartment. He zoned out in front of the TV after eating, and she woke him at 2 PM.

"Time for you to leave, Mr. Crabbe," she said, gently shaking his shoulder.

"Call me 'Sean', won't you?" he smiled up at her. Mrs. Gomez smiled back.

"Si … yes," she answered. "But only if you call me 'Maria'."

Back at the club it was more of the same, with some roadwork thrown in. At 5 PM Manny came in.

"How's it goin'?" he asked Louis and Sean. Sean was sweating and puffing. He blew out his cheeks.

"Goin' well," he answered. "I've gotten a bit out o' shape. Too much o' the good life last week!"

"Why don't we knock off," Manny suggested to Louis. Louis nodded, and Manny turned to Sean.

"I'm joinin' you for dinner."

Sean nodded agreeably, but voiced concern that Mrs. Gomez might have already fixed something.

"Nah, nah, I already called her. She's fixin' extra. We're eatin' at your apartment."

"Oh! Great!" Sean exclaimed. He showered, got into his street clothes, and they drove back to the apartment in Manny's car. When they arrived, Manny was pleased to note that Sean and Mrs. Gomez were on a first name basis.

Over coffee Manny told Sean that they were going to have visitors on Wednesday morning.

"Carbino and company," he said. Sean looked puzzled.

"Vito Carbino … Tony's boss," Manny clarified.

"Tony's *boss*?" Sean exclaimed. "Then Rocky is still part of this … our organization. I thought…"

"You thought right," Manny interrupted. "Carbino is Tony's boss. But as far as the fight game goes, they're different outfits."

Sean nodded and arched his eyebrows.

"So it was Carbino that wooed Rocky away," he mused.

Manny nodded sardonically.

"Wooed, stole, somethin' like that," he smirked.

"And what's the purpose o' the visit? Just to get acquainted, or…"

"I don't know, exactly," Manny admitted. "But I can guarantee you it'll be more than just gettin' acquainted."

Manny left and Sean spent the rest of the evening turning things over in his mind. There were obviously political nuances that he was only beginning to sense. Carbino was Tony's boss, but in what capacity? Each has his own fight group. Maybe Rufus would know something.

Tuesday passed without incident, and the first hour and a half of Wednesday morning seemed to be business as usual. But then, at 10 AM, Manny and Skopelli came into the club. Manny motioned for Sean to join them at ringside.

"How are yuh?" Skopelli greeted. "Dey keepin' yuh busy?"

"Aye," Sean smiled.

"You eatin' good?"

"Oh yes. Mrs. Gomez is a great cook," Sean exclaimed.

"Good! You eat what she fixes. She knows what we want. No between meal snacks, *kapeeshi*?"

"Yes, sir," Sean promised.

"OK," Skopelli continued. "You know we're getting' company this mornin', right?"

Sean nodded but said nothing.

"You get to meet the current champ," Skopelli said.

Sean waited for Skopelli to continue, and when he didn't Sean concluded that Tony didn't know anything more than Manny did.

"Go ahead and keep workin' out," Skopelli grumbled. "We'll call yuh when our visitors get here."

A little after 11 AM a group of men entered the club. Skopelli and Manny hurried over to greet them while Sean and Louis watched from the heavy bag.

"Take yer gloves off," Louis whispered.

Sean could guess which one was Vito Carbino. He was well dressed, rather short, and quite lean. It seemed incongruous that he would be big Tony's boss. His dark eyes scanned the big, open room, and it occurred to Sean that he'd never seen a more mirthless countenance. Carbino said something to Skopelli, and Skopelli shouted across the room to Louis.

"Everybody out! Except you and Fiddler!"

Louis hastened over to the equipment room window and told Seth to go find some coffee somewhere. Seth seemed to understand.

"Rufus too?" he asked. "He's workin' in the locker room."

"Yeah, the man says everybody," Louis answered.

Manny motioned for Sean and Louis to join them at ringside.

"OK," Skopelli barked, "Fiddler, dis is Rocky. Rocky, Fiddler Crabbe."

Rocky smiled slightly and nodded, but didn't extend his hand.

"And dis is Rocky's trainer, Vic," Skopelli continued. "He's gonna explain why we're here."

Vic nodded to Skopelli's people and hopped up into the sparring ring.

"We all know what to expect in July," he began. "What we need to do is work out how Round 11 is gonna go. It's gotta be convincin' on the one hand. But," he added, looking squarely at

Sean, "we can't have any real damage done. We all know by now what you're capable of, Fiddler. And we respect that. But o' course the big money comes in the rematch. And with all due respect to Rocky's ability to take a punch, we want him in one piece after the knockout in July. Understand?"

Sean nodded and glanced at Rocky. He didn't like what he saw in Rocky's eyes. He could only imagine that Rocky despised the idea of faking a defeat. He couldn't blame him.

"This is the only time we'll be meetin' before the bout," Vic went on. "But both you guys are gonna practice what I show you today. We don't want any screw ups."

Again Sean looked at Rocky, but Rocky refused to look back. He did, however, grudgingly nod his head at Vic.

"OK, come up here," Vic told them. Sean and Rocky climbed up into the ring, and Vic commenced showing them how Sean was going to take Rocky down.

"I'll motion like this from ringside, when there's only a minute left in Round 11," he told Rocky. "You'll say to Fiddler, 'Do it', just in case he ain't lookin' at me. Got it?"

Fiddler and Rocky both nodded.

"OK, turn around and face each other," Vic commanded, taking the two fighters by their arms.

"You watchin' this?" Vic asked Louis.

"Yep," Louis nodded from ringside.

"OK," Vic continued. He took Sean's right wrist.

"As soon as you hear Rocky say 'do it', you're gonna throw a round house, loopin', overhead right at Rocky's head like this. You, Rocky, are gonna raise both hands to block. Go on and do it."

Rocky cynically raised his hands.

"Then you, Fiddler, are gonna give him what appears to be a hard shot to the gut. But of course it ain't *really* gonna be all that hard. Go ahead and do it."

Sean faked driving his left into Rocky's gut.

"Bend over," Vic chided Rocky. "He just hit you with a punch that could kill a cow."

Rocky smirked but complied.

"And now, the knockout," Vic said excitedly. "This'll bring the crowd to its feet. You, Fiddler, slam the back of Rocky's head with your left. It drives Rocky right down into the canvas and out cold. Just fake it for now. Rocky, you don't have to go down here, but I want you to practice bein' slammed to the canvas durin' practice, got it?"

Rocky and Sean both nodded.

"OK," Vic said, turning away and addressing the men at ringside. "After the takedown, we're gonna rush into the ring and protest that it was a foul. But the ref … he's in on this … is gonna rule it's a legitimate knockout and give the win to Fiddler. Rocky's gonna swear revenge in the months before the rematch. There's gonna be lots of public interest. Does everybody understand?"

All of the men at ringside nodded, save for Vito Carbino.

"So that's it," Vic concluded. He turned back to Sean and Rocky. "Both o' you guys are gonna be drilled on this, and we expect your full cooperation. It's gotta look convincin'."

Sean and Rocky both acknowledged that they understood.

"And remember," Vic added, poking his index finger into Sean's chest, "it's only for show! No rough stuff! OK, Big Guy?"

"OK," Sean answered softly.

"One final thing," Vic said. "You can mix it up … put on a good show in the first ten rounds. Fiddler, you can use your left, but always on Rocky's shoulder and arm. We'd like to see Rocky knocked down a couple times from those arm and shoulder shots. Your ability to do that is a real big buzz in the fight world. It'll get the crowd juiced up big time."

"Aye, it's OK with me," Sean grinned, casting a glance at Rocky.

Rocky smiled, but with a look that seemed to say, "In your dreams!"

Sean got a cold feeling in the pit of his stomach. Rocky's mouth was saying 'Yes', but his eyes were saying something else. Again Sean chalked it up to Rocky's reluctance to fake a defeat.

"All right," Vic concluded. "You two shake hands and come out swingin' in July."

Sean extended his hand and Rocky took it. On his part, Sean imagined that they shared a certain kinship. He was guessing that Rocky didn't like rigging a fight any more than he did. He hoped that the shaded look in Rocky's eyes reflected that. But of course, known only to Vito Carbino and Rocky, the reality was quite something else.

Carbino and company departed, leaving Tony and his crew standing at ringside. Tony seemed out of sorts.

"Well, dat's dat," he growled. "You got dem moves down pat?" he asked Louis

"Yeah, I think so," Louis nodded.

"You *t'ink so*? You better *know*!" Skopelli shouted. Louis winced abjectly.

"I do … I know," he apologized.

"OK. We don't want no foul ups," Tony said in a gentler tone. "Anybody got any questions?"

No one was inclined to respond.

"OK, den," Tony said, motioning to Manny. "Come on, we got stuff to do."

Tony waddled out of the club with Manny obediently in tow.

"Well," Louis said in a shaky voice, "Let's break for lunch. I think I'm gonna see if I can find Seth and Rufus."

For the first time Sean found himself alone in the club. It gave him an eerie feeling and he hastened toward the door still wearing his sweats. Presumably the place didn't need to be locked up. In any case, it wasn't his problem.

On the walk home it occurred to him that he hadn't heard Vito Carbino's voice once that morning. The man was something of an enigma; he seemed to be surrounded by an aura of evil. And then there was Rocky. Sean's instincts told him that none of them … not even Tony … really knew what the bottom line was. He'd have to be careful … *very* careful … on fight night.

Chapter 40

The rest of the week passed without incident. Louis made Sean and a sparring partner take a couple of practice runs through the knockout that Vic had choreographed. During coffee break Sean told Rufus that Carbino and company had come in Wednesday.

"Yeah, Seth tole me," Rufus said somberly. "How did Rocky look?"

"He looked good," Sean answered. "I'm not certain he much likes takin' a dive though."

Rufus nodded but said nothing.

"I don't know what all the secrecy is about," Sean continued. "You all know what the story's gonna be in July."

"I ain't sure Seth does," Rufus murmured. "And dat's prob'ly a good thing, him bein' a family man and all."

"*Is* he?" Sean asked brightly. "Any young 'uns?"

"Yeah, he got two," Rufus grinned. "They's like my own."

"So what's the relationship between Carbino and Tony?" Sean asked. "Manny says we're independent camps on the one hand, but that Carbino is Tony's boss on the other."

Rufus looked at him with round eyes.

"You kiddin', man? Skopelli and Carbino is Mafia. They's part o' the mob."

Sean nodded soberly.

"I wondered about that back in Europe," he murmured. "And how about Manny?"

Rufus shook his head.

"He ain't Mafia … can't be. He ain't Italian."

"So he's more like us … one of Tony's employees," Sean mused.

"Yeah, I guess," Rufus replied. "But higher up."

Thursday evening Sean called Sam and Julie. Sam asked him if he'd decided on anything, and Sean suggested they go to the top of the Empire State Building.

"You know, I've lived here all my life and I haven't visited it," Sam confessed. "Let's do it!"

They agreed to meet at the diner for breakfast on Saturday morning. Sean was there at 9 AM and Sam and Julie were already waiting for him inside.

"How does it feel to be waited on?" Sean asked Julie when a waitress brought their breakfasts.

"It feels good," Julie smiled. "I could get used to this!"

"What made you pick the Empire State Building?" Sam asked. "Did you hear or read about it in Ireland, or…"

"Actually, I've wanted to see it ever since watchin' the movie, 'An Affair To Remember', Sean answered. "Did yuh ever see that movie?"

"Have we ever!" Julie gushed. "With Cary Grant and Deborah Kerr? We watch it every time it comes on cable."

"And Julie bawls her head off at the end, without fail," Sam teased.

Julie protested, but Sean admitted that he got teary the one time he'd watched it.

After breakfast they walked to the train station.

"Would you like me to push?" Sean asked Sam.

"Yeah, thanks," Sam agreed. "It'll probably be faster."

They took a train into 5th Avenue and walked to the Empire State Building. The sidewalks were already jammed with throngs of pedestrians.

"What an amazin' city!" Sean marveled out loud. Sam asked him about Ireland, and they made small talk on the way up to the observation deck.

The view from the top took Sean's breath away. As they worked their way around, Sam pointed out various landmarks. By 11:30 they were back down on 5th Avenue and moving along with the river of humanity. Sam preferred wheeling himself along. Sean could sense how strong his arms and shoulders were from the ease with which he maneuvered along in the crowd.

It was lunchtime and Sean asked Julie and Sam to pick out a restaurant, his treat. Sam thought for a moment.

"How about Broadway Joe's?" he suggested. "I hear they've got really good steaks and seafood, and it's a sports hangout."

"Sounds good!" Sean said. "Do we walk to it or…?"

Sam frowned.

"We should probably take a cab," he muttered. Sean could tell that Sam was fretting over the logistics of his wheelchair. He stepped to the curb and flagged down a taxi. When one pulled to the curb, Sean bent over and spoke to the driver.

"Could yuh pop your trunk?" he asked.

"Sure thing," the cabby exclaimed, jumping out and hurrying around to the back of his taxi. Sean bent over Sam.

"Grab a hold," he murmured, not looking at Sam.

"Like this?" Sam asked, putting his right arm around Sean's shoulders.

"Aye," Sean replied, effortlessly lifting Sam out of his wheelchair and swinging him into the cab. Julie wheeled the chair around to the back of the cab and expertly collapsed it. The cabby put it in the trunk.

Sean sat in up front, next to the driver.

"Where to?" the cabby asked. Sean shrugged and looked back at Sam.

"Broadway Joe's," Sam said. "I think it's on 46th Street, between 8th and 9th Avenue."

"You're right," the driver answered, tripping his meter and pulling into the traffic.

Sean was bowled over by the restaurant. He learned that it had a long history of entertaining show business and sports folks. The food was superb. Their waiter was very attentive and recognized Sean right off. Sean introduced Sam and Julie, and told the waiter that his friends were showing him the sights.

"Have you seen the Statue of Liberty yet?" the waiter asked.

"No, I've only been here in the states a couple o' weeks," Sean answered. "How about you two?" he asked Sam and Julie.

Again Sam had to admit that he'd never been, despite his lifelong residency in New York.

"You're not alone on that one," the waiter smiled. "If you all want to go, you should have plenty of time to catch the Circle Line out to the island."

So everyone agreed that they'd do that after downing some New York Cheesecake and coffee.

It was a beautiful day and Sean enjoyed the boat trip out to Liberty Island. It felt good to be out on the water again. He was moved by the poem at the statue's base. He and Julie passed on climbing up inside, despite Sam's urging. By 4:30 they were played out and headed back to Brooklyn.

"Sam, Julie, this has been one o' the greatest days o' me life," Sean exclaimed back in the diner's parking lot.

Sam beamed and shook Sean's hand vigorously.

"We had a ton of fun too, Sean. Can we drop you anywhere?"

"No, thanks. It's only a short walk from here," Sean declined. "Shall we do this again sometime?"

"The sooner the better," Sam grinned. "Why don't you give us a call."

"I'll do that," Sean promised. "Here, let me give yuh my cell phone number."

He didn't have anything to write on, so Sam jotted the number down on the back of one of his business cards.

Once back at the apartment, Sean heated a frozen dinner in the microwave and settled down in front of the TV. The Saturday night fights were on, and he kicked back and studied the techniques of some of his peers.

"I wonder how much o' the fight game is fixed?" he thought to himself. At the end of one bout, which he found too close to call, one of the boxers raised his hand in victory and the other all but climbed through the ring ropes before the winner had been announced.

"It's gettin' more and more like wrestlin', isn't it?" he thought to himself cynically. "It's become show business, and a cash cow for them on the inside."

Chapter 41

Louis worked Sean as hard as ever on Monday and Tuesday. Manny came into the club midmorning on Wednesday. He asked Sean whether he'd seen Madison Square Garden, the scheduled site of the title match in July. Sean told him he hadn't had the pleasure, and Manny suggested that Rufus take him there for a get-acquainted look-see.

Rufus of course agreed. He called a Garden caretaker named 'Chazz' on his cell phone.

"How you doin', man?" Rufus spoke into the phone. "Guess who I's bringin' over this mornin' to check out the Garden."

"Fiddler Crabbe?" Chazz answered.

"Yeah! How'd you know?"

"Jus' a lucky guess," Chazz laughed.

"We gonna be gettin' there aroun' noon. You want me to pick up some chicken?"

"Man, that sounds good to me," Chazz said. "I be waitin' for you down in my hideaway."

"OK, Bro'. We see you there."

Sean showered and changed into his street clothes, and he and Rufus took a train into Manhattan. Outside their destination Rufus bought a bucket of fried chicken.

"Here she is," Rufus said, leading the way into an alley. "Madison Square Garden."

Sean wondered why they were going into what appeared to be a blind alley. But Rufus paused before a steel doorway, fished a ring of keys out of his pocket and unlocked the door.

"I ain't s'posed to have keys to this place," he said quietly. "But I used to work here, an' I never gave my keys up."

Rufus led the way through a maze of hallways and out into the Garden's main floor. A dog show was in progress.

"Here's where you and Rocky does it," he whispered.

"They'll set up a ring?" Sean wondered.

"Oh yeah. They plays basketball in here, has concerts, you name it," Rufus continued. "Some o' them pups gonna get wind o' this chicken. Shall we go find Chazz?"

Sean nodded and Rufus led the way back through a locked door, into the restricted area.

"Dey's dressin' rooms down there," he said, pointing down one hallway. "We's goin' down to the basement."

Rufus unlocked another door and he and Sean descended a flight of stairs to the enormous subterranean area of Madison Square Garden. Rufus clearly knew his way, and at length they entered a well-lit lounge. Rufus' friend, Chazz, was slouched on a sofa, watching TV.

"Hey, Chazz, come meet de Fiddler!" Rufus greeted. Chazz walked over and shook Sean's hand.

"Glad to meet you, champ," he grinned. Sean wondered if that was just a figure of speech, or if Chazz knew about the pre-arranged outcome in July.

"Man, what you got here?" Chazz asked Rufus, taking the large paper sack from his arms. "You all want a beer or soda, he'p youselves," he said, gesturing toward a refrigerator. Rufus went over and got a beer, and Sean followed suit.

Chazz unloaded paper plates, side dishes and the bucket of chicken from the brown paper sack, and all three men dove hungrily in, breathing grunts of approval.

"So, you gonna be the champ," Chazz smiled after eating his fill. Sean glanced at Rufus.

"Oh yeah, Chazz knows," Rufus volunteered. "Ain't nothin' goes on here in the Garden he don't know 'bout."

"Aye, it appears I will be," Sean confessed. Chazz noted the troubled look on Sean's face and liked him for that.

"How many fixes you seen here since takin' over from me?" Rufus asked Chazz.

"More'n I can remember," Chazz snorted. "It gettin' to be a way of life. It gettin' to be like rasslin'."

"That's just what I was thinkin' Saturday night, watchin' the fights on TV," Sean said. "It seemed obvious in some cases that the fighters knew who won the match even before the announcement.

"Oh yeah, I's seen some climb through the ropes and get pulled back into the ring before the decision's announced," Chazz said.

"You'd think they'd know better," Rufus muttered.

"They prob'ly would under normal circumstances," Chazz answered. "But after twelve rounds, even puttin' on a show, they sometimes don't know which way is up."

"I 'spects so," Rufus nodded. "How's old Sonny doin'? I ain't seen him in quite a spell."

"Oh, he's fine," Chazz replied. "He's still workin' at the News Stand over yonder a block."

Rufus looked at Sean, who didn't have a clue who Sonny was.

"Sonny most got hisself killed ten, twelve years ago right here in de Garden," Rufus explained.

"Yeah, he was s'posed to become middleweight champ," Chazz added. "That was the understandin'. But he got double crossed."

"Double crossed?" Sean pressed.

"Yeah," Rufus said. "The champ was s'posed to lose to him in de ninth, but he caught old Sonny in de seventh. He scrambled his brains before he could go down."

"That was the end o' him," Chazz interjected. "He never fought again. He been sellin' papers an' magazines ever since."

Sean nodded his head somberly.

"Why would they do such a thing?" he wondered aloud. "I thought the whole idea was to maximize profits."

"Ordinarily, I s'pects it is," Rufus answered. "But ever' now and then … who knows? Maybe one capo don' like another … wants him to lose some big bets laid off aroun' the country. Could be a lot o' things."

The three men continued talking about things they'd witnessed in the fight game. At 1 PM Rufus rose.

"Well, I s'pects you gotta get back to work," he said to Chazz.

"Oh yeah," Chazz groused. "Ain't no tellin' what dem mutts gonna leave on the floor upstairs."

Rufus laughed and made several quick hand clasps with Chazz. Sean couldn't follow them or duplicate them in his mind.

"Hey, Fiddler, you play poker?" Chazz asked Sean.

"Aye, I've done me share," Sean smiled.

"What you think?" Chazz asked Rufus. "We take this chile's money Saturday night?"

"I's all for it," Rufus grinned, looking at Sean. "You want to join us Saturday night for some penny ante at Seth's place?"

"Sounds good," Sean agreed.

"All right! Dat's cool, man," Chazz said, shaking Sean's hand. "I see you suckers then."

Rufus led Sean off in a different direction through the maze of underground hallways. They emerged into a large storage room where hundreds of cardboard boxes were stacked.

"Step in here," Rufus suggested, lifting a wooden gate. "We ride back up to de street in style."

Rufus pushed a button and Sean felt the elevator floor push up against their feet. Above them two rusty steel plates opened upward and they could see blue sky. Once they'd stepped out into a broad alley way, Rufus sent the lift back down.

"Deliveries," he grunted in explanation.

"Where does Sonny work?" Sean wanted to know.

"Not far from here," Rufus answered. "You want to walk over to his stand?"

"Aye," Sean said. "I'd like to meet him."

"They ain't much to meet," Rufus nodded. "He got hurt in the head, that last fight. But he be a good soul."

Rufus led the way, and in less than ten minutes they were at Sonny's newsstand.

"Hey, Sonny!" Rufus greeted. "Shake hands wid Fiddler Crabbe. He fightin' for de heavyweight crown in July!"

Sonny grinned and shook Sean's hand, but said nothing. Sean estimated he was in his forties, but he looked older. His hair was mostly white, and it was clear that he wasn't quite right in the head. He didn't seem to recognize the name 'Fiddler Crabbe' despite the numerous ring magazines on his stand.

Rufus picked out a magazine and handed Sonny a five dollar bill.

"We be goin' now," he said. "Take care o' youself, Sonny."

Sonny nodded and added the fiver to a roll of bills he pulled from his pocket.

"A double cross, huh?" Sean mumbled, once he and Rufus had moved out of earshot.

"Dat's what I hear," Rufus confirmed. "It happens. Sometimes I don' know what holds de mob together."

"Only their common hate for the cops, I expect," Sean nodded.

"Yeah, dat's it all right. But you be careful in July, Irish. Hear? They ain't nothin' certain in the fight game."

"I plan to be," Sean answered. "Frankly, I didn't get a warm feelin' when Carbino and his crowd visited the club."

"Yeah, I can dig it. Dat Carbino is one spooky dude. Here," Rufus muttered, handing the magazine to Sean. "You can have this. I ain't got time to be doin' much readin'."

Chapter 42

Sean invited Rufus and Chazz to come over to his apartment Saturday afternoon and watch a ball game. They barbecued up some steaks for dinner.

"Man, this is *nice*!" Rufus said when he and Chazz first arrived and looked around. "And dey pays for all this?"

"Aye, I guess it's all part o' the trainin' package," Sean grinned. "O' course they get it all back, plus several million to boot."

Rufus nodded his head.

"I s'pose I oughta be jealous," he sighed. "But you know sump'n, Irish? I wouldn't know what to do wid dat kind o' money. I don' even play de lottery for fear I wins it."

Sean laughed and said he wasn't in any better shape. He told Rufus he was going to have to get some professional advice on how to invest his winnings.

"Yeah, Seth an' me got a liddle inves'ment club goin'," Rufus said. "We tries to buy some stocks or bonds ever' month."

"Good for you!" Sean exclaimed. He wanted to ask Rufus how much they had, but decided not to pry.

Chazz was less inhibited.

"You buyin' stocks?" he cried, clearly flabbergasted. "How much you got?"

Rufus grinned and shrugged.

"I don' rightly know. Seth is de brains. I jus' kicks in some money ever' month."

"How much you kick in?" Chazz pressed.

"Not much," Rufus demurred. "Only $200 lately. But it add up in time."

"Don' it jus'," Chazz thought aloud. "Man, I got to start doin' sump'n like that."

"Yeah, a man can't retire jus' on Social Security in *this* town, that's for sure," Rufus observed.

The three men kicked back and enjoyed the ball game. By mutual consent they drank soft drinks, knowing they'd be going to Seth's house after dinner.

None of the three owned a car, so after dinner Sean called for a cab to take them over to Seth's home. Rufus had wanted to clean up the dishes after they finished eating, but Sean insisted on leaving everything in the sink.

"Mrs. Gomez'll take care o' that Monday mornin'," he explained.

When they arrived at Seth's house, Seth introduced Sean to his wife, Beulah. She was a pleasant, plump woman, and Sean guessed she might be a few years older than her husband. Their son, the older of their two children, was clearly fascinated by Sean. When Beulah took Sean's jacket, the boy looked at Sean's lopsided physique with eyes of wonder.

"Uncle Rufus says there ain't no man in the world stronger than you!" he exclaimed.

"Isn't," his mother corrected. "There isn't *any* man in the world…"

The boy nodded, but couldn't tear his eyes away from Sean.

"Uncle Rufus say you can kill a grown bull with one punch," the youngster continued.

"I expect I could make one blink, all right," Sean grinned. "What's your name, lad?"

"Oh, I'm sorry," Beulah interjected. "This is Danny. And this," she continued, pulling a shy little girl out from behind her skirts, "Is Shilah."

"Shilah … what a pretty name," Sean said. "And Danny … that's a fine Irish name!"

"How about Fiddler?" Danny asked. "What kind o' name is that?"

"Danny!" Beulah scolded. Sean laughed.

"It's OK," he said. "It's a good question. 'Fiddler' is me ring name. Me real name is 'Sean … Sean Crabbe'."

"So how come they nickname you Fiddler?" Danny wondered. "You play the violin?"

"No," Sean laughed. "It's after these little crabs that have one enormous claw. They're called fiddler crabs, and someone thought that would be a good name for a fighter."

"Oh-h-h," Danny murmured, "now I get it."

Sean spent some more time getting acquainted with Danny and Shilah, and won Beulah over in the process. They were both cute kids, and Sean could understand why Rufus loved them like they were his own.

After a while Beulah took the children into the living room to watch TV and the men sat down at the kitchen table for a night of poker. Seth had the refrigerator well stocked with beer, and they drank straight from the bottles. It was strictly penny ante and for fun. It occurred to Sean that even the worst bad luck case wouldn't be able to lose more than $10 in the course of an evening.

Beulah had set out a couple of bowls of pretzels, and would come out into the kitchen every half-hour or so to see if the men needed anything. On one such occasion the topic of 'most memorable person' had just come up.

"Who was your most memorable person?" Seth asked Rufus.

"Shoot, Bro', you know who dat would be," Rufus answered. "It was our Mama."

"Yeah, I 'spects for me too," Seth agreed.

"How 'bout you, Irish?" Rufus asked. "Who done have the greatest effeck on you?"

Sean peeked at his hole card and took a pull from his bottle of beer.

"Well," he murmured, "there's been a few. I'd say me late Grandma Mary was one."

"That's nice," Beulah commented. "She'd be happy to hear you say that."

"What you remember 'bout her?" Seth asked.

"Oh, many things," Sean said. "She and Grandpa Shamus used to come to me parents' house for Sunday dinner. I remember one Sunday, not long before she died, she told me that my wanderin' would cease the day I looked into the right woman's eyes."

"That's so roMANtic!" Beulah cried. "What a beautiful thought!"

"Aye," Sean continued. "She said that every man has one special island he calls 'home', and that he knows the island when he gazes into his love's eyes."

"Well, I don't know about dem eyes," Chazz snorted, "but I sho' 'nuff agree wid de island part."

"Oh yeah?" Rufus challenged. "An' how's dat?"

"'Cause I knows what *my* island home is," Chazz grinned, "an' its name is Ma-a-anHATtan."

Everyone laughed.

"I'll drink to that," Seth said, raising his bottle in mock toast.

"Hear, hear!" Sean chimed in, following suit.

"Yeah, I'll sho' 'nuff drink to Manhattan," Rufus said, glancing at Chazz. "Man, is your ante in de pot?"

"No," Chazz shot back, "but I b'lieve my Uncle Bubba's in dere."

Chapter 43

Sean called a taxi again after the poker game broke up. He dropped Chazz off at the trains into Manhattan.

"This be good for me too," Rufus said, following Chazz out of the cab. "I can walk to my place from here."

Chazz bent over and peered back into the taxi at Sean.

"Hey, man, thanks for the sody pop and steak," he grunted. "Dat was a lot o' fun."

"Same goes here, Irish," Sean heard Rufus chime in.

"Thank *you* guys, for invitin' me," Sean answered. "Rufus, I'll probably see you on Monday."

"I be dere," Rufus called back. "Be good!"

That night, as he lay waiting for sleep to claim him, Sean wondered how Sam and Julie had spent their day. He debated whether to give them a call in the morning, but finally decided that perhaps Sunday was family time for them. The next day he took a train into Manhattan and re-visited The American Museum of Natural History. This time he took in The Hayden Planetarium. It was astounding how realistic the show was. He'd never seen anything like it in Ireland. And of course only light from the brightest stars made it through New York's air at night.

The next week went by rapidly, with Louis keeping the pressure on. Were it not for his misshapen form, Sean could have been a contender in any body builder contest. His young body responded quickly to the rigors of weight training and the healthy meals prepared by Mrs. Gomez.

There was an article in Sunday's paper about himself and Rocky. Among other things it said that Fiddler Crabbe's share of the gate in July would be ten million dollars (with Rocky getting fifteen million). Sam read the article with interest and left the paper folded open and on the floor with the rest of the news and features.

Julie ordinarily didn't even glance at the sports pages, but when she gathered the scattered pages up to put into the trash that night, the article caught her eye.

"Ten million!" she thought to herself as she lay in bed next to Sam that night. It was more than she and Sam might expect to earn in one or two hundred years! Of course the reality was that Sean himself would receive only a fraction of the ten million. But Julie didn't know about such things and took the article at its word.

Thursday evening she helped Sam pack, and Friday morning she drove him to JFK airport to catch a flight to Atlanta. Sam had worked his way up in the Amway network and was expected to attend their conventions whenever possible.

"See you Sunday night," he told her at the passenger drop-off area, pulling her down for a goodbye kiss.

"I'll be here," she answered. "If there's any problem, give me a call."

Julie drove back to Brooklyn and went to work for the day. That night she was restless, and finally had to admit to herself that she yearned to see Sean.

The next morning, at around 9:30, the phone rang.

"Hello," she spoke into it, fully expecting to hear Sam's voice.

"Hi, Julie, it's me, Sean," she heard instead. "Did you have a good week?"

"Oh, Hi!" she answered, feeling her heart pound in her chest. "Yes ... pretty much the usual. We missed you last weekend."

"Yeah," Sean apologized. "I got roped into a Saturday night poker game with some o' me cronies. I thought I'd call and see if you two wanted to do anything today."

Julie paused, but then caved in (she didn't know to what).

"Why don't you come over for lunch? You know the address, right? We can ... go on from there."

"Great!" Sean answered. "Any special time?"

"Oh, say 11:30?" she suggested.

"I'll be there," Sean promised. He didn't have a clue what they'd be doing, but decided to let Julie and Sam make the decision this time. At 11 o'clock he had a cab take him around to a bank teller machine, withdrew a couple hundred dollars, and continued on to the address on Sam's business card.

"Very nice," he mused, eyeing the big apartment building. He went inside, found their apartment door and knocked on it. Julie opened it. She looked very pretty and her eyes were sparkling with excitement. For an instant, pangs of jealousy stabbed at Sean.

"Hi," he began. But she took his hand and pulled him inside. Sean thought that perhaps they were going to surprise Sam as she closed the door. His head went numb when she grasped him by the back of his neck and kissed him on the mouth.

"Are yuh crazy?" he whispered hoarsely, pulling back and looking down the apartment's hallway over her head.

"Sam's not here. He's away at a convention for the weekend," Julie whispered.

Sean's first impulse was to bolt. But she pulled his head down toward her face again.

"I want you," she whispered, "and I know you want me."

Her eyes closed and her lips parted, begging to be kissed again. His head spinning, and unable to think straight, Sean pulled her tightly against himself and kissed her passionately. His hands ran over her body. It had been so long! He swept her up into his arms, kissing her again, and carried her into the apartment's living room.

"The couch, the couch," she whispered huskily, kissing his neck with a desire that matched his own.

Later, while he could hear her taking a shower, Sean began to experience feelings of remorse. He didn't really know Sam that well, he argued to himself on the one hand. Yet he couldn't help feeling guilty on the other hand. His one overriding thought now was to get out of there. He had no idea what the outcome of all this was going to be. If only Sam was ... whole! It would be so much easier!

Julie emerged from the bedroom that she shared with Sam. It was clear that she was confused too. Sean smiled sheepishly at her. Even now he wanted to remove the terry cloth robe she'd put on.

"We need some time to think, don't we," he suggested softly. Julie only nodded.

"I think I'm fallin' in love with you," Sean murmured, rising to his feet. Julie's brow wrinkled and tears brimmed in her eyes.

"What should I do?" Sean asked, looking down at the floor. She walked to him and kissed him on the cheek.

"I don't know," she whispered. "I don't know what any of us should do."

Sean put his hands on her and felt her soft body through the robe. But she stepped back, her eyes pleading 'No'.

"You're right," she murmured weakly. "I need time."

Sean nodded and walked to the door. Julie followed him as far as the hallway.

"Call me," he called, turning to look back at her. "Let me know what you want."

Julie seemed to think for a moment, and then answered him.

"If I call, it'll be because I want … us to happen," she promised.

Sean walked outside and scanned the street for a cabstand.

"And if she doesn't call…" he thought morosely. Part of him hoped she would, and another part feared that she would. What a bag of snakes adult life could be! The old saw, 'There are no snakes in Ireland', drifted through his mind. He thought of Lillian Scully and Peter Connolly and the way things had worked out for them. Had they been intimate as High School sweethearts?

"Probably," Sean thought. "Face it. Like every race on earth, the Irish have their share o' snakes."

Chapter 44

Julie spent a troubled Saturday afternoon in her apartment, and after dinner she called her widowed mother, Alice, who lived in Queens. She told her that she needed to talk, and asked if she could come over the next day. Alice of course said 'yes'.

A little before 9:30 the next morning Julie rang her mother's doorbell. Alice hugged her daughter and took her into the kitchen to have some light breakfast.

Julie told her mom the whole story and Alice listened quietly.

"What should I do, Mom?" she pleaded.

Alice rose and freshened their cups of coffee, marshaling her thoughts.

"I can't tell you what to do," she began. "You're a grown woman. But how about if I ask you some questions?"

Julie nodded eagerly.

"First off, I don't think you should be consumed by a lot of guilt," Alice said. "You haven't broken any vows to Sam."

"I know," Julie agreed lamely. "But still…"

Alice shook her head negatively. She wasn't budging on this one.

"Sam, and every young man who lives with a woman, should know that he doesn't have any right to expect exclusive access without a ring. If the two of you were married, this would be a different story. But as things stand, you don't need to beat yourself up for considering a sincere offer from another man."

Julie pondered that for a few moments.

"Should I tell him?" she wondered.

"Tell Sam?"

Julie nodded.

"Well, let's look at that next," Alice answered. "Who do you want to be with? If you want Sam out of your life, then telling him will probably accomplish that. If you want to continue on with him, then I don't recommend it. Your big problem right now is to make a choice. I don't really think a woman can have it both ways, no matter what the modern hype says."

"That's just it," Julie complained. "I don't know."

"If you never called this fighter back, would you spend the rest of your life worrying about what became of him?"

"Probably not," Julie admitted. "I've only seen him, what … four times."

"And how about Sam? What if you walk away from him?"

Julie's eyes misted over.

"How could I?" she murmured, hanging her head. "Sam is such a part of me."

Alice nibbled on a piece of toast and said nothing.

"We've become such good friends," Julie continued. "We're so … *comfortable* with one another."

"You know, unless he wins the lottery he's probably never going to be a millionaire," Alice prodded, playing the devil's advocate.

"I know, I know. But he's a fighter too, in his way. I think he'll always do well."

"Where do you think your best long term prospects lie?" Alice asked. "Will Sam still be with you ten years from now? How about the prize fighter?"

Julie knew, then, that she had her answer. She looked at her mother and her face relaxed for the first time.

"Thanks, Mom," she said, squeezing Alice's hand.

"Why don't you go to church with me this morning, and we'll go out for some lunch afterward?" Alice suggested.

"I'd better not," Julie replied. "I've got to pick Sam up at JFK by 3. And I'm not really dressed for…"

"Nonsense," Alice said. "You're dressed better than a lot who go to services these days. I'll settle for church. That'll leave you plenty of time to get to JFK."

Julie agreed, and they went to her old church … the one her parents had always attended. On the way, Julie thought about her mother's situation. Although widowed, Alice seemed to be comfortably well off. She owned her house and car free and clear, and between 401K's, investments that she and her late husband had made over the years, plus Social Security, she had an adequate income. Julie knew that her dad had never done any better than Sam was doing. So obviously great wealth wasn't the key to happiness. The secret to Alice's security seemed to be that she and Julie's dad had stuck together and worked as a team for more than forty years.

It had been quite a while since Julie had been in *any* church, and feelings of peace enveloped her when they entered and sat down in one of the pews. There was a subtle fragrance in the air that she'd never found anywhere else.   When she and Alice had seated themselves, Alice's chin dropped to her chest in silent prayer. Julie wondered what her mother's thoughts were. Was she talking to Dad, now gone for more than seven years? Was she praying that her daughter would find happiness as she had?

Julie closed her own eyes and wondered what she should be thankful for. And then, without really thinking about it, the words were there in her mind.

"Thank you, God, for Mom."

Julie kissed her mother goodbye when they returned to Alice's home.

"Thanks, Mom," she whispered. "Thanks for listening."

Alice smiled and smoothed her daughter's hair.

"I know you'll do the right thing," she said softly. "Don't be a stranger."

"I won't," Julie promised. "I'd better be going."

On the drive back from JFK, Julie told Sam that Sean had called.

"No kidding! I was beginning to wonder what'd become of him," Sam exclaimed.

"I told him you were out of town," Julie said quietly. Sam sensed there was more.

"And?" he murmured.

"And he wanted to come over. I … don't think we should see him anymore, Sam."

Sam grew silent. At first he was awash with disappointment. He wasn't usually wrong about people that way. Then other thoughts … darker thoughts … began creeping into his mind.

"And did he?" he asked at length.

"What? Come over?"

Sam nodded.

"No, of course not," Julie muttered.

That night, after dinner, Julie did what she'd thought she never would. She handed Sam an ultimatum.

"Sam," she said in a determined tone, "I don't want to live like this anymore."

Sam's first reaction was that he was losing her. But, he was no fool and he rarely fell victim to self-doubt. Just when Julie was becoming exasperated by his non-responsiveness, he spoke to her again.

"Will you marry me?" he asked softly.

Julie looked at him with startled eyes. Suddenly she began to weep and laid her head on his shoulder.

"Yes," she whispered, turning his face toward her and kissing him again and again. "Yes, Yes! When?"

"Whenever you say," he smiled, kissing her back. "But not before we buy you an engagement ring."

Other than having legs that ended in stumps above the knee, there was nothing wrong with Sam Steadman. And that evening, after they'd gone to bed, the future Mrs. Steadman gave him a night he'd never forget.

Chapter 45

By Sunday evening Sean was pretty much hoping that Julie wouldn't call. Was he ready to complicate his life, given everything else that was going on?

Throughout the following week he continued feeling the same way, but by week's end he was starting to wonder why she *hadn't* called. His pride couldn't accept that she might have chosen Sam over himself.

"The man's a bloody *cripple*," he thought spitefully. A heartbeat later he couldn't believe the thought had crossed his mind. He was filled with self-loathing to the depths of his soul.

He knew that any chance for a friendship between himself and Sam was gone forever. He waxed hot when he thought about his interlude with Julie. But he as quickly turned cold when he wondered about her motivations. After all, she barely knew him! Was the attraction physical? Was she a gold digger?

He'd said he was falling in love with her. What a joke!

"Amazin', what desire will lead a man to say," he thought cynically.

Midway through the second week, he had convinced himself that she wanted to contact him but didn't know how. Obviously she wasn't going to ask Sam for his phone number, any more than he was going to call her for fear that Sam would answer.

"You're a dirty rat," he upbraided himself, "but you're not rotten enough to feign friendship under the current circumstances."

By Thursday of the second week, Sean had decided that he absolutely had to know what the score was. By now he was well aware that it was his own vanity that drove him. Yet he felt he had to be certain. And so, after lunch, he bypassed his usual snooze in front of the TV and set out on foot for the diner.

He decided that if Julie was working behind the counter, then he'd go to a booth. The important thing was that she'd get a chance to talk to him if she wanted to.

As luck would have it Julie *was* working behind the counter when he came in. At first she didn't see him, and he sat down at a booth where she couldn't miss him.

"Just coffee and a piece of apple pie," he told his waitress quietly. Before his order arrived, Julie began wiping the countertop and noticed him. He put on his most benign face, neither smiling nor scowling. She frowned, looking him straight in the eye, and shook her head 'no'.

Sean felt the blood drain from his head. It was Lillian Scully all over again. Yet he knew in his heart that Julie was no mean-spirited shrew. It was quite simple, really. She had chosen Sam.

Sean's eyes stung with mortification. Julie turned her back to him and began brewing a fresh urn of coffee. Two minutes later, when she glanced back at the booth, it was empty. A five-dollar bill lay on the table.

The waitress came to the empty booth and looked around, bewildered. She waltzed over to the counter.

"Did the guy in that booth go to the john, did yuh notice?" she asked Julie.

"He left," Julie answered quietly.

"*Left*?" the waitress exclaimed. "What am I supposed to do with this?"

"Dump it," Julie shrugged. "He paid for it, didn't he?"

"Well, yeah," the waitress said, glancing back at the table. "But what…I don't get it! People are crazy these days!"

Sean walked back to the fight club, numb with embarrassment.

"So now yuh know, stupid. Any questions?" he self-flagellated himself. He changed into his sweats and attacked the heavy bag savagely. By the time Louis returned at 2:30 he was sweating profusely.

"What's goin' on? How long you been here?" Louis asked.

"I can put in some extra time if I want, can't I?" Sean snarled.

Louis arched his eyebrows. Wow!

"Sure, champ," he said. "You can do anything you *want*."

Sean continued pushing himself to the max for the next two weeks. At least he slept well on weeknights. On the weekends he began haunting strip joints in Manhattan. His dampened spirits suppressed his immune system, and with only two weeks until the title bout he developed a nasty and persistent cough. Louis told Manny about it. Manny came in late Thursday morning and told them to knock off…he was taking Sean to the doctor. Sean protested, but Manny told him he didn't have a choice.

"Any fever? Chills? Sweats?" the doctor asked Sean, once he was seated on the table in an examination room.

"I don't think so. O' course I sweat a lot when I'm workin' out," Sean said.

"Yes, of course," the doc nodded. "But not at night?"

"Nah, I sleep like a dead man at night," Sean answered.

"You're eating good…no loss of appetite?"

"No, I eat like a horse," Sean smiled wanly. "I feel fine."

The doctor studied Sean's face. He sensed that Sean was hiding something…probably emotional.

"How's your love life?" he asked quietly.

"What love life?" Sean snorted, hanging his head.

"OK!" the doc said. "Put your shirt on. Let's go talk with Liebowitz."

Sean complied and found the doc conversing with Manny at the prescription counter.

"Probably an allergy," he overheard the doc say. "We're into July now, you know."

"Should he be takin' anything?" Manny asked.

"I could prescribe something," the doc answered. "But it would make him lethargic."

"What if I just ride it out?" Sean asked, approaching the other two.

"Most people do," the doc responded. "It's not a serious condition."

"I think I should just do that," Sean said to Manny. Manny nodded agreeably.

"Let me know if anything more than the dry cough develops," the doc said. "Itchy, watery eyes, rash, or anything of that nature. Barring that, I think you're OK."

On the drive back to Sean's apartment, Manny breathed a sigh of relief.

"Man, all we need right now is for you to get sick," he muttered.

"I'm *fine*!" Sean reassured him.

"Only two weeks from this Saturday," Manny said. "You're gonna be a rich man! Heavyweight champ of the world! Are you ready?"

"Aye, ready as rain," Sean answered. "All things considered, how can we miss?"

Manny nodded and studied Sean candidly. He seemed down, and Manny chided himself for not having noticed earlier.

"You ever been upstate…to the Catskills?" he asked.

Sean shook his head 'no'.

"Except for our New England trip, I haven't been out o' the city. What are the Catskills… mountains?"

"Yeah. You know, we always have a contender take some time off before a title bout," Manny lied. "I think you and I will take another trip. Upstate New York this time. We could leave Saturday…day after tomorrow."

Sean nodded agreeably.

"Sure, whatever," he mumbled.

Manny pulled his Lincoln up in front of the apartments.

"On second thought, I got nothin' goin' on tomorrow. Let's leave tomorrow mornin'. We'll beat the weekend traffic."

Sean glanced across at Manny and again nodded.

"I'll pick you up tomorrow at 9, OK?" Manny continued. "Tell Mrs. Gomez she has next week off."

"Sounds good," Sean smiled weakly, reaching for the door handle.

"Stay out o' trouble, huh?" Manny said, giving Sean a mock punch on the shoulder. "Pack for five days. I think we'll do Grossingers. It's a big resort up north. We'll get some fresh air."

"Somethin's buggin' that boy," Manny thought as he pulled away. "A week in new surroundin's might be just what he needs."

Manny knew from experience that, despite the resort's rural setting, a man didn't need to forego the pleasures of female companionship.

"Oh yeah," he grinned, "he's gonna be a new man after a week in that mountain air."

Chapter 46

Manny was right. A change of scenery was just what Sean needed. The Catskills were lovely, and Grossingers Resort was a blast. There was nightly entertainment, and Sean laughed at the featured comedian until his sides ached. Grossingers had entertained many fighters over the years, and Sean and Manny received the royal treatment. They swam, played golf (Sean did remarkably well), and of course ate and ate some more. But Manny adroitly assured that they ate healthy.

After three days at the resort, Manny suggested that they check out and work their way back to New York City by way of eastern Pennsylvania. Manny himself had never been there and he wanted to have a look at the Amish country.

Both of them got a huge kick out of the horse-drawn buggies with electric taillights and turn signals. And even Sean, with his rural Irish background, wondered at the austere lifestyle of the Amish.

"Belief systems … humans live in a world of belief systems," Manny exclaimed. "Models of reality … of what's right and true … of what's worth fightin' for."

"An interestin' thought," Sean murmured. "These Amish people do seem to have their own set o' beliefs about how men and women should live, don't they?"

"Don't we all," Manny grunted. "I'd bet almost every war ever fought was fought over clashin' belief systems."

"Aye, that and real estate," Sean added.

"Even the game we're in … the fight game … prospers because of people's desire to fight for a cause," Manny mused.

"Playin' on the warrior spirit in every man," Sean murmured.

"Yeah. Blood sports are probably the oldest of all the sports. I bet they go back to prehistoric times."

"I expect they do," Sean agreed. "Men hackin' each other up for the release and amusement of other men."

"It seems to be as good a way as any to fill in the lulls between wars."

"And it doesn't even have to be real, does it?" Sean thought aloud.

"Heck, no. Every kid knows that movies are only make believe. Not to mention pro wrestlin'. People in wrestlin' openly admit that it's bogus. Yet audiences flock to the matches. It's bigger than ever!"

"And now it's happenin' to boxin'," Sean said.

"Yeah … some of the time, for sure," Manny admitted. "But not always."

"Aye, I can vouch for that," Sean murmured, feeling the scar on his cheek. "What d' you think I should do if Rocky goes for the win?"

"Whadda yuh mean? If he doesn't lie down like agreed?"

"Aye. It's been known to happen."

"It ain't gonna happen in your fight," Manny said. "I know Rocky from way back. Independent thought ain't his strong suit. The only way that would happen would be if Carbino wanted it to happen. And Vito Carbino ain't walkin' away from the kind o' gate that your rematch is gonna generate."

Sean nodded. But he silently resolved still not to take anything for granted on fight night.

Manny and Sean made it back to Brooklyn by suppertime on Friday night.

"Stay out o' trouble," Manny charged Sean when he dropped him off at his apartment. "Business as usual on Monday. Tuesday we got weigh-in. I think Tony's gonna be goin' with us."

Sean relaxed over the weekend, and Louis went easy on him all day Monday. By then the goal was limited to keeping Sean limber and looking good. At the weigh-in on Tuesday, Sean and Rocky indulged the press and posed with Sean's left side prominently displayed. Rocky was cordial and pleasant for a change. As Manny had guessed, Skopelli accompanied them. Tony took Sean, Manny and Louis out to dinner afterward.

"Nothin' too strenuous dis week," Skopelli told Louis. "And Friday off."

Louis nodded obediently. Later, Tony spoke to Sean.

"How you feelin'? You ready for Saturday night? What's dat cough I been hearin' all night. You ain't gettin' sick, are yuh?"

"No, I'm fine," Sean reassured him. "Manny already took me to the doctor's. It's just the air here in New York … an allergy, the doc said. Nothin' to worry about."

Skopelli looked at Manny and smiled approvingly.

Louis went easy on Sean for the rest of the week. Manny insisted on treating Sean to dinner and a Broadway show on Friday night. The show was enjoyable, but for the most part Sean was preoccupied with the fight, now less than 24 hours away.

Manny picked Sean up at 2 PM Saturday afternoon and they swung by the club to pick up Louis, Rufus and Sean's fight gear. Someone … Skopelli or Manny (Sean didn't know who) … had ordered a new robe made up. It was a gorgeous thing, like silk, with a colorful picture of a fiddler crab embroidered on its back.

"You gonna knock their eyes out wid dis baby," Rufus grinned when he had Sean try it on for size. It was a perfect fit, and Sean had to agree.

For Sean, everything seemed to happen in a blur from that point on. It was rather like he was being prepped for surgery. Everyone around him seemed to know what they were doing, and he was along for the ride.

Somehow Manny's car got parked and they all ended up in a spacious dressing room at Madison Square Garden. Rufus helped Sean get dressed for the fight. Manny was popping in and out of the dressing room, growing more and more excited as the minutes ticked away. It was contagious, and Louis began to get juiced up too.

"You know what to do," Louis coached Sean. "Some arm and shoulder shot knockdowns in the early rounds."

"Do I hold back?" Sean asked him.

"Well … we don't wanna break his arm," Louis answered. "Don't end the fight before it's s'posed to end. But no, go ahead and give him some good punches. He's in shape. It's gotta look convincin'."

Sean nodded and smiled ever so slightly. He looked forward to seeing Rocky's eyes when he unloaded on him. Rufus took note.

"Um Hm-m-m, Oh Yeah, He got dem cattle punch blues," he sang. Sean smiled at Rufus and Rufus grinned back.

"It be payback time in de Rockies," Rufus continued singing. This time Louis smiled, but said nothing.

Manny burst back into the dressing room.

"Come on, you guys, let's get his gloves on!" he shouted. "It's almost show time!"

Rufus checked his cut kit out while Louis pushed the gloves onto Sean's hands and laced them. Manny was babbling advice, but Sean found it hard to concentrate on what he was saying. He felt like he was in the best shape of his life, and knew he'd be able to take Rocky even without things being rigged. To be sure, it would still be rough and tumble. And that was fine with him. The thought of slugging it out with Rocky roused his blood lust. The moment was at hand. The time had arrived to do battle with the heavyweight champion of the world, and to give him a taste of Irish justice.

Chapter 47

Sean and the rest of the team were met at the restricted area's exit by eight security guards. They formed a circle around the fight team and escorted them to ringside. It was a sellout crowd in the Garden and, although not the favorite, Sean received lots of encouragement as they made their way down the aisle.

Once inside the ring, Sean did some dancing and shadow boxing, showing off his new robe. When Rufus removed it the crowd's excitement audibly increased. The musculature of Sean's left side was truly massive and spectacular … not unlike the bull he'd dropped back in Ireland.

Sean stole candid glances out over the sea of faces. There were several show business personalities at ringside, and he also recognized the mayor of New York. Tony Skopelli and Vito Carbino were there too. Carbino was seated within eyesight of Tony, but on an adjoining side of the ring.

Several men at ringside were smoking cigars, and Sean couldn't help coughing every minute or so. He knew from the roar of the crowd when Rocky entered the auditorium. The uproar continued when Rocky climbed into the ring and danced with his gloves above his head. Vic was putting on a good show of giving last minute instructions to Rocky. When one of his seconds removed Rocky's robe, the crowd cheered even more loudly. Rocky did some shadow boxing, smiling at the crowd, and there was no question that he too was in terrific shape.

Sean and Rocky were introduced to the audience, and Sean got more applause than he'd anticipated. The ref gave the two fighters the usual lecture at center ring and the fight was on. Rocky and Sean put on a good show. Sean swung his left several times, but was careful to miss or only graze Rocky. Rocky danced and boxed confidently, as befit a world heavyweight champion.

Manny had suggested that Sean knock Rocky down with body shots in rounds 4 and 7. When the bell for round 4 sounded, Sean came out boxing and a minute into the round he landed Rocky a crushing blow on his right shoulder. It sent Rocky careening into the ropes and he lost his footing. Sean retreated to a neutral corner while Rocky took the standing eight count. The crowd went ballistic. This was what they'd been hearing about for more than a year and had come to see.

Rocky came out of the eight count smiling ever so slightly at Sean. His face seemed to acknowledge Sean's awesome power and Sean actually began to like him. Rounds 5 and 6 came and went, and in round 7 Sean gave Rocky another sledgehammer blow on the shoulder. This time Rocky went down, tumbling across the mat. He felt like he'd been blindsided by a loaded eighteen wheeler. Sean played to the crowd, standing menacingly over Rocky for a few seconds before retreating to a neutral corner.

By now it seemed clear to Sean that everything was going as planned. He relaxed his defense imperceptibly and let Rocky land some shots to his head. It looked good to the audience, but he could tell that Rocky was holding back.

At the bell for round 9 the two fighters came out and mixed it up. Rocky backed Sean into a corner and Sean feigned going for some body shots, giving Rocky an opening to his head. And then … the unexpected … out of the blue. Rocky unloaded a vicious left hook at Sean's jaw. Had Sean not coughed and bent forward at just that instant, the punch would have found its target and Rocky would have finished him off before his head cleared. But, thanks to Sean's sudden lurch forward, the punch caught him on the right ear.

Between the sheer force of the blow and the inordinate weight in the left half of his torso, Sean was sent spinning over the ring's top rope. He hooked the rope with his left arm as he cartwheeled over the top, and ended up sitting on the ring apron. Rocky sprang on him, trying to punch his head through the ropes. The ref grabbed Rocky and pushed his own body between Rocky and Sean. He was in on the fix, and was as confused as everyone except for Rocky and Carbino.

Manny and Louis were immediately in front of Sean, looking up at him from ringside.

"You OK?" Manny asked him, staring anxiously up into his eyes. Sean's right ear was ringing, but other than that he felt all right.

"Double crossin' scum," Louis hissed, looking malevolently at Rocky. Rocky, ordered to a neutral corner, was crossing the ring, shaking his head up and down in angry paroxysms and audibly cursing.

Manny glanced at Tony Skopelli. He couldn't see Vito Carbino from where he stood. Ordinarily Skopelli would have been on his feet in a state of rage. But in this case he was evidently looking over at Carbino in confusion.

"Is Louis right?" Sean asked. "Are they double crossin' us?"

Lacking feedback from Skopelli, Manny didn't know what to answer.

"Can you go on?" he muttered, looking back at Sean.

"Aye, I can and will," Sean growled.

"Get back in there then," Manny said. The ref had already counted to 3.

"Kill the rat, Fiddler. Take him down," Louis whispered hoarsely to Sean as Manny returned to his seat. Sean nodded and grinned.

"Aye, I will that," he promised, climbing back through the ropes.

The noise from the crowd was deafening. Rocky's initial rage at having missed his window of opportunity had passed, and his eyes had taken on a hunted look. When the ref waved them together, Rocky rushed Sean and clinched him.

Even now Sean was inclined to give Rocky the benefit of the doubt, and was going to ask him what he was doing. But before he could speak, Rocky snarled into his ear.

"'Bye 'Bye you Irish turd." And with that, Rocky gave Sean a vicious head butt. Sean felt like his forehead had been caved in. Head buzzing, he instinctively hooked his left arm around Rocky's right elbow and lunged upward, thinking to push Rocky's right arm up and away so that he'd have a clear, steer-killing shot. But Rocky's right glove and wrist were under Sean's armpit. So prodigious was Sean's strength that he lifted Rocky entirely off the canvas a good three feet. And then there was a loud snap and Rocky's body came back down, his right arm broken completely backward at the elbow and still draped grotesquely over Sean's massive forearm.

Sean was aghast and disengaged his own arm with a mixture of terror and disgust. Rocky lifted his right upper arm in disbelief, staring at the dangling forearm. The crowd hushed. The pain was more than Rocky could endure. He staggered backward a few steps and fainted.

The fight doctor rushed into the ring, beckoning frantically for a stretcher. The ref, as stunned as the crowd, wasn't sure what to do. Louis was the first of Sean's team to enter the ring. He pulled Sean to their corner.

"His boxin' days are over," Louis crowed. Rufus was next through the ropes, but he said nothing. Manny climbed up onto the apron, but was intently looking at Skopelli. Tony, in turn, was staring bug-eyed at Vito Carbino, who was returning his stare with the eyes of a snake. Skopelli's face and raised hands seemed to be telling Carbino that he didn't have a clue what was going on. And the truth was that he didn't.

Manny looked over at Carbino in time to see four well dressed but bad looking thugs bent over him. Carbino looked up into the ring at Sean and made a kissing motion with his hand. The four thugs nodded and moved away. Manny could literally see the big handguns bulging under their suit jackets. He glanced back at Skopelli and Skopelli motioned with his head for him to come down by him. The look on his face seemed to be saying 'Get away from him!'

With knees turning to rubber, Manny knew that Sean had been marked for death. He reached over the ropes and grabbed Sean's hair in both hands. Pulling Sean's head close to his own, he whispered into Sean's ear.

"Run, man. Get away from here. Get out of America if you can. I can't protect you. Even Tony can't protect you. I'm sorry. Good luck."

Manny jumped down to the floor and motioned for the security guards to get into position. He gestured to Rufus, and then moved away toward Skopelli.

"Come on, Irish, let's get out o' here," Rufus said, holding the ropes open for Sean. Louis followed Sean through the ropes. Once down on the arena floor, Sean, Rufus and Louis were surrounded by security. They began the trek out of the arena. Midway to the restricted area doors Sean saw Louis push through the ring of guards and run toward a public exit.

"Pay him no mind," Rufus said. "He just be gettin' in our way."

Chapter 48

The security guards delivered Sean and Rufus to the restricted area entry, but that's as far as they went.

"Here we are, champ," the squad leader said, unlocking the door. It seemed like he wanted to say more, but given the bizarre turn of events he appeared to be at a loss for words.

Rufus and Sean entered the restricted area and waited for the door to click shut behind them. It was eerily quiet in the hallways, and Rufus put his finger to his lips signaling that they should keep it that way. Midway down the hall he took out his keys and opened a door to the basement. He clearly knew where he was going and Sean followed quietly.

They entered a room where dozens of paint buckets and other painting paraphernalia were lined up along the walls. Rufus grabbed an extension ladder and motioned for Sean to hold the door open for him. They walked down the hall, around a corner, and Rufus motioned for Sean to open another door.

The door opened into a cavernous room with a 6-foot pit at its center. Around the pit was a concrete walkway. A couple of stairwells led down into the pit where there were large boilers. At first Sean thought that they were going to hide behind the boilers. But Rufus set the ladder on a walkway, 16 or 18 feet below a large, 3-foot square grate.

"It be hinged on de top," Rufus whispered. "I hid money up in dere once. Climb up. I be back in a few hours to get you out o' here."

"You think I'm in danger?" Sean whispered. Rufus looked at him with compassionate eyes.

"Irish, if Carbino's boys catch up wid you, you in danger all right. You a dead man!"

Sean nodded and climbed the ladder. He lifted the grate and could see about ten feet into a large, square duct. Once inside, he scooted around and looked down at Rufus.

"Stay put," Rufus whispered. "I be back later."

He carted the ladder back out the door, and Sean settled down behind the grate with a view of most of the boiler room. He was still in his fight togs, but it was pleasantly warm in the duct.

Sean was mentally, if not physically exhausted. But, unlike when he'd broken Smythe's ribs in Dublin, he felt no compassion for Rocky. He still wasn't sure that Rocky hadn't fractured his skull with the vicious head butt, and wondered if Rocky's head was in similar shape.

With a sigh he laid his chin on his forearm, trying not to doze off. At 11:45 he was jolted awake from a dream. The door to the boiler room had opened and he could hear voices. Chazz came in with two swarthy men. Each man held a big, 9mm automatic pistol in his hand. They scanned the boiler room.

"What's down there?" one of them asked Chazz.

"Gas-fired boilers," Chazz answered nervously.

"Watch the stairs," the man told the other, descending into the boiler pit with gun at the ready. A minute later he emerged from between two of the boilers, shaking his head.

"Nothin'," he grunted.

"What's that?" the other man asked Chazz, pointing up at the ventilation shaft with the barrel of his gun. Sean's heart pounded in his chest. Both men were looking right at him! Yet they didn't seem to make him out behind the grate.

"Ventilation, I guess," Chazz said. "It gets hot in here."

"Whadda yuh think?" the man asked the other. They both considered the height of the grate above the walkway.

"Nah," the other man answered. "Let's keep movin'."

The men motioned to Chazz, and they all filed back out of the room. Sean was drenched in sweat, and didn't have any trouble staying awake after that.

At 2 AM the door opened and Sean could hear an aluminum extension ladder rattling. Rufus came into view.

"Irish?" he whispered.

"Aye, I'm still here," Sean whispered back, pushing the grate outward on its hinges.

"I got clothes for you in de paint room," Rufus said while Sean climbed down. They returned the ladder to the paint room and Sean changed into the clothes Rufus had brought. They made their way out to the freight receiving room that Sean had been in once before. Rufus pulled a stack of cardboard boxes aside.

"Hide in here 'til I sees if de coast be clear," he whispered. Sean edged into the opening and Rufus slid the stack of boxes back, hiding him from view.

Sean heard the elevator go up and then come back down.

"Come on," Rufus whispered. "Nobody in sight."

Up in the alleyway Rufus motioned toward a beat up Pontiac.

"Seth's car," he whispered. "I got no license, but I drives pretty good. You hide on de back floor."

"Where are we going?" Sean asked as Rufus started the engine.

"Seth's," Rufus whispered back. "My place prob'ly bein' watched."

"No way," Sean answered. "It's too dangerous for Seth and his family."

Rufus seemed to be at an impasse. He appreciated Sean's concern.

"What you suggest?" Rufus whispered. "You wants to chance my place?"

"No, you're probably right. Chances are it's bein' watched. I think I should get down to the waterfront … maybe hide there or stow away on a ship."

Rufus couldn't think of anything better, and he eased out of the alleyway. Less than twenty minutes later the Pontiac was slowly cruising along the wharves, with Sean peeking out of a back seat window.

"Here! Stop here!" he whispered as they approached what appeared to be a blue-water fishing boat. Rufus could make out the boat's name in the dim light.

"What be its name?" he whispered. "Can you make dat out?"

"Aye. She's the Gypsy Queen," Sean answered. "I think I can shinny up her moorin' rope."

Sean climbed out of the car and bent over at the driver's open window.

"Thanks, Rufus. If I make it, I'll get word to you somehow."

"Good luck, Irish," Rufus whispered, extending his hand out of the window. Sean thought about slapping it, but then took it in his own and squeezed warmly.

"I owe you me life, Rufus," he whispered.

"You don't owe me squat," Rufus grinned. "We be brothers!"

"Don't count me out," Sean grinned back. "Never underestimate the luck o' the Irish."

And then, with a little wave, Sean crept to one of the big boat's mooring lines. He swung down under it, hooking his left leg over it, and began shinnying up effortlessly.

"Dat boy can climb like a monkey," Rufus thought.

Once over the rail, Sean disappeared from view. But a minute later Rufus could see one of the covered lifeboats rocking slightly from its supports.

With a sigh Rufus put the car in 'Drive' and pulled quietly away.

"Lord, I never ask you for much," Rufus prayed silently. "But I's askin' you now to keep a eye on de Fiddler."

Chapter 49

Sean curled up on the lifeboat's floor. Despite himself he began to doze off again. Just before daybreak he was jolted awake by the sound of men coming aboard. He guessed that they were conversing in Italian. Within half an hour he heard the rumble of the big boat's engines and sensed that they were getting underway. An hour later he could smell the open sea and feel the boat rise and fall as it plowed out into the Atlantic.

He decided to stay put for as long as he could. Perhaps the boat's crew would fish for a day and return to New York. Or perhaps they'd put in at another port. All he knew for certain was that he was still alive and, for the time being, out of reach of Carbino's soldiers.

The ship remained underway all that day and the following night. At about 2:30 AM Sean crept out from beneath the lifeboat's canvas cover. The deck was deserted. He could see lights on up in the bridge. A radar dish on top of the bridge whirled 'round and 'round, scanning the open sea.

Up in the bow was a mast with a running light at its top. Sean crept around in the darkness and eventually came upon a water tap with a cup hanging next to it. He drank greedily. He was hungry, but decided not to risk going below decks.

He repeated the same routine the next night. Still the ship kept plowing along, he had no idea where to. By the afternoon of the third day he was frantic with hunger and decided he'd have to reveal himself. At about 4 PM he lifted the lifeboat's tarp and climbed out. A deck hand looked at him with startled eyes. He began to shout in Italian. Other deck hands materialized. They were all shouting wildly, and one of them ran up to the bridge.

Seconds later the captain rushed out and stared at Sean in disbelief.

"D' yuh speak English?" Sean called up to him, putting on his least threatening face. The captain nodded and Sean continued.

"I came aboard your vessel in New York. I'm very hungry and would be glad to work for a bit o' food."

The captain shouted something to the deck hands and two of them stepped forward, taking hold of Sean's arms. They seemed friendly enough and Sean didn't struggle.

Now the reality was that Sean could not have picked a worse ship to stow away on. It was registered to a phony front company owned by Vito Carbino and two other New York capos. It wasn't a fishing boat at all; it was used to smuggle contraband. On the present voyage it was carrying a load of weapons across the Atlantic to the IRA in Ireland.

The captain recognized Sean at once and placed a ship-to-shore call to Carbino's New York offices. One of Carbino's top lieutenants answered the phone.

"Guess who's stowed away on the Gypsy Queen," the captain said in Italian.

"Who, the pope?" the lieutenant wisecracked.

"No. Fiddler Crabbe."

There was a stunned silence on the other end of the line.

"Are you sure?" the lieutenant asked.

"On my mother," the captain said. "I'm looking at him this very minute."

"Hold on," the lieutenant exclaimed. Moments later Vito Carbino came on the line.

"Did you know we're looking for him?" Vito asked in Italian.

"No. But that makes sense. He's obviously on the run."

"That's right," Vito said. "There's a bounty on him."

"Mama Mia," the captain exclaimed. "What do you want me to do with him?"

"How far from land are you?" Vito asked.

"A hundred miles … maybe a little more … west of Ireland," the captain replied.

"And you're out of the shipping lanes?"

"Oh yeah. Like always. We haven't seen another ship since leaving New York. You want he should go overboard?"

"I want him dead," Vito answered. "I don't care how. There's five hundred for every member of your crew, and five thousand for you."

"Consider it done," the captain promised, signing off.

The skipper came back out on the bridge and again shouted something to the deck hands. They looked at one another, shrugged, and advanced toward Sean. Three of them took hold of Sean's left arm, and another three took hold of his right. They walked him toward the rail. When they tried to lift Sean over it, he suddenly realized what was happening. With a lunge he easily lifted the three deck hands hanging on to his left arm, tossing them against the three holding on to his right. Four of them fell to the deck. The others drew knives and advanced toward him.

With a leap Sean vaulted over a large container on the deck and scrambled up the mast in the bow. There was a small lookout platform near the mast's top and he perched there, hanging onto the mast with one arm. No one seemed inclined to go up after him.

The captain stared at Sean, went back into the bridge and re-emerged holding a rifle. He worked the bolt action and took aim. Sean heard a rifle slug sizzle by his ear an instant before hearing the rifle's report. The captain cursed, worked the bolt action, and took aim again.

Sean gave a mighty leap to the side of the ship. He flew through the air with arms and legs flailing. Clearing the ship's gunwale by a yard, he slammed into the ocean and was pulled under by the turbulence of the ship's propellers. He could see the blurred shape of the hull and the churning screws slide by. Fiercely he clawed his way up and broke the surface with a gasp. He reeled around in the water and watched the ship pull away. The captain fired again, and a slug zinged into the sea two feet from Sean's head.

"Shall we go back and finish him?" the first mate asked.

"No, we're a good hundred miles from land and these waters are shark-infested," the captain decided. "He's a dead man."

With panic-stricken eyes Sean watched the boat's stern recede. He reeled around in the water, scanning the horizon. There was nothing but blue sea in every direction. The only visible object was the ship, already growing smaller.

Sean got control of his emotions and checked the sun's position. The boat was clearly headed eastward. How far from landfall could he be? Could he make it? Would he find something to keep him afloat?

He took a deep breath and went under, taking off his fight boots and socks. The afternoon sun's rays penetrated obliquely into the depths, with no bottom in view. His mind played tricks on him and he imagined seeing great dark forms moving below him.

With a cry he broke the surface again, gasping for air. He wriggled out of the trousers and shirt Rufus had given him. Naked except for his jock, he began to sidestroke after the ship, already nearly gone from view.

He marked the sun's position again. Would he be able to maintain his bearings long enough to get a fix on the stars when they came out? It was his only hope. He had no knowledge of where in the sky the constellations were. And besides, he knew that they rotated around the pole star in the course of a night.

How long could he swim? He was as strong as he'd ever been. Yet he knew he was weak from hunger. He swam and swam, trying not to swallow seawater. It was rough going. The waves were eight to ten feet high. One moment he'd be struggling along in a trough, and the next he'd be riding a crest. Every time he crested he looked at the horizon in front of him. Suddenly he realized that the boat had entirely disappeared from view. He was alone, far out in the Atlantic. The waves seemed to be coming at him from the east. Was he actually losing ground, being pushed back toward the west?

He remembered his last words to Rufus: 'Don't count me out.' With tears squeezing out of his eyes, mourning the imminent end of his life, he resolved to keep swimming until he sank.

Part 5

A Woman's Eyes

Chapter 50

After three hours in the water, Sean was barely moving. He was chilled to the bone. The sun was sinking below the horizon. This time, he thought, his soul and countless others would go with it.

His mind ranged back over his brief life. There wasn't much to be proud about. Manny had told him from the start that he was getting into a crooked business. And he had only too eagerly gone along, drooling over the riches he thought would be his. Sam could have been a good friend … even a best friend. But despite the fledgling bonds of trust they had begun to forge, Sean knew he had never really stopped lusting for Julie. He had never killed another human being, but murder was in his heart only a few nights before. Had Rocky's arm not snapped, he'd almost surely have killed him or crippled him for life.

Sean was jolted back to reality by a movement in the corner of his eye. Something big had rolled at the sea's surface. With terrified eyes he looked around in every direction. There! A fin! And another! Barely five feet away a blue shark rolled at the surface. It was at least eight feet long. For an instant Sean could see its eye staring at him.

Sean wheeled around in a circle, frantically treading water. He ducked his head under and saw the blur of a big shark pass beneath him. The fins circled him, tightening the noose. Then suddenly, for some unknown reason, they canted over and with splashes scattered in every direction.

Sean could scarcely believe it. Had they realized he wasn't their usual prey? Had they lost interest? Just when he was beginning to rejoice that he'd drown instead of be eaten alive, an enormous fish rolled only a few feet in front of him. It was a 20-

foot Great White shark. Its dorsal fin dwarfed those of the blue sharks. Sean instantly knew why the blues had fled the scene.

He ducked his head beneath the surface. He had seen on a TV show how Great Whites often attack from below. But he couldn't make out anything in the fading light. Then, about 30 yards away, he saw the big dorsal fin accelerating toward him. This was it!

"God forgive me," he cried. "Take care o' Ma and Da'."

His mind was racing! Frantically he kicked in the direction of the charging fin. With horror he waited for the gaping mouth. And then … And then … Sean got his miracle. It all seemed to happen in slow motion. There was a bulge in the sea, and a snub-nosed head knocked the Great White completely out of the water! Sean recognized the markings immediately. It was an Orca … a Killer Whale!

As if in a dream he watched the huge shark's body hang suspended for an instant in the air. Great ripples shuddered down its abdomen. The Orca's head sank below the waves but another Orca, at least ten feet longer than the Great White, exploded out of the sea, arching over the submerged one. Sean could see its jaws open and hit the Great White as it fell back into the waves. There was a tremendous thrashing and then … silence.

Suddenly the shark rose only four feet from Sean. It was on its side, and one of its lateral fins quivered in the air. Sean backwatered frantically, but then realized that the shark's head hung grotesquely down into the sea. Its neck was more than half-bitten through. As Sean watched, its great tail flapped the surface a few times, driving it feebly forward. And then it nosed down and sank into the depths.

Sean again spun around in the water. There was only silence. Would the blues be back, attracted by the Great White's blood? Would he be dinner for the Orcas? He could barely move his arms and legs. They seemed to be all but paralyzed. The cold and exhaustion had come full circle.

"'Bye, Mommy," he whispered, ceasing his struggling. His head slid beneath the surface. But his feet touched bottom! His mind dimly sensed the bottom rising beneath him! And then he lay sprawling on the back of an Orca. He stretched his arms and legs out, trying to keep his perch on the leviathan's back. It was like trying to hold onto the hull of a capsized ship.

Sean craned his head upward and stared at the enormous dorsal fin in front of him. It was at least 6 or 8 feet tall. There was a sound, and another Orca surfaced beside them. Its dorsal was smaller, although it appeared to be as long as the one beneath him. The second Orca made some noises and Sean saw the fin above him curve and straighten, curve and straighten, beckoning to him. Somehow he got the message. Like a turtle he crawled forward and grabbed the front of the fin with his left hand. He felt the huge beast begin to move. The sea washed over the whale's back and into his face. He couldn't breathe. He was drowning. Just as he began to loosen his grip, the leviathan stopped. The one next to them chattered away, and again the fin beckoned. Sean crawled to his knees and reached up higher, wrapping both arms around it. His mighty left hand locked onto his right wrist with a grip that only death could loosen.

Again his steed got under way. This time Sean hydroplaned on top of the water. In the fading light he could see the Orca's blow hole breach and expel mist, only to suck in fresh air and submerge again. The smell of the great beast's breath made Sean giddy.

"My God! My God!" he shouted. Above him the first stars were coming out. On each side, other Orcas porpoised along. He thought there must be a dozen in all. The memory of what Grandpa Joe had told him drifted up from memory into what remained of consciousness.

"Every God fearin' man gets a miracle."

Grandpa was right! Sean didn't know where the pod of Orcas was taking him. But he knew that nothing would tear him away from the fin that sliced through the waves. It was his ticket to someplace else, away from this place of sharks and death, and that was enough!

The great porpoise and his companions continued on into the night. Slowly but inexorably Sean sank into delirium. He sang wildly at the stars ... *My Wild Irish Rose ... When Irish Eyes Are Smiling...*

The Orcas seemed to appreciate his serenading, and even to expect it. It was a clear night out in the ocean, far from the belching gas pipes and stacks of civilization. The sky was filled with stars. Sean hallucinated madly, imagining that he himself was a creature of the sea.

The wild ride ended a little more than six hours after it had begun. At first Sean didn't realize it. But then he sensed that he wasn't hydroplaning. All around him the Orcas lolled in the waves, chattering to one another. And there was a sound ... a familiar sound. It was the sound of surf! Sean raised his head and looked past the great sail of a fin. There, in the starlight, he saw a beach nestled in front of towering cliffs.

"Whoa!" he cried as the great form below him submerged. He could feel the fin slide down out of his arms. He tried to swim, but he couldn't unlock his arms! Indeed they felt like lead. No matter how his mind willed them to move, they refused to respond. His legs were no better.

In despair he looked up as the sea closed over his face. So close, only now to drown! His mind began to shut down ... to go somewhere else. But then he felt a great pad of warmth lift him. He was raised up to the surface. As in a dream he realized that he was in an Orca's mouth. His arms unlocked and flopped out between the great conical teeth in the behemoth's lower jaw.

It was the pod matriarch who had realized Sean's final peril and was rescuing him. With a great rush she accelerated toward the beach. And then Sean felt the huge tongue thrust outward. He was catapulted into the surf. Grunting and sobbing, on the fringe of insanity, he pulled himself up the slope of the beach.

He looked back over his shoulder and could see the mother Orca, thrashing back and forth and inching back into the sea.

"Shank you!" he cried, unable to make his swollen tongue work. "Shank you berry much! God blesh!"

He inched himself higher.

"Arive! Ruck o' the Irish," he exulted feebly. And then, a strange buzz in his head. The sound of the surf fading into the distance. And then ... nothing.

Chapter 51

It was a stroke of good luck that Sean's wild ride ended at high tide. While he lay unconscious at the ocean's edge, the tide receded. The sun rose, and gulls began to sail up and down the beach, eyeing the strange apparition lying in the sand.

In the distance there was a sound of bells. William O'Ryan walked alongside his old horse, picking up pieces of driftwood and throwing them into a two-wheeled cart. At first he couldn't make out what he saw in the distance. And then, as he drew nearer, he couldn't believe his eyes.

Leaving the horse, he hurried along the beach toward the human form. Pain stabbed in his left arm. When he reached Sean he looked down in utter amazement. What kind of a strange man was this, all but naked and drowned? He knelt down and felt Sean's wrist. A pulse! The poor bloke was alive!

"Wake up! Wake up!" O'Ryan intoned, rolling Sean over and gently slapping his face. Sean's eyes opened. His face relaxed in a look of complete peace.

"Are you God?" he grated, barely able to make a sound.

"No, laddy, I'm Bill O'Ryan. You've washed up on the shores of Ireland."

"Alive? I'm still alive?" Sean croaked.

"Aye. But not by much, from the looks o' yuh. We'd best be getting' you into a warm bed!"

O'Ryan hurried back to the cart and pulled the driftwood out of it.

"Come on, girl," he said to the horse, taking her by the halter and leading her toward Sean.

"You're a big man," O'Ryan said, lifting Sean to a sitting position. "I don't think I can get you into the cart alone."

Sean nodded and willed his body to assist the old man. He was so weak that he couldn't stand by himself. O'Ryan pulled him to the back of the cart and sat him on its edge. He gently pushed Sean down onto his back, leaving his legs dangling over and his feet dragging the sand.

The old man led the horse back along the beach and up a rocky path slanting up the cliff's face. Sean lay staring up at the blue sky, punctuated here and there with fluffy white clouds. Occasionally a gull swept overhead, looking curiously at the cart and its occupant.

"Betsy! Betsy!" he heard O'Ryan call. "Make ready the bed in the spare room. I've a near-drowned man here!"

Sean was only vaguely aware of what was happening as O'Ryan half dragged him into a farmhouse. He nodded at a young woman, vaguely embarrassed at his nakedness. O'Ryan helped him down a hallway and into a small bedroom. The old man sat Sean down on the bed's edge, pushing him sideways. Sean's head toppled onto a soft pillow. He moaned as O'Ryan lifted his feet into the bed and pulled a sheet and a couple of blankets over him.

"He's half froze," the old man muttered to his granddaughter. "I'm goin' to fetch Doc Anderson. Don't worry. I don't think he's gonna move."

O'Ryan hastened out of the house and Betsy knelt at the bedside, reaching under the covers to rub heat into Sean's arms. She was all but blind, but she was able to make things out when they were only inches in front of her face. She could feel what a mountain of a man Sean was. It was the first time in her twenty years that she'd ever felt a man's body, other than her grandfather's.

"You'll be all right," she whispered over and over again. Sean moaned and seemed to hear her voice as if through a fog.

"Cold. So cold," he slurred through chattering teeth, shivering violently. Betsy's hands ran down his torso to the wet jock.

"Best if this comes off," she whispered. She tugged it down and off under the covers.

Sean continued to shiver in spasms. On an impulse, Betsy lifted the covers and crawled into bed with him. His entire body was as cold as ice. She pressed her own body against him and placed her mouth close to his. Each time he inhaled she tried to exhale, breathing her own warmth into his lungs.

Slowly Sean's shivering abated. He opened his eyes and found himself staring straight into hers. It was the most beautiful face he'd ever seen.

"Are you an angel?" he whispered with effort.

"No. Don't you know where you are?" she whispered back.

In a state of delirium, Sean pulled her face toward his own and kissed her on the lips. His hand cupped her breast and he moaned. She shrank away, but he complained like an infant, not wanting to let go of its mother. Somehow she knew that she was in no danger. She placed her own hand over his and pressed it more firmly against her bosom.

"Uh-h-h," Sean moaned, tears streaming out of his eyes. "Uh-h-h."

"You're all right," she whispered to him. "You've had a rough time of it, but you're safe now."

Sean's eyes opened for an instant, slightly crossed and unfocused. Then they closed again and he began to snore lightly. Betsy moved her hands over his body, gently rubbing warmth and life back into him. It was difficult to believe that any man could be this strong.

"You're goin' to be all right," she whispered again, kissing his cheeks and eyes.

"Thank you," he slurred, only half awake.

"Rest. You need rest," she murmured, rubbing his massive torso.

Chapter 52

Bill O'Ryan chased Doc Anderson down and returned to the farmhouse an hour later, followed by the doctor in his own car. Betsy heard them coming and slipped out of the bed. The two men entered the bedroom on tiptoe. The doc bent over Sean, feeling his forehead and lifting his eyelids. Sean's eyes were rolled back and only the whites showed.

Doc began to pull the covers back, and could see that Sean was naked. But, he knew that Betsy was functionally blind. O'Ryan noticed the wet jock kicked halfway under the bed, but said nothing.

"He's already warmin' up," the doc muttered, feeling Sean's body carefully. He scanned the misshapen form before him.

"You know who this is, don't yuh?" he asked O'Ryan. The old man shook his head 'no'.

"I'd bet fifty quid this is Fiddler Crabbe. He's a fighter … a boxer who just fought a championship bout in America."

"How ever did he end up washed ashore here?" O'Ryan wondered aloud.

"I have no idea," Doc replied. "Whatever, he's a tough customer."

"Should you be givin' him anything … a shot or somethin'?" O'Ryan asked.

"No, not for the present," Doc answered. "He's runnin' no fever. We'll wait and see what develops."

Sean was dimly aware of the sound of strange men's voices and forced his eyelids open.

"Well, now," Doc exclaimed, smiling down at Sean. He pulled the covers back up to Sean's chest.

"It looks like you've had quite a time of it," he continued. "How long were you in the sea?"

"All night, I think," Sean croaked. "I haven't eaten in several days."

The doc gave a little start. Sean *did* seem to be somewhat emaciated.

"Can he have anything?" Betsy whispered.

"Aye. Somethin' warm if you have it," Doc replied.

Betsy nodded and felt her way out of the bedroom. Minutes later she came back in with a plate piled high with steaming mutton. Sean had lapsed back into a slumber.

"Laddy, Laddy, here's some food for yuh," Doc said, gently shaking Sean by the shoulder. Sean's eyes opened with a start.

"Let's get you sittin' up," the doc said, motioning for Bill to help him. They got Sean propped up against the bed's headboard and handed him the plate of meat. Sean began shoveling forkfuls into his mouth and swallowing without chewing. He wolfed the meat down like a ravenous beast.

"More?" O'Ryan asked after he'd cleaned the plate. Sean nodded gratefully.

"Maybe some bread. And a glass o' milk if you have it," the doc again said to Betsy.

While she was gone the doc asked Sean if he was Fiddler Crabbe. Sean's eyes became guarded.

"It's all right. You don't have to talk now if you don't want to," Doc said gently.

"Where am I?" Sean asked. It seemed like the food was already having an effect. Color was coming back into his cheeks.

"You're on Achill Island," O'Ryan said. "I found you near drowned, washed up on the beach."

Sean's eyes glazed over as his mind went back over his time in the sea. Had it really happened? Or was it a dream?

Betsy came back in with half a loaf of bread and a glass of milk. Sean took them from her gratefully. He gazed at her face. She looked familiar. He watched the way she felt the furniture as she moved back away from the bed. Her eyes looked normal, but he guessed that she was blind. It occurred to him that he was naked under the covers.

"Well," the doc said as Sean tore bites out of the loaf of bread and washed them down with gulps of milk. "I think it's safe for me to be goin'. I'd like you to stay in bed for a few more hours, young man. If you feel like gettin' up this afternoon, that'll be fine."

As an afterthought, the doc turned to O'Ryan.

"D' you have any clothes for this lad to wear?" he asked.

"Aye," O'Ryan nodded. "We'll make do for now."

As the doc left, O'Ryan walked him out to his car.

"A fighter, isn't he?" O'Ryan said in a low voice. "Such a strange … build."

"Aye. I've read about him," the doc replied. "Lopsided from birth, he was. The strength in his left side is legendary … more like that of a gorilla than a man."

"Is he the lad who killed that bull a few years back?" O'Ryan asked.

"Aye, I believe he is," Doc answered. "From stunnin' steers with his punches, he got into boxin'."

"I didn't know…" O'Ryan murmured. "I don't follow the sports that much."

"If it's him, then his real name is Sean … Sean Crabbe," the doc said.

"Yes … I recall now," O'Ryan murmured. "What d' you think we … me and Betsy should do?"

"Well," Doc answered, "I think you're safe enough, if that's what you mean. From all I've read, he's a decent enough chap. But if you're worried or don't feel up to keepin' him here…"

"No, No, we're happy enough to have him until he's up and about," O'Ryan said. "I guess we'll just have to wait a bit and see what he wants to do."

Doc nodded and squeezed the old man's shoulder.

"I'll be back out tomorrow afternoon," he promised. "Phone me if you need me sooner."

"Aye, Doc. Thanks for comin'," O'Ryan said, taking out his wallet. "How much do we owe yuh?"

"*You* don't owe me a pence," Doc said. "If he's who I think he is, he's more than able to pay his own bills."

Doc got into his car and drove off. O'Ryan waved and winced at the pain in his chest and shoulder. He took out the small vial of nitroglycerin pills that Doc had given him and placed one under his tongue. There was no telling when the clogged arteries in his heart would close down completely. He'd been worried about Betsy. What would become of her if he suddenly joined her grandmother in the family plot? Her father … his son in law … had died in Belfast, fighting with the IRA. And her sainted mother, his lovely daughter, had succumbed to cancer not long after They both shared the family plot with his departed wife..

Would this strange young man play a role in Betsy's future? Who could say? More than seventy years of living had taught O'Ryan that life is never without its little surprises. Men could only guess about their futures, not to mention the future of the entire earth. Many a night he'd prayed for Betsy's security and happiness after he was gone. And now, out of the blue…

"Mysterious are the ways o' the Lord," he murmured, turning back into the farmhouse.

Chapter 53

Sean was out of bed by noon, and put on the clothes that O'Ryan had stacked on a rocking chair next to the bed. They had belonged to Betsy's father, and they weren't a bad fit. A little snug on the left side, but at least he was decently covered.

"Hello," he said softly, entering the kitchen. Betsy was seated alone at the table, peeling potatoes. Sean could see, by the way she held the potatoes up close to her face, that she wasn't completely blind.

"How are yuh feelin'?" she greeted. "Help yourself to some pie if you like."

"Thank you. I think I will," he said gratefully.

"There's dishes and glasses in the cupboard to the left o' the stove," she said. "And silverware in the top drawer below. Feel free to have a glass o' milk too."

Sean was cutting a wedge of pie when O'Ryan came in from outside.

"Well," the old man smiled, "you're up and about. The clothes seem to fit all right."

"Aye," Sean smiled back, extending his hand.

"D' you remember me name?" O'Ryan asked. Sean shook his head 'no'.

"I remember next to nothin'," he admitted. "I guess I was out o' me head."

"Aye, a fair assessment," O'Ryan answered. "Sit down, lad, and tell us who you are."

Sean took a seat at the table and told O'Ryan and his granddaughter who he was and how he'd stowed away on the Gypsy Queen.

"Filthy blighters. And they left yuh in the sea to drown," O'Ryan growled. "How far d' you figure you had to swim?"

Sean shrugged. He felt that the story about the Orcas was too farfetched to tell to strangers. He wasn't even sure that he hadn't dreamed it.

"The Mafia," O'Ryan mused. "I've heard tell o' *that* lot. What are you gonna do?"

"Oh, lay low for a time, I think," Sean shrugged.

"O' course you could stay here. I could use a hand," O'Ryan said casually. "I'm gettin' on in years, don't yuh know."

Sean's ears pricked up.

"I'd be happy to earn me keep," he said eagerly.

"I'm thinkin' you'd be safe enough here," O'Ryan continued. "There are no criminals on the Isle of Achill."

"Achill …" Sean murmured. "To the west of the mainland, isn't it?"

"Aye," the old man agreed. "We're mostly farmers and fishermen here, with a bit o' the tourist trade."

And so the deal was struck. Sean pitched in and more than earned his keep. It was a beautiful and peaceful place. O'Ryan owned over a hundred acres, all fenced by stonewalls. Behind the farmhouse was a medium size barn where sheep were shorn. O'Ryan's flock numbered over 300. The sheep spent their time in the well-grazed pastures that sloped down from the front of the farmhouse, to the cliffs at the edge of the sea.

O'Ryan suggested that Sean grow a beard, and stay there at the farm until it grew in. In his second week at the farm, Sean asked permission to call his parents in County Louth. O'Ryan readily agreed. Sean called in the evening, when Lester and Emma would both be at home.

His disappearance had been in all the papers, and it was a great mystery what had become of him. Rufus had told no one but Seth how Sean had stowed away on a ship. And Seth had told no one else.

Emma wept openly on the phone when she heard her son's voice. Sean didn't want to go into details about how he'd wound up back in Ireland. He asked them not to tell anyone but his grandparents that they'd heard from him.

"When will we see you?" Emma asked.

"Soon," Sean promised. "I'm growin' a beard and shouldn't be so easy to recognize in a few months."

Emma made him promise to write, and they rang off.

Two months after going to work for O'Ryan, Sean accompanied the old man into the nearest town. Betsy had taken Sean's measurements, using pieces of string, and had altered some of her father's old clothes to better fit Sean's odd shape. Sean watched her at work. She was, in fact, a good seamstress.

O'Ryan suggested that Sean might like to use a different name as they drove into town. Sean knew that Crabbe was a common name in Ireland. His middle name was 'Peter', and he suggested that he be introduced as 'Peter Crabbe'. The few people he was introduced to marveled afterward at Bill O'Ryan's good luck to find such a stout hired hand.

"I shouldn't be surprised if he and Betsy ..." the wife of the general store's owner mused to a friend.

"D' you think so?" the other lady exclaimed. "He seems nice enough."

"Sure, and he is."

"Wouldn't that be a relief to Bill O'Ryan?" the other lady thought aloud.

"Aye, I should think so. Bill has a heart problem, you know."

"So I've heard. And he *is* in his seventies ..."

In the weeks after Sean's first trip to town, Betsy continued to alter clothes for him.

"What a fine figure of a man you are," she'd murmur, feeling around his torso with her measuring strings.

Sean gazed at her pretty face gratefully. Where others saw a freak of nature, she saw ... or felt ... only strength. Her eyes were as blue as Grandma Mary's had been. Looking at them, one would never guess that she was severely impaired. Sean began to feel stirrings for her.

One day, while she was fitting an altered shirt on him and chattering away, he bent toward her on an impulse and kissed her. She was still talking when he did it. There was a stunned silence, and tears welled up in her eyes. Sean immediately thought that she had wanted only to be friends, and that he had ruined everything.

"I'm sorry," he muttered. "Truly I am."

"Why?" Betsy asked.

"I shouldn't o' done that."

"I didn't mind," she whispered.

"But … you're cryin'," Sean murmured.

"I'm cryin' because it's the first time I've been kissed," Betsy explained.

Sean looked at her in astonishment.

"But … you're so *pretty*!" he exclaimed.

Betsy put her hands to his face, exploring his lips and cheekbones with her fingers.

"Nobody wants a blind girl," she said.

"That's not true," Sean whispered huskily. He put his arms around her and pulled her to him, kissing her mouth until her lips parted. When he drew his face back, she grabbed his head in her hands and kissed him hungrily on the mouth.

"Sweet Jesus," she murmured, pressing her cheeks against his chest. "I never thought this would happen to me."

"Nor did I," Sean answered gently, stroking her hair.

That night Sean lay awake until after midnight. He felt that he was falling head over heels in love. Old Bill seemed happy enough to have his help. Achill Island was beautiful and peaceful. He realized that he didn't miss the life he'd left behind in the slightest. Who needed to be a millionaire? For some … for many … great wealth could be more a curse than anything else.

Betsy's handicap was a blessing in disguise. She would never see him as something grotesque. He remembered the conversation he'd had with Grandma Mary so long ago. What was it she'd said? 'You'll know you've found your island home when you gaze into the right woman's eyes.'

Had the Orcas brought him home? Sean thrilled at the prospect. He had enough money stashed away in English banks to buy his own farm. Were he and Betsy destined to be mates? It had never occurred to him that the right pair of eyes would be blind to his deformity. Was that what Grandma Mary had in mind?

"How did she know?" Sean whispered into the darkness. "How did she know?"

Chapter 54

It was autumn and the days were beautiful on Achill. Sean rediscovered the secluded beach where Bill had first found him. It was nestled at the foot of the cliffs in front of the farm. One Friday he walked down the path that O'Ryan used when he went and gathered driftwood. The cliffs curved in a crescent along the coast, effectively isolating the beach entirely from the rest of the shoreline. At one point the rocks were somewhat hollowed out, no doubt by eons of high tide surf. Sean stretched out on the sand in the hollow, looking alternately up at the vaulted rocks above and out across the broad Atlantic. He could see the cliff's rock face above the hollow, but it occurred to him that no one topside could see down into the hollow without tumbling over the cliff's edge. A plan began to form in his love-struck mind.

He suggested that night, when he and Betsy were alone, that the two of them go for a picnic on the beach the following day.

"How will I get down there?" she asked

"You'll ride the horse and I'll lead the way," he answered.

"It sounds like fun," she mused. "I'll wear me swim suit. It's been more than a year since I was in the ocean over on the Eastern Shore."

Sean frowned. He of course had no swim togs there on the farm.

"What'll I wear?" he asked.

"Nothin'," she whispered in his ear. "You said it was secluded. And *I* won't be able to see yuh!"

Sean's heart thumped at the prospect. He was a little taken aback at her suggestion. He had thought of taking a blanket and lying on it with her, kissing her and seeing where things would lead. But the thought of being naked when he did it made him skittish.

"But, what the hey? What're you afraid of?" he asked himself. That evening he asked Bill if he'd be able to take Betsy away for a few hours the next day. He managed to explain, with only moderate blushing, that they planned to go on a picnic down on the beach.

"Aye, it sounds like a nice outing," Bill slyly agreed. Sean breathed a sigh of relief, awash now with mixed feelings of deserving Bill's trust on the one hand, and passion for Betsy on the other.

The next morning he and Betsy had their chores done by 11 AM, and Betsy had packed a picnic basket. Sean put a bridle on Bill's old horse, but no saddle at Betsy's request. He helped her mount the steed and called to Bill.

"Well, I guess we'll be off then. We should be gone only an hour or two."

"Aye, off you go," Bill answered. "Take your time and have fun. I'll hold things down here for the afternoon."

They set off, with Sean leading the old horse with one hand, and carrying the picnic basket with the other. Betsy grabbed a handful of mane and seemed to be enjoying the ride. She wasn't the least bit apprehensive as they wended their way down the path to the base of the cliffs.

Once there, Sean led the horse over to the secret hollow in the cliffs and helped Betsy down. He took the blanket Betsy had packed in the basket, and spread it out on the sand.

"Would you care to sit down for a bit before goin' in for a swim?" he asked innocently.

"Aye, that sounds good," she answered.

Sean kneeled down and took her hand. She sat down on the blanket and Sean stretched out beside her. He could feel her swimsuit beneath her dress.

"What a beautiful day," she murmured. "Tell me what you see."

Sean stared up at the cliffs and out over the water.

"Well, the Atlantic stretches to the west as far as the eye can see," he said softly. "It's as blue as the sky and sparklin' in the sun. Above us rise the cliffs. There's grasses and mosses sproutin' higher up, and it looks like some birds are nestin' in the cliff walls here and there."

"Let's go in," Betsy said of an instant, rising and lifting her dress up and over her head. Sean's heart thudded in his chest. She had a beautiful figure. He wanted to pull her back down onto the blanket but she held her hand out and asked him to lead her into the surf. When he rose and took her hand, she could feel that he was still fully clothed.

"Faith and you can't be goin' into the sea like that," she scolded. Sean looked around uneasily. There wasn't a soul in sight.

"Well, why not?" he told himself. "She clearly doesn't mind. If Bill is lookin' over the cliff's edge, so be it."

He shrugged out of his clothes and dropped them on the blanket. The sea was cold when they waded into it. Chest deep, sudden feelings of terror gripped Sean. Betsy seemed to sense his unease.

"What is it?" she murmured, turning to face him.

"I don't know," he answered. "Maybe it's the memories of the night I spent out there, alone…"

Betsy put her arms around his neck and kissed him. He could feel her body pressing against his own. And she could feel his manhood responding to her.

"I want…I want…" he mumbled thickly.

"I do too," she whispered. "Let's go back to the blanket."

Sean lifted her up into his arms and carried her out of the surf. When he set her down on the blanket, she kneeled and pulled him down in front of her. She put her arms around his neck and lay down. He kissed her passionately and pulled the top of her swimsuit down. She was so full breasted and beautiful it made his head swim. He put his hand on her and she moaned.

"Oh, my love, my love," she whispered.

Sean could tell that he was her first, 'though she did no more than cry out once. As far as he was concerned she was his first also.

Afterward, when she lay next to him basking in the autumn sun, he kissed her softly and asked her to marry him.

"I will, Sean Crabbe," she sighed. "I will, and that's for sure ."

They lay there holding each other until passion awakened again in Sean. When it was time to go back, Betsy stuffed her still damp swimming suit into the picnic basket and pulled her flimsy dress on over her head. To Sean it seemed obvious that she had nothing on under the dress. He worried that O'Ryan might notice and he resolved to talk to the old man that very night.

Once back at the farmhouse Betsy took a shower, explaining that she needed to rinse off the sea salt. Sean went outside and busied himself with the sheep. After a time Bill came out and joined him. Sean decided that the head-on approach was best.

"I'm in love with your granddaughter," he blurted.

"Are yuh now?" Bill answered. "Well, that's fine. I've a feelin' she fancies you too."

"I asked her to marry me, and she said 'Yes'," Sean continued.

Bill looked up at Sean and his eyebrows arched.

"I'd like your permission," Sean continued nervously, looking old Bill squarely in the eye. "I accumulated a tidy sum durin' me fights in Europe, and I can afford to buy me own farm."

"Well, well," Bill said, clearly impressed and pleased. "If Betsy said 'yes' then I've no objection. But why don't you work this place? It'll be hers soon enough. If the two of you want, I'll sign it over to her now, as a weddin' gift, provided you keep me on as a hired hand."

Sean grinned widely and his eyes glistened. He stepped toward Bill and extended his hand.

"This place is yours for as long as you live," he said.

Bill nodded and returned Sean's handshake.

"When did the two o' yuh want to tie the knot?" Bill asked.

"I don't know," Sean answered. "It's all up to Betsy. As far as I'm concerned, the sooner the better. I'd like to go see me Ma and Da' and transfer some funds to a bank here on Achill. And o' course they'll be comin' to the weddin'."

"Aye, absolutely," old Bill said. "I look forward to meetin' them."

Bill grinned absently as a devilish thought seemed to occur to him.

"By the way," the old man said, I've a bottle stashed in the house. Will yuh join me for a drop o' the Irish?"

"Aye, I will that," Sean said. "It's been a while since I've had a taste. Will Betsy be joinin' us?"

"I don't know," O'Ryan smiled. "Let's go ask her."

Chapter 55

Betsy, Sean and O'Ryan had a rousing good time of it that night. They all got into Bill's bottle of Irish whisky and it had the desired effect. Sean told Betsy that he'd gotten her grandfather's permission to marry her.

"He wants to know when we'll tie the knot. I told him the sooner the better," Sean slurred.

Betsy grew serious for a moment.

"I think…I'd like to wed durin' the holidays," she announced.

"What a grand idea!" Sean cried. "Before or after…"

"Between Christmas and New Years," Betsy decided.

And so the date was set. The next morning Sean's head felt like concrete, but nothing could dispel the warmth he felt at how well things had gone.

He discovered that his funds could be transferred from England without his leaving the island. He had O'Ryan take some pictures of himself and Betsy. And he in turn took pictures of her and Bill. He spent an extra hour or so roving the farm, taking pictures of it and of it's lovely setting. That evening he wrote a long letter to Emma and Lester, filling them in on his good fortune and of the impending nuptials.

Emma was in seventh heaven when she read Sean's letter. She had the grandparents over for Sunday dinner and passed the letter and pictures around.

"Ain't that the limit?" Grandpa Joe exclaimed. "What a pretty colleen Sean has snagged.

"Aye, she is, isn't she?" Lester chimed in. "She's blind, yuh know."

"No! How ever?" Grandpa asked.

"We don't know," Emma answered.

Emma and Lester announced their plans to travel across Ireland during the Christmas season. It was decided that the grandparents were too old for the trip. And so Emma wrote a long letter back to Sean and Betsy, telling them of their plans. Betsy made reservations for them at the best hotel on the Eastern Shore.

Autumn slipped by in silent grandeur there on Achill. It seemed that the betrothal of Sean and Betsy had a near mystical effect on Sean. It was as if a door clicked shut on his past, and the years he'd spent in the fight game became more and more a curious memory.

He took a new interest in the farm's operation, and by November was pretty much running things alone. Bill made heroic attempts to pitch in, but the simple truth was that he could do little. With each passing day the angina pains in his shoulder and arm grew more frequent. Doc Anderson quietly shook his head when he listened to the old man's laboring heart.

Betsy sensed her grandfather's weakening state, but with quiet resolve carried on. She dug her late mother's wedding gown out of a trunk in a spare room and made alterations to it befitting her own full figure. Tossing old superstitions to the wind, she had Sean help her each time further alterations were called for. It was pleasant work for him, and as the alterations took shape she looked more beautiful every time she put the dress on.

Sean's family had never attended church regularly, but Betsy and Bill went every Sunday. At first Sean had stayed there on the farm. But once they had become engaged Betsy insisted that he accompany them at least one Sunday to meet their priest. Sean agreed readily and following services they gathered in the priest's place for Sunday dinner. Sean enjoyed the whole affair, particularly the church services. He had a fine baritone voice and enjoyed singing the hymns. Betsy was happily surprised when he announced the following Saturday that he'd like to go to services again. And so he became a Sunday regular along with her and her grandfather.

The other farmers on their side of the island visited the O'Ryan farm occasionally. And gradually, between the visits and the church going, Sean made the acquaintance of many men and even of their families. With each new friendship he felt his roots sinking deeper into the island's soil. December came, and then the day of their wedding was practically at hand.

Emma and Lester arrived by train from County Louth and Sean picked them up at the station. On the drive out to the farm Emma waxed enthusiastic about how beautiful the countryside was. The western coast of Achill was of course a good deal more rugged than the eastern one was, and Emma and Lester were virtually enchanted when they arrived at the farm. There was the usual feminine fuss when Emma met Betsy. They had dinner there at the farm, and then Sean took his parents on a walk around the property. Both lovers of the sea, Lester and Emma were enthralled by the view to the west.

"It's such a beautiful place, son," Emma murmured, taking Sean's arm.

"Aye, it is that," Lester heartily agreed.

Sean recounted his misadventures in America and told them of his deliverance from the sea. Lester listened in near disbelief.

"So Jonah and the whale is a true story," he murmured after Sean had finished.

"Aye, I hadn't thought of that. But it probably is," Sean agreed. "I don't know whether he spent a full three days in the beast's mouth, but…"

"Probably a less than perfect translation of the ancient texts," Lester allowed. "I don't always feel that the English version of the scriptures accurately reflects the original writers' meanin's."

Sean and Betsy drove his parents back to their hotel late in the afternoon, and Lester treated them all to a fine meal in the hotel's dining room. Later, after Sean and Betsy had said their good-byes and returned to the farm, Lester and Emma lay in the dark in the strange hotel room, marveling at how things had worked out.

"Did I ever tell you what my mother said to Sean once?" Emma asked.

"About every man findin' his island home?" Lester asked.

"Yes," Emma answered, wondering how Lester had heard the story.

"I'd say she somehow knew, wouldn't you?" Lester asked.

"Yes, it's uncanny isn't it?" Emma replied. "Sean knew he'd come home when he looked into the right woman's eyes. Who ever would have guessed those years ago that they'd be eyes unable to see his deformity?"

"Yes, things do have a way of workin' out, don't they?" Lester answered, pulling Emma to himself and kissing her on the cheek.

Everyone had to gather at the church the next day for a rehearsal, and Emma and Lester had dinner out at the farm that night. Sean and Betsy were wed the next day, on December 30th. It was decided that they'd forego a honeymoon for the present, and that Emma and Lester would leave following the ceremony in order to be back at their own home for New Year's eve with the grandparents.

"Be happy, Seanie," Emma whispered as she kissed her boy goodbye. "And know that your Da' and I are happy for you. You've married a beautiful girl."

"Aye, that's for sure," Lester agreed. "May shamrocks and bluebirds be with you all the days of your lives."

And then they were gone.

That night Bill O'Ryan settled back into the soft pillow on his bed with a happy sigh. It was as if his work on earth was done. Betsy would be taken care of. He had long since lost any dread of his own end. If anything, he believed that he'd be reunited with his wife and looked forward to the final curtain.

He wanted Betsy and Sean to take over the master bedroom. But Sean would have none of it. He reminded old Bill that the place was still his. But the truth was that Bill was letting go. By the following spring it was clear that the old man was fading. One day in April he failed to come into the house when Betsy rang the lunch bell. Sean went looking for him and found him laid out in the shearing barn. He was still alive, but he was wheezing and his lips were blue.

Sean carried the old man to the truck, shouting to Betsy to call the medical center. Bill had tried nitroglycerin tablets under his tongue, but this time they hadn't seemed to help.

"I fainted dead away," he murmured to Sean as they sped toward the medical facilities. "It was like the bloody ground rose up and hit me in the snoot."

In the medical center Doc Anderson's face grew somber as he listened to Bill's irregular heartbeat.

"He's had a heart attack," he told Sean when they were alone. "We'll keep him here for a day or two. It's touch and go."

Sean nodded gravely.

"Will he recover?" he asked quietly.

"It's hard to say," Doc answered. "His EKG is erratic, but that's to be expected. If he comes home, I recommend that you rent a hospital bed. He'll be more comfortable with his upper body elevated."

"Aye, I'll do that," Sean promised.

That night he and Betsy lay quietly in their bed. Sean had arranged to pick up the hospital bed the next morning.

"We'll put it in the front room. He'll like that," Betsy stated.

"Aye. He'll be able to hear you workin' in the kitchen and the like," Sean agreed.

Chapter 56

Two days after going to the hospital, Bill was brought back to the farm in an ambulance. Sean explained to him that they'd set an adjustable bed up in the front room, and Bill seemed to be happy about that. But there was a certain vacant look about the old man. It was as if the fight had finally drained out of him.

They got Bill settled into the bed and Betsy prepared a supper for him in accordance with Doc Anderson's instructions. Bill picked at it but ate little. That night Sean told Betsy that he was going to stay up at least part of the night. She kissed him and went to bed. The spring air was moist and chilly, and Sean lit a fire in the hearth.

"Many a fire the ocean has provided us fuel for," O'Ryan rasped, turning his hoary head and looking across the room at the flames.

"Aye, the driftwood always burns well," Sean agreed. "I'm gonna stay out here for a while and keep it goin'. Try to get some sleep."

O'Ryan looked into Sean's eyes.

"I'm grateful you washed up on our beach," he whispered. "You've been a great help to me, and I know you'll take care o' Betsy."

"Aye, we'll take care o' her together," Sean smiled. "Rest now."

Sean walked back to the hearth and threw a large chunk onto the fire. He slumped down into a chair and gazed into the whispering flames. Bill's labored breathing was the only other sound in the room. Every now and then it seemed to stop and Sean would tense. But then it would resume with a gasp.

Sean became contemplative as he gazed into the flames. Every now and then a log would pop and send sparks up the chimney. Were they souls leaving the earth? He knew that every day thousands upon thousands of new lives begin on the planet, and other thousands end. One day it would be his turn. How would he

feel? Bill seemed to be not at all afraid. It was all such a mystery.
Perhaps the deepest mystery the human mind must deal with.

The longer Sean stared into the flames, the more his eyes
seemed to tire. He closed them and continued thinking about the
changes that seemed to be in store for all of them. Imperceptibly his
thoughts drifted into dreams. The fire gnawed away at the big
chunk of wood. Pieces fell away, adding to the bed of embers under
the grate. Slowly the flames died down, and finally the log broke in
half. The noise partially roused Sean, but his mind clung to sleep.
A shower of sparks wafted up the chimney.

At 3 AM the sound of soft weeping roused Sean with a start.
The fire had gone out and the room was cool. He heard Betsy
sobbing across the room by the hospital bed. Kneeling beside her,
he felt Bill's hand. He was gone.

Somehow all of the arrangements got made and after a day and
an evening in the funeral home, Sean and Betsy drove to the church
for the funeral services. Bill lay in repose at the front of the church.
Sean was awestruck by the number of people who attended.

"He touched many lives during his own lifetime," the priest
said. "And not just here on Achill."

It was the truth. Dozens … perhaps a hundred or more people
drove across the Island Bridge from the mainland.

Betsy wept silently, but already with acceptance as the priest's
voice gently read the mass. Following the services they met with
many people in the church's vestibule and then they left for the
farm. It was decided that no one but Sean and Betsy would attend
the graveside services such as they were. Bill was laid to rest beside
his wife of 53 years.

Less than two weeks after the burial Betsy announced that
they'd be moving into the master bedroom. Bill's bed was moved
out and their furniture was moved in. Betsy's period of grief was
brief. It was as though she had let go of the old man while he was
still alive. Late in the summer Sean drove her into town to see Doc
Anderson. She informed Sean that night that they were about to
become a family of three. Like his father had done before him, Sean
nearly fell to the floor when she gave him the news.

Little Mary was born in the spring along with the lambs. Sean looked at the baby anxiously in the hospital nursery. She seemed to be perfect.

"D' you think there's any chance that my…condition…"he began to ask Doc Anderson.

"I don't, I surely don't," the Doc replied. "I'd say that your asymmetry isn't an inherited trait. She looks to be perfect to me. I shouldn't worry about givin' her lots of brothers and sisters."

The Doc was right. In the first few years that followed, Mary grew straight and even. She had Sean's red hair, and her eyes were as blue as her mother's. But there was no sign of blindness. Betsy conceived again when Mary was three years old.

As the Christmas holidays drew near, Sean got to thinking about his escape from America and how Rufus had saved his hide. He decided to somehow let Rufus know that he had made it. Presumably the old boy was still a cut man at the fight club, and would get a letter if it were mailed there. But how could Sean get the message to him without compromising his own existence. And then it hit him.

Sean held Betsy in his arms the night she told him that Mary was getting a brother or a sister. The air wafting through the cracked bedroom window was crisp and smelled of the sea. Outside he knew that the sheep were bedded down, warm in their wool and waiting for the morning sun. Sean felt that he must be the luckiest man alive. Only a few years ago he'd been driven to accumulate great wealth. And now he thought he understood why.

"The matin' game," he thought to himself. "We all think we're unique. And to be sure we are. But we're also part of a grand process… a process that's been goin' on since life began in the sea."

Reproduction of the species. He knew it was one of the most fundamental instincts that man shares with all the other creatures of the earth. How many other lives had preceded his and Betsy's, back through the mists of time? Like he and she, they'd had their dreams. But always they'd been driven by the same imperative he now felt…to raise their progeny…to leave someone behind when their time came.

"Men need a cause to live for, and even to die for," he mused. "And raisin' a family's the most tried and true cause of all."

He realized now that the quest for riches had, in the final analysis, been a desire to attract a mate. Was it not that way with all men? Yes, they wanted wealth and power. But why?

With a sigh Sean pulled Betsy closer to him and kissed her mouth. He breathed in the fresh scent of her hair.

"I feel like we've been so blessed," he whispered into the darkness.

"And so we have," she murmured, snuggling closer to him.

Epilog

Six weeks after Sean disappeared from New York, Tony Skopelli concluded that his Mafia boss wasn't his friend after all. He secretly arranged to have Vito Carbino assassinated by some out-of-town guns. Tony planned to be in Los Angeles when it happened. But he never made it. Carbino got wind of the hit, and Skopelli's body surfaced in the Harlem River two days before his scheduled flight to LA.

Manny was shocked at first, but he was too pragmatic not to recognize an opportunity. He had been laying off sure bets for years and had accumulated a hefty chunk of working capital. He took over Skopelli's lease on the fight club and started his own stable of fighters. Rufus and Seth were kept on the payroll.

The years slipped by and the operation flourished. During the Christmas season four years after Sean's disappearance, Seth called Rufus over to the equipment room window.

"You got a letter or Christmas card, man," Seth grinned. "It looks like it come from across the pond. What you been up to over there in England?"

Rufus took the envelope from Seth's hand and stared wonderingly at it. He hadn't been in England for nearly a year. And not knowing how to write, he had *never* gotten any letters.

"And what kind o' name is that?" Seth demanded, pointing to a couple of words written where the return address would normally be.

"What's it say?" Rufus mumbled.

"Ain't no address. Just what look like a crazy name."

Rufus gave his younger brother a look that seemed to say, 'If you don't tell me what it say, I gonna slap you up side the head!'

"I never see a name like that before," Seth grunted. "Uca somethin'."

"*Uca? Uca?*" Rufus cried, tearing the envelope open with trembling fingers.

Inside there was only a photo. It showed a red haired man and a pregnant woman holding a beautiful little girl in her arms. The man had a bushy beard and his left half was hidden behind the woman. He looked perfectly normal except for the hand resting on her shoulder. It was as big as a frying pan.

Green fields sloped down and away behind the couple. Beyond the fields blue ocean stretched away to the horizon where it met the sky.

"Who is it?" Seth asked, grabbing Rufus' wrist and looking at the photo.

"Don't you recognize dem eyes?" Rufus asked.

"No, man, who that be anyway?"

Rufus looked away. In the sparring ring two young hopefuls practiced on each other. In the corner another rising star made the light bag move in a blur.

Ratta Tatta Ratta Tatta the bag went. Rufus sighed and tucked the photo into his shirt pocket.

"I'm dogged if it ain't de Fiddler," he murmured. "Irish done foun' his island."

The End